Today's Homeowner®

Essential Home Tips

500 SOLUTIONS FOR PROBLEMS AROUND YOUR HOME

CREATIVE PUBLISHING international

MINNETONKA, MINNESOTA

Credits

Creative Publishing international, Inc.
5900 Green Oak Drive
Minnetonka, Minnesota 55343
1-800-328-3895

President: Iain Macfarlane
Group Director, Book Development: Zoe Graul
Director, Creative Development: Lisa Rosenthal
Executive Managing Editor: Elaine Perry

Editorial Director: Bryan Trandem
Associate Creative Director: Tim Himsel
Managing Editor: Jennifer Caliandro
Lead Writer/Editor: Jerri Farris
Writer/Editors: Christian Dick, Carolyn Witthuhn
Copy Editor: Janice Cauley
Technical Photo Editor: Joel Schmarje
Senior Art Director: Gina Seeling
Lead Mac Designer: Phyllis Lee
Mac Designer: Laurie Kristensen
Project Manager: Jill Anderson
Illustrators: Andrew Christie, Bryan Chrisyie, Mario Ferro, Trevor Johnston, Narda Lebo, Tom Moore, Chad A. Peterson, Richard Stromwell, Ian Warpole

Vice President of Photography & Production: Jim Bindas
Studio Services Manager: Marcia Chambers
Photo Services Coordinator: Carol Osterhus
Photographer: Rebecca Schmitt
Scene Shop Carpenter: Troy Johnson
Production Manager: Kim Gerber
Purchasing Manager: Dave Austad
Production Staff: Curt Ellering, Laura Hokkanen, Kay Wethern

Today's Homeowner®

VP/Editor-in-Chief: Paul Spring
Design Director: Murray Greenfield
Executive Editor: Bob Markovich
Managing Editor: Steven H. Saltzman
Senior Editors: Leslie Plummer Clagett, Fran H. Donegan, Lynn Ocone, Joseph Truini, John Wagner
Associate Art Director: Nancy Stamatopoulos
Editorial Assistant: Kerstin Sabene

VP/Publisher: John W. Young
General Manager: Jill Raufman
President, Today's Homeowner: Jason E. Klein

Printed in U.S.A. by World Color
01 00 99 98 / 5 4 3 2 1

Library of Congress Cataloging-in-Publication Data

Essential home tips : 500 solutions for problems around your home.
p. cm.
At head of title: Today's homeowner.
Includes index.
ISBN 0-86573-758-4
1. Dwellings--Maintenance and repair--Amateurs' manuals.
I. Today's homeowner.
TH4817.3.E84 1998
643' .7--dc21 98-19038

Contents

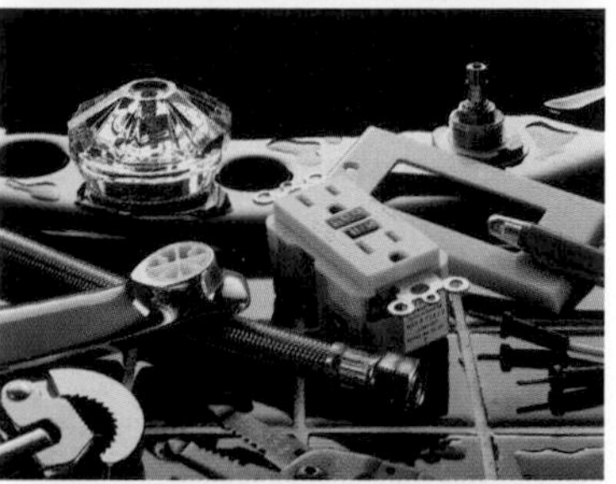

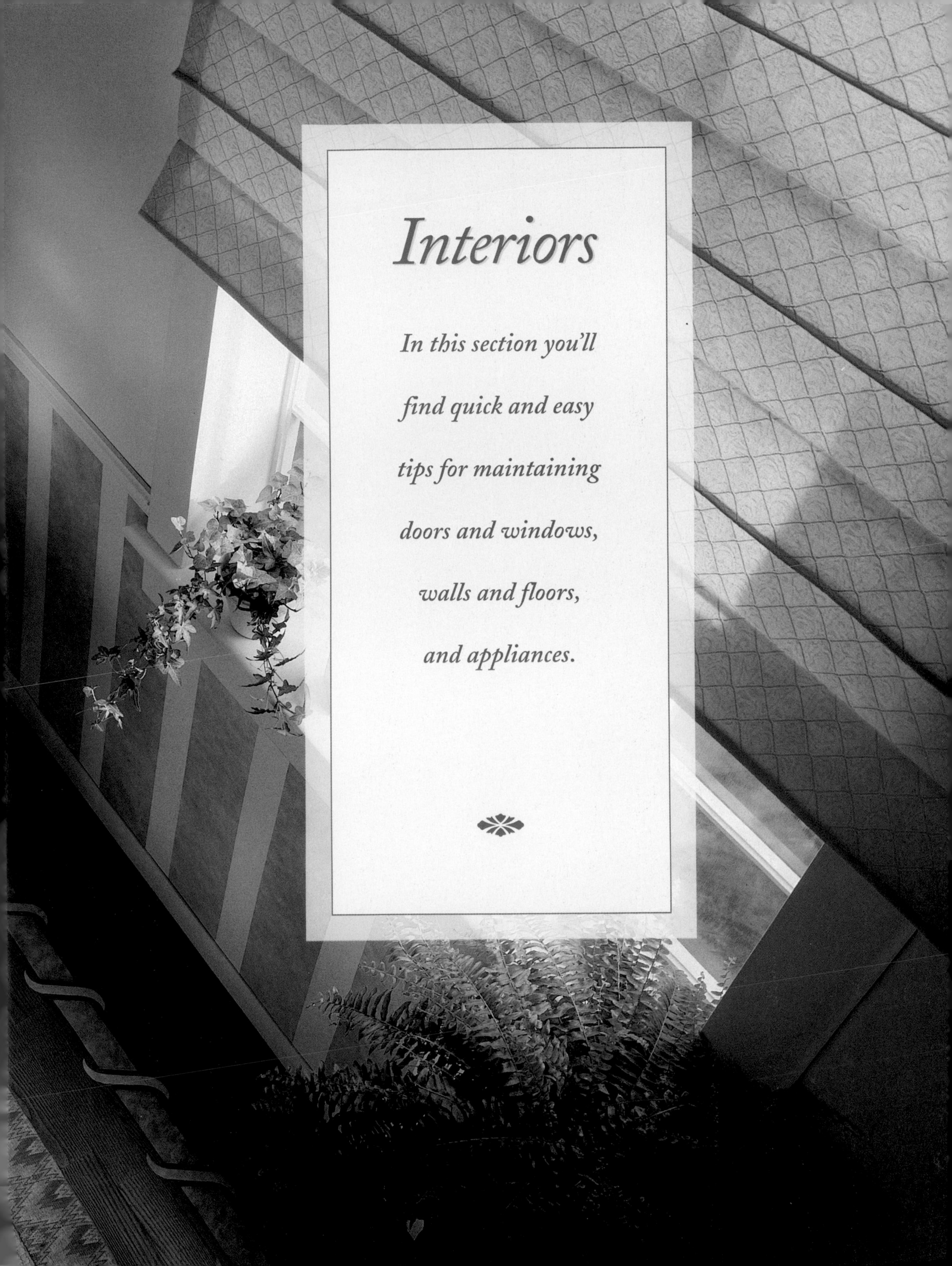

Interiors

In this section you'll find quick and easy tips for maintaining doors and windows, walls and floors, and appliances.

Doors & Windows

Doors and windows provide access to your home and a view of the outside world. They also play key roles in energy conservation, safety and home security.

The amount of energy wasted through poorly insulated doors and windows is roughly equal to the energy transported across the Alaskan pipeline each year. This statistic, reported by the U.S. Department of Energy, points out the importance of selecting appropriate doors and windows and maintaining them properly.

Other door and window problems—hinges that shriek when you open the door, latches that won't catch, windows that resist even the most determined efforts to open them—may not have such obvious consequences, but they can become real problems if left unattended, especially in regard to safety. The National Safety Council reports that each year, approximately 4,000 Americans perish in household fires. Making sure that doors and windows function correctly is an essential part of providing an escape route in the event of fire.

Doors and windows also have a substantial impact on the security of your home. Unsecured doors and windows are an invitation to burglars, but outfitting them with some simple, inexpensive hardware can significantly improve your home's security.

Helpful Terms

Balance: Weights or springs hidden behind the jamb and attached to double-hung windows to make them slide up and down

Casing: Trim around the perimeter of a door or window opening

Dead bolt: A bolt on a lock that is moved by turning a key or knob; more secure than a spring-activated lock

Glazing: Material used to seal the glass pane in the window sash

Jamb: Sides and top of a door or window opening

Mullion: Vertical strips that separate the panes of a window

Sash: A frame that holds the glass panes of a window or door; the sliding section of a window

Sill: Flat bottom edge of a window or exterior door frame

Strike plate: A brass or steel plate mortised into the doorjamb, surrounding the hole for the door latch

doors

Doors come in many different styles, each with its own shape and method of operation. Recognizing the strengths and weaknesses of various styles is helpful when you replace doors and their hardware.

Types of Doors

Replacing the doors in your home is one of the simplest ways to improve its appearance and energy efficiency.

Choosing the right doors requires some thought and evaluation. Doors should complement the architectural style of a home, as well as meet the specific needs of their locations.

Exterior doors, for instance, provide security and a barrier to the outside elements, while interior doors define boundaries and offer privacy.

Doors define the entrance to your home and can significantly enhance the look and feel of a room. The material that you choose is just as important as the style.

The descriptions below of the most common household doors will help you evaluate the doors currently in your home and those you may consider purchasing in the future.

Entry: An entry door should be at least 36" wide and at least 80" high. The best entry doors are either solid wood, steel or fiberglass shells filled with insulation. Such doors are strong, durable, energy efficient and secure when equipped with appropriate hardware.

Combination storm: A storm door is always used in combination with an inner entry door and can roughly double the insulation value of the entry.

Passage: Used only in a home's interior, passage doors range from 30 to 34" wide and are usually less substantial than entry doors. Commonly, passage doors are hollow-core and come prehung in frames. However, solid-core interior doors are preferable for rooms that require soundproofing.

French: These are double doors, often glass-paneled, that open from the center. They offer elegance and plenty of light but are less secure than standard entry doors.

Patio: Patio units have one fixed and one sliding glass panel. They provide good light and ventilation but can be drafty and less secure than other door styles.

Passage Door

Combination Storm Door

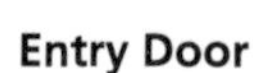

Entry Door

French Doors

Patio Door

Free at Last

Doors stick when the hinges sag or when the wood of the door or frame swells or shifts.

To free a sticking door, first make sure the hinge screws are tight. When tightening hinge screws without removing the door, prop up the bottom of the door using shims.

You may find that a door continues to stick during unusually wet weather even though the hinges are tight. If this is the case, wait for a dry period and seal all edges of the door.

If a door sticks constantly and tightening the hinges doesn't help, try sanding the edges of the door. To quickly sand the bottom of a door without unhinging it, tape a piece of coarse sandpaper to a section of newspaper. Stack a layer of newspapers on the floor under the door, placing the sandpaper on top of the stack. Then open and close the door repeatedly, dragging the low spot across the sandpaper. Once the low spot has been sufficiently sanded, the door will swing freely.

If a door continues to stick after you've tried this method of sanding, wait for dry weather, and take the door off the hinges. Sand or plane the door to fit; then seal the edges.

QUICK TIPS

To prevent warping as wood expands and contracts, use the same type of sealant (paint, polyurethane or lacquer) on all six sides of a door. Seal the inside and outside faces as well as the top, bottom, left and right edges. Without this protection, doors swell and eventually warp.

Doorknob Secrets

You don't need a locksmith to replace a faulty lockset on an interior door. It's a simple job anyone can finish in less than 15 minutes. For many novice do-it-yourselfers, however, the most difficult part is the first step: removing the doorknob.

On most simple passage locks, the mounting screws are concealed, so at first glance there doesn't seem to be a way to disassemble the knob. Here's the secret: look closely at the shank of the interior doorknob and you'll see a tiny slot or hole. Push the tip of a narrow-blade screwdriver or nailset into the hole. Tug on the knob and it will slide right off. Then pry off the round decorative plate, called the rose, to expose the screws that hold the lockset on the door.

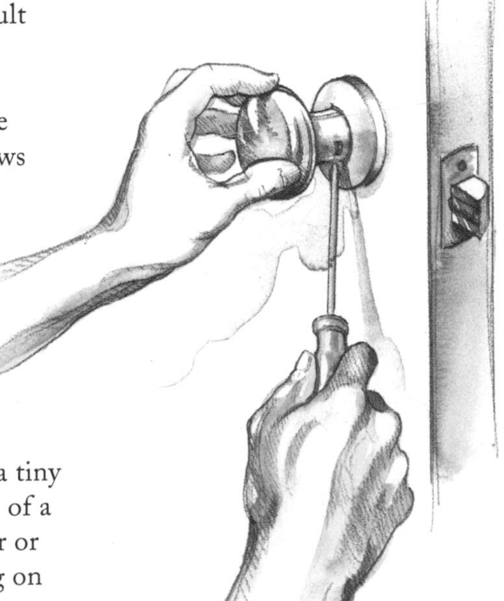

A router is the ideal tool for cutting mortises for hinges or locksets. The challenge when using a router is holding it steady on the narrow edge of a door. If the tool tilts, even slightly, the resulting mortise will be uneven. Here's an easy way to steady the router.

Clamp a board to each side of the door to create a wider base for the router. Make sure all three edges are perfectly flush. Besides preventing the router from rocking, the wider base also prevents any tear-out and splintering as the router bit exits the workpiece.

Pencil Trick

Graphite powder is the obvious solution for a door lock that sticks. If you're having trouble with a lock and don't have graphite powder on hand, a pencil with a soft lead will help.

Rub a pencil lead up and down and all around the key, transferring graphite to the key's surface. When you have a fairly good buildup of graphite, put the key in the lock. Move the key in and out several times; then, turn it back and forth several times in the lock. Just that simply, the sticking problem should disappear.

Tee It Up

Loose butt hinges are a common cause of sticking doors. Tightening the hinge screws often fixes the problem, but you may find that the screws can't be tightened because the holes are stripped. One solution is to fill the stripped holes with a golf tee and carpenter's glue.

Open the door wide and insert a wedge under the bottom outside corner to hold it. Remove the screws that hold the loose hinge leaf to the doorjamb. Swing the leaf away from the jamb.

Spread carpenter's glue onto a golf tee. Tap the tee into the worn screw hole. Let the glue dry for the recommended time; then, cut off the excess wood. Plug each of the stripped screw holes in the same way.

Reposition the hinge leaf and drill 1/8"-diameter pilot holes. Secure the hinge by driving screws into the reinforced holes.

Chisel It Out

One of the simplest ways to cut a mortise for a hinge or strike plate is with a chisel. To score the outline of the cutting area, hold the beveled side of the chisel toward the inside of the marked area, and tap the butt of the chisel lightly with a mallet.

Make a series of parallel cuts, 1/4" apart and about 1/4" deep, as shown below. Hold the chisel at a 45° angle with the blade perpendicular to the wood grain.

Now chisel in the opposite direction to remove the wood chips. Repeat until the cut reaches the desired depth, and trim to the marked lines.

MARKING STRIKE PLATE LOCATION

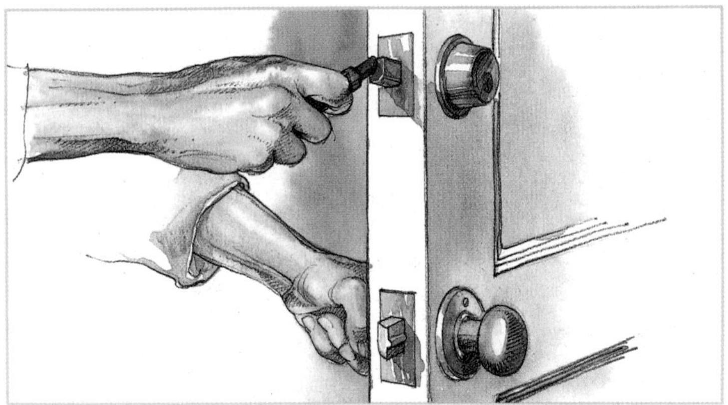

If you've ever installed a lockset or dead bolt on a door, you know how hard it is to accurately mark where the strike plate goes on the doorjamb. One solution is to use a little lipstick.

First, open the door and rub the lipstick onto the latch or dead bolt. Any color will do, but bright red works best. Turn the knob to retract the latch; close the door; then, release the knob just enough for the latch to "kiss" the jamb. The resulting imprint indicates exactly where you need to mortise in the strike plate.

Smooth Sailing for Sliding Doors

The best time to take care of a sliding glass door is before it starts sticking or hopping out of its track.

Begin by checking the adjustment: stand back and look at the door from the outside. There should be a uniform gap along the bottom and top edges of the door. If the side with the adjusting screw is too high, turn the screw counterclockwise. If that side is too low, use a flat pry bar to raise the door while you turn the adjusting screw clockwise.

Next, check the metal track that forms the threshold. If this track is bent and crooked, you need to straighten out the bends, bumps and wrinkles. Lay a wooden block into the track, place one foot on top and tap the block with a hammer to bend the track back into shape.

Vacuuming the track regularly will help keep the door sliding smoothly. So will periodic applications of powdered graphite or silicone spray.

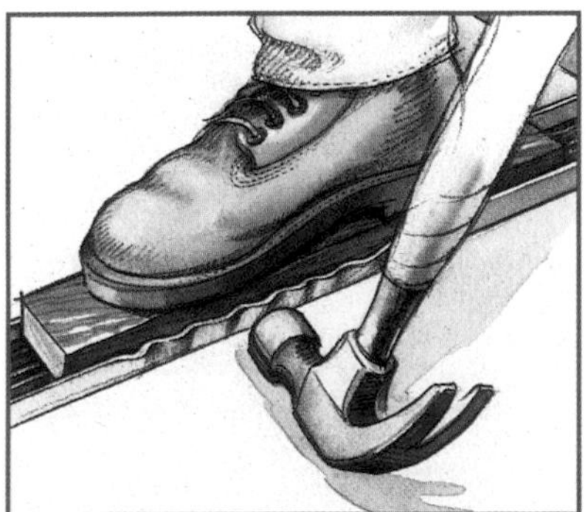

Filing a Strike Plate

If a door won't latch unless you slam it, the strike plate mounted on the doorjamb is probably out of alignment.

Instead of moving the strike plate, which often requires you to increase the size of the mortise, try this trick:

Take the strike plate off and clamp it in a vise, making sure to pad the clamp's jaws with cloth to protect the strike plate's finish. File the interfering edge of the plate to enlarge its opening slightly so the latch bolt can enter properly. Reinstall the strike plate, and test the door.

A Show of Hands

When ordering prehung doors, it's imperative to know the "hand" of the door.

To determine the hand, stand facing the inside of the door opening. The hinged side of the door defines the door's hand—right or left.

QUICK TIPS

To remove a stubborn hinge pin, insert the top of a nail into the hole from the bottom of the barrel. Tap the nail with a hammer, forcing the pin up and out of the hinge.

To straighten out a slightly warped door, place it across sawhorses with the convex side facing up. Set weights, such as concrete blocks, in the center of the bowed area, and leave them until the door returns to its proper shape.

All Lined Up

When the handle of the garage door is rotated to the locked position, two horizontal steel bars slide out in opposite directions and pass through slots in the door track.

If locking your garage door has become increasingly difficult, the locking bars probably are misaligned. Misaligned bars often hit the track and prevent the lock from catching.

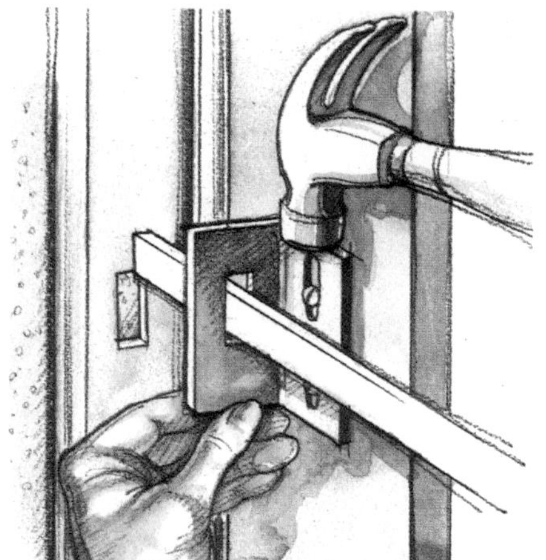

The solution is to adjust the two L-shaped guide brackets mounted to the door near the outer end of each locking bar. Loosen the screws on one bracket and use a hammer to tap it either up or down until the bar is aligned with the center of the slot. Tighten the screws, and then readjust the other guide bracket.

SAFETY FIRST

Keypad entry systems are popular and can be very convenient for you and your family. But don't let the keypad give burglars any clues to your code.

Clean the keypad periodically to remove fingerprints and smudges that might provide an advantage to someone trying to decipher your code.

QUICK TIPS

If you're away from home on an extended trip, reinforce your overhead garage door with a long-shackle padlock. Before leaving, place the padlock through the door track, just above one of the door rollers, to prevent entry.

A Little Less Noise

Automatic garage-door openers often transmit noise and vibration, especially to a room above. To reduce this problem, use the thick reinforced-rubber strap from a muffler hanger to connect the ceiling-mounted angle iron to the support for the opener motor.

Unbolt the rubber strap from the metal portion of the muffler hanger. Then cut out short sections of the opener's support straps, and bolt the rubber pieces in their place. Check the rubber connections several times a year for signs of deterioration.

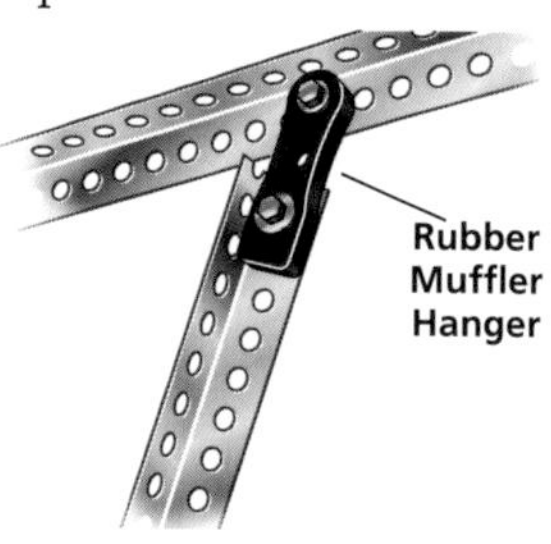

Testing Automatic Garage Doors

The National Safety Council recommends that to protect yourself and your family from garage door related injuries you should conduct the following tests each month:

Reversal Test: Federal Law requires that all garage doors manufactured since 1993 come equipped with a reversing feature. To test your reversing feature, start by opening the door. Place a 1½"-thick piece of wood on the ground directly below the center of your garage door. Push the transmitter button, and watch as the door closes. When the door makes contact with the wood block, it should immediately reverse and begin rising.

Force-Setting Test: Stand outside your garage door as it's closing, and hold the bottom of the door. If the door does not automatically reverse, the door may be exerting excessive force. Consult your owner's manual for instructions on adjusting the door's force.

Door Balance: Stand outside the door when it is closed. Activate the release mechanism by opening the door with the remote control. If the door balance is properly aligned, you should be able to lift the door without resistance, and it should stay open around three or four feet above the ground. If your door does not pass this test, have a qualified technician adjust the balance.

The variety of window styles and options seems endless. Recognizing the options simplifies repairs and makes it easier to purchase replacement parts.

Windows

The windows shown below are the most common types found in homes. Windows should match your home's architectural style and the specific needs of a room. Understanding how each type works and the window's advantages and disadvantages may help you select the most appropriate windows for a new home or choose a more practical model to replace your current windows.

Double-hung windows: These have two sash that move up and down, one behind the other. Most new double-hung windows are made so that one or both of the sash tilts in for easy cleaning. Their traditional styling makes double-hungs suitable for many homes.

Single-hung windows: These are the same as double-hung units, except the top sash doesn't move. Usually not the best choice, because they lack the flexibility of double-hungs.

Casement windows: These are hinged on one side, like a door, and operate with a crank. Look for multipoint locking, especially on tall casement windows. In bedrooms, you may need to specify optional "egress" hardware that opens the window wide enough for emergency evacuation.

Sliding windows: These units have two or more panels that slide open and overlap—like a sideways double-hung. They're durable and easy to open and close, but difficult to clean.

Awning windows: These resemble casement windows turned sideways. They're hinged at the top and open from the bottom.

Bay windows: These units are a combination of three windows that protrude from the house. The center unit is parallel to the house, while the side units sit at an angle. Bay windows make rooms seem larger, seeming to bring the outdoors into the room.

Double-Hung Window

Single-Hung Window

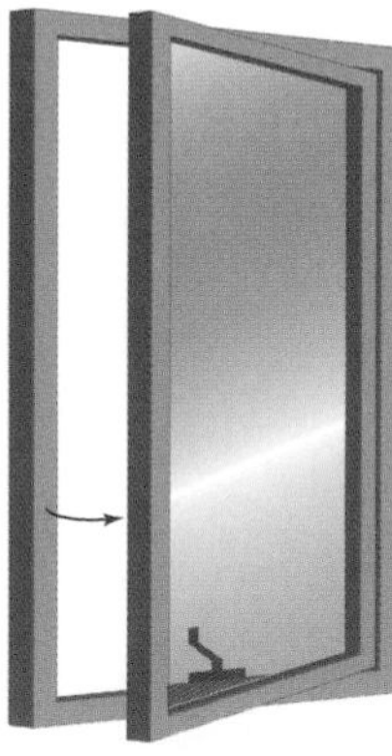

Casement Window

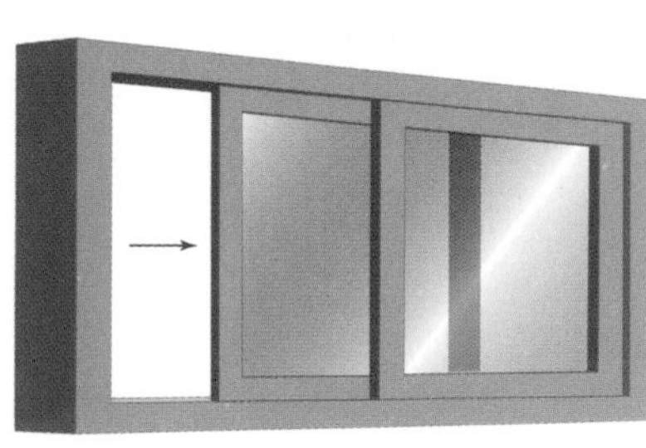

Sliding Window

Awning Window

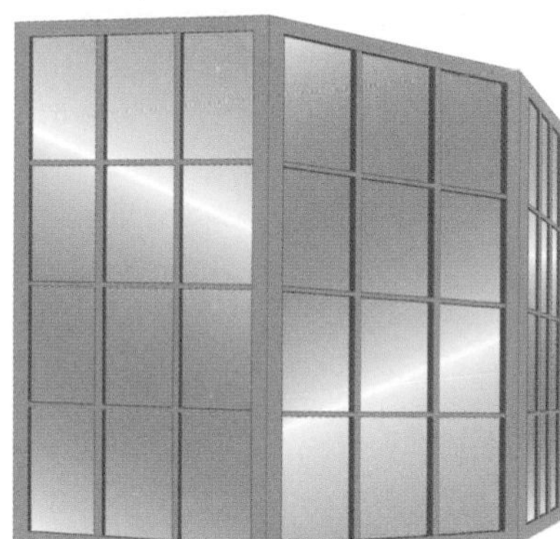

Bay Window

New Life for Old Windows

There truly is no need to put up with double-hung windows that refuse to open or that slam shut unless you prop them open. Repairing broken sash cords is easy and requires only a few basic hand tools and a pair of safety goggles.

To reach the weights, which are concealed inside the wall, you'll have to partially disassemble the window, which may chip the paint. The paint in most homes built before 1978 may contain lead, so take proper precautions.

Disassembly

Slice through the paint film with a utility knife or pizza cutter if the sash has been painted in place. Then use a thin, flat pry bar to carefully remove the wooden stops that hold the lower, interior sash in place. Tilt the window toward you, and cut any sash cords that are still attached to the window. Lift the interior sash out of the window opening, and move it to a safe place.

Pry out the parting beads—the narrow vertical strips of wood that separate the two windows. The beads fit into grooves in the side jambs, so be careful. If a parting bead does break, don't panic; they are available at most home centers and lumberyards.

With the parting beads removed, pull the upper, exterior sash from the window opening.

If the window won't budge, it's probably painted in place. Cut through the paint seal around the outside of the sash. Then, gently tap the sash with a wood block and a hammer until it's free from the frame. Remove any cords that are attached to the window, and keep these for reference.

Retrieve the sash weights inside the wall. The majority of double-hung windows have a small access panel cut into each side jamb. In most cases, you can simply remove the nail or screw holding the panel closed, reach into the wall cavity and pull out the weights.

Check the pulleys near the top of each side jamb to make sure they spin freely and aren't clogged with dust, dirt or paint. Scrape off any dried paint; then, apply a few drops of light machine oil to the pulley axles.

Replace the broken rope. Use 1/4"-diameter nylon rope, which lasts much longer than cotton cord. Tie one end piece of string to a small nail, and tie the other end to the new sash cord. Feed the new ropes over the pulleys and down into the wall cavity. Tie the rope ends to the weights; then, slip the weights back into the wall cavities.

Scrape off any dried paint and grime from the side jambs. Then sand these surfaces smooth with 100-grit sandpaper wrapped around a small wood block. If you want to paint the sashes, do it before you put them back into the frame. Do not paint the vertical edges that slide against the side jambs, however; the finish will make the sash stick and bind.

Reassembly

Apply a coat of wax to the edges of each sash. If you notice any dried paint drips or rough spots on the edges, sand them smooth.

Trim cords to size for the upper, exterior sash. Use the old cords as a reference for length. Tie knots in the sash cords, and press the knots into the holes bored in the sash edges. Be sure to locate the knots so the sash can travel freely from fully open to fully closed. If necessary, change the position of the knots to lengthen or shorten the cords.

Locate the knots, then drive a small nail directly through each of them to hold the cord in place. Reinstall the access panel or interior trim. Push the sash into the jambs, and replace the parting bead. Then install the lower, interior sash in the same way.

Replace the interior stops to hold the sash in place. The stops should be close enough to the sash to keep it from rattling but not so close that they bind the sash. Attach the stops with small wood screws or finishing nails just long enough to pass through the stop and jamb. (Long fasteners will protrude into the wall cavities and catch on the sash cords as the weights travel up and down.) Make sure that each sash slides smoothly and closes tightly.

Fast Fix for a Stubborn Sash

You can usually improve the movement of an obstinate double-hung window by widening the channels the sash slide in. The channels are formed by the vertical stop molding and parting bead (the strip located between the two sash).

First, raise or lower both sash. If the stops are thickly coated with paint, use a utility knife to score the joints where they meet the side jambs. Wearing safety goggles, hold a wood block against one of the stops and give it a few solid whacks with a hammer. Try moving the sash up and down. If it slides a little easier but is still tight, repeat this procedure on the opposite stop.

FREE A/C

Double-hung windows are designed to provide instant relief in hot summer weather. Before you race to turn on the air conditioner, try taking advantage of the efficient design of your double-hung windows.

To pull hot air out of the room and draw in a breeze, adjust the window so that the top sash is one-quarter open and the bottom sash is one-third open.

Replacing Broken Window Glass

The sound of glass breaking doesn't have to be followed by an expensive repair bill. With the advent of new glazing compounds applied with a caulk glue, it's not difficult or expensive to repair a broken window yourself.

Note: Wear heavy gloves and eye protection when working with broken glass.

To hold the broken glass in place until you're ready to remove it, put strips of masking tape across the window.

Measure the window opening, and order new glass from a hardware store (to allow expansion space, the replacement glass should measure 1/4" less in each direction than the actual opening).

If you're repairing a spring-loaded, double-hung window, remove the sash by pushing against the flexible vinyl channels to release the channel pins. Then pry out the vinyl glazing strips. If you're working with an older double-hung, you can repair the glass with the sash in place.

Use a heat gun or torch to soften the glazing compound; then, scrape it away with a putty knife.

Remove the broken glass and metal glazing points from the frame; then, scrape the L-shaped grooves to clean away old paint and putty. Coat the bare wood with sealer, and let it dry.

Apply a thin layer of glazing compound in the primed grooves. Press glass lightly to bed it. Press in new glazing points every 10 inches with the tip of the putty knife.

Apply glazing compound. Move the tube tip along the edge of the glass while steadily squeezing the trigger. Smooth the glazing compound with a damp cloth.

Paint the sash when the glazing compound is dry, overlapping the paint onto the glass by 1/16".

Securing Doors & Windows

Research shows that most burglars are willing to work no longer than 60 seconds to break into a home. Therefore, homeowners who fortify their doors and windows greatly reduce the risk of being burglarized. Try these suggestions.

Exterior Doors	Select solid hardwood or steel doors with peepholes. Fit exterior doors with dead bolts that have a full one-inch throw and three-inch-long strike plate screws.
Garage Door	Install a separate keyed lock; don't rely on an automatic garage-door opener for security. If you're away for an extended time, place a padlock through the door track, just above one of the door rollers, to prevent entry. Any time you're away overnight, secure the door leading from an attached garage into the house with a padlock and hasp.
Sliding Patio Doors	Install a keyed lock or security bar on each patio door.
Windows	Install a lock on every window. Consider keyed locks—some varieties let you open windows for ventilation.

Beautiful Thresholds

Oak thresholds for exterior doors often suffer from heavy use and exposure to the elements, but a periodic bath in linseed oil will protect them.

Strip or sand the threshold. Saturate the wood with boiled linseed oil, and let it sit for about 30 minutes. Wipe the linseed oil away, and let the wood dry completely. Another option is to apply several coats of exterior polyurethane to the threshold.

A Recipe for Clean Windows

To make an effective window cleaner, add a half cup of ammonia, one cup of white vinegar and two tablespoons of cornstarch to one gallon of warm water.

Wait for a cloudy day to wash your windows. On sunny days you'll fight streaks because the cleaner dries before you can shine the glass.

A Little Dab'll Do Ya

Here are two quick fixes for screens that have holes and tears less than 1/2" in diameter.

- Start by using a darning needle or ice pick to pull the wires back into place as much as possible. Apply clear fingernail polish or clear acrylic glue in layers until the hole is solidly covered. Give each layer time to dry before adding the next one.
- Cut a small patch and place it over the torn area. Use acrylic glue or clear fingernail polish to secure the edges of the patch to the screen.

The Mystery Unfolds

To keep bifold doors working smoothly, clean and lubricate them. Open or remove the doors, and wipe the tracks with a clean rag; then, spray the track and rollers with silicone spray.

To align the doors, adjust the pivot blocks with a screwdriver or wrench until the gap between the closed doors is even. Pivot blocks are commonly found at the top of the door but may be located at the bottom of some doors.

Maintaining Crank-Operated Windows

Most problems with crank-operated windows center around the crank and track. Simple maintenance will help keep problems at bay.

To keep the track clean, open the window and disengage the sliding arm. Clean the track and arm with rubbing alcohol and a cotton swab.

Maintain crank-operated windows by lubricating the crank, extension arm joints and track with silicone spray. Work the crank by opening and closing the window until the spray has penetrated completely.

QUICK TIPS

To dust louvered doors, wrap a cloth around a ruler and run the flat side along each louver.

Rub a candle or block of paraffin wax along the tracks of double-hung windows to make them slide more easily.

To free a window that is painted shut without damaging the sash or sill, run a utility knife or paint zipper tool along the groove between the sash and the sill and along the sash channels until the sealed paint is broken.

SCREEN REPAIR

If a screen has been damaged by a large hole or tear, simply replace the screen in the original frame.

Use a screwdriver to pry the vinyl spline from the grooves around the edge of the frame. Save the old spline if it is still flexible, or replace it if necessary. Stretch the new screen fabric tightly over the frame so that it overlaps the retaining grooves. Use a spline roller (available at hardware stores) to press the spline and screen into the grooves. Cut away excess screen fabric with a utility knife.

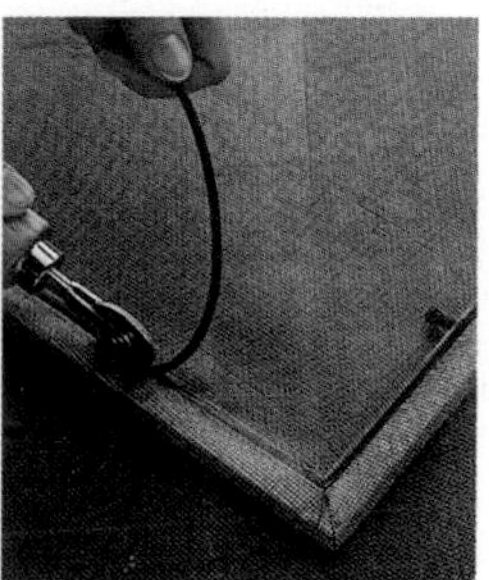

Walls & Floors

Well-built, well-maintained walls and floors define the boundaries of a room. They also conserve energy, muffle sound and create an attractive atmosphere.

Although the basic framing style of walls and floors is usually consistent within a home, the wall and floor coverings vary widely from room to room. From ceramic tile bathroom walls to fabric-draped bedroom walls, painted drywall to plaster, each type of wallcovering has a specific look and purpose.

Floor coverings also vary throughout a house, usually coordinating with each room's specific use and traffic patterns. From durable hardwood to elegant stone or comfortable carpeting, floor coverings set the tone and provide color, style and a backdrop for the room's furnishings and activities.

Due to the heavy traffic of everyday living, walls and floors can really take a beating. Occasional accidents also leave their marks. As your home ages, cracked walls, damaged corners and marred or squeaking floors become common problems. If left unaddressed, these ailments can lead to structural troubles and expensive repairs.

Fortunately, caring for and repairing your walls and floors involve tasks you can easily tackle. By arming yourself with the following tips and techniques, you can ensure the beauty and function of your walls and floors for years to come.

Helpful Terms

Corner bead: The metal strips used to reinforce exterior drywall corners

Insulation: Material used in walls and floors to limit the transmission of thermal energy or sound

Joint compound: A plasterlike substance used to smooth the surface of drywall joints

Joist: A horizontal piece of lumber used to support a ceiling or floor

Mastic: An adhesive compound used for securing tiles and paneling

Stud: A vertical framing member, usually made of wood or steel, used in framing walls

Tongue and groove: A style of flooring in which neighboring strips interlock as the grooved edge of one board accepts the protruding tongue of the next

Vapor barrier: Material used to discourage moisture flow from a home's interior into exterior walls where it can condense

Wall Crack Cover-Up

Hairline cracks that appear above windows and doors are caused by framing lumber that dries out and shrinks, or by settling of the structure. Although the fractures are small, they can be persistent; simply spackling over trouble spots seldom hides them for long.

For a more permanent repair, scratch along the crack with the pointed tip of a can opener. Hold the tip at a slight angle to undercut and widen the crack.

Cover the crack with strips of adhesive-backed fibermesh wallboard tape.

Next, spread a thick coat of joint compound over the taped crack with a 4"-wide putty knife.

To even the surface, let the compound dry completely; then, sand it lightly. Apply at least two more coats of joint compound, feathering each one slightly to blend it into the surface of the wall. Paint the surface once the compound dries completely.

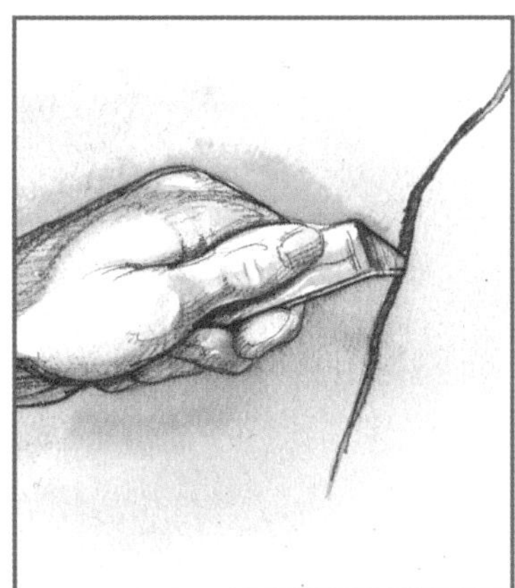

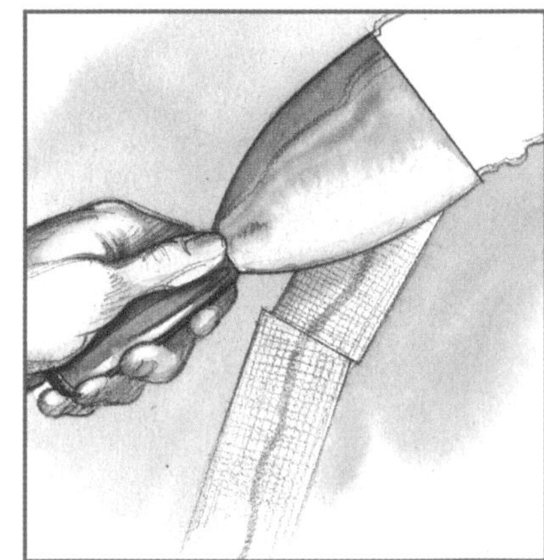

It's in the Bag

To fill holes in drywall finished with textured paint, fill a small, resealable zipper-style plastic bag with joint compound. Snip off one corner of the bag with a pair of scissors. Then place the cut corner over the hole in the ceiling or wall and squeeze the bag to deliver precisely the right amount of compound.

TOOL BOX

Tools used for joint taping can rust easily if they aren't properly cleaned. To protect these tools, wash and dry them thoroughly. Then spray all the metal parts with an all-purpose metal lubricant, such as WD-40. The lubricant will also make the tools easier to clean after the next use.

BATTLE OF THE BULGE

You've seen it—that ugly bulge caused when a nail "pops" from a wall. You can hammer the nail back in and spackle over it, but inevitably, the nail will loosen up and pop again. For a permanent fix, make repairs with wallboard screws, which have threaded shanks that resist popping.

Lean against the wall to press the drywall tightly against the stud or joist. Drive a 5⁄8" screw about two inches away from the popped nail. The screwhead should be indented slightly but should not tear through the paper surface.

Pound in the popped nail, leaving a slight indentation. Fill the dents with taping compound. Let compound dry; then, repaint.

Use a wide-blade putty knife to apply two or three coats of spackling compound over the fasteners. Allow each coat to dry completely before spreading the next. When the last coat is dry, lightly sand the patch with fine sandpaper. Then prime and paint the repair to match the rest of the wall.

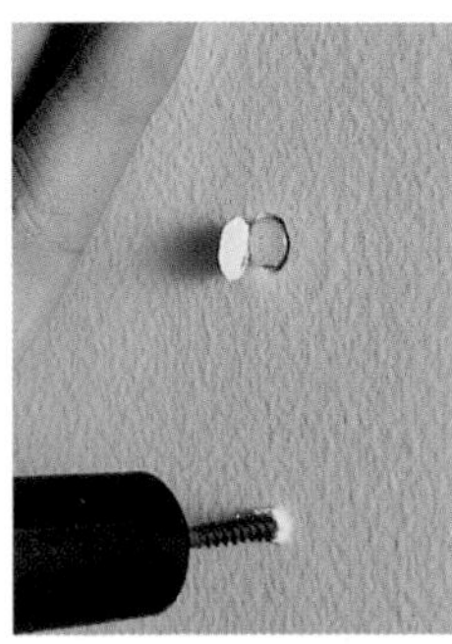

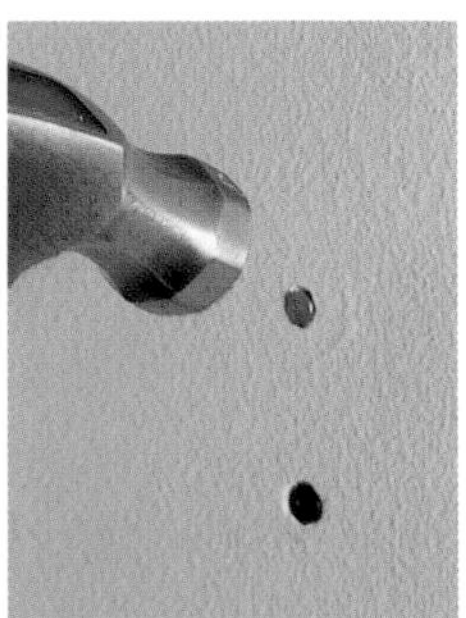

Chip Off the Old Block

Chips along the edge of the outside corners of drywall or plaster walls look shabby, and paint alone will not fill them. Luckily, it's not hard to rebuild a corner with joint compound.

Use coarse sandpaper to rough up the damaged surface on each side of the corner. Brush away any dust or chips, and dampen the area with a wet sponge.

Next, hold a flat piece of plastic or wood against one side of the corner while you apply joint compound to the other side, using the guide to form a precise edge.

Continue adding thin coats of joint compound until the damaged area is flush with the surrounding wall. Sand between coats, and seal the patch with primer before painting.

How Dry Is Dry Enough?

Applying paint before wall repairs are completely dry is a sure path to paint failure. Here's an easy way to make sure plaster repairs are ready to be painted:

Tape a square of plastic over the area. After 24 hours, remove the plastic and check for signs of moisture. If you detect dampness, wait another day, and retest.

When the plaster is completely dry, prime and paint the area.

QUICK TIPS

When filling holes or dents in drywall, you can reduce the sanding required by rubbing the dried joint compound with a damp towel or sponge. The texture created will help blend the patch into the rest of the wall.

Dip screws in water before you drive them into a plaster wall. The damp plaster sets up around the screws and holds them firmly in place.

Just Around the Corner

If a wallboard corner is so badly bruised that the metal corner bead is damaged, your best option is to cut out and replace the damaged section.

Begin by chipping out the area with a chisel to expose the metal corner bead. Use a hacksaw to cut through the bead a few inches above and below the damage. Then remove the nails or screws and pull out the damaged section.

Use tin snips to cut a replacement section from a new piece of metal bead. To avoid flattening the bead, make a cut from each outer edge toward the center spine; then, bend the new section back and forth to snap it off cleanly. Fasten the new piece with wallboard screws, making sure it aligns with the existing corner bead. Use a file to smooth out any roughness across the joints where the new corner bead meets the old one.

Apply three coats of joint compound over the repair with a 6" taping knife, allowing the compound to dry between coats. Lightly sand each coat; then, prime and paint the new bead to match the walls.

Let Your Light Shine

It's tough to avoid ridges and depressions when applying joint compound to an outside corner. Next time you're in doubt, try this simple trick:

Position a bright light so it shines up toward the wall. Hold a straightedge horizontally across the drywall surface. If you can see light between the straight-edge and the corner's edge, add joint compound, or sand to feather the edges of the patch.

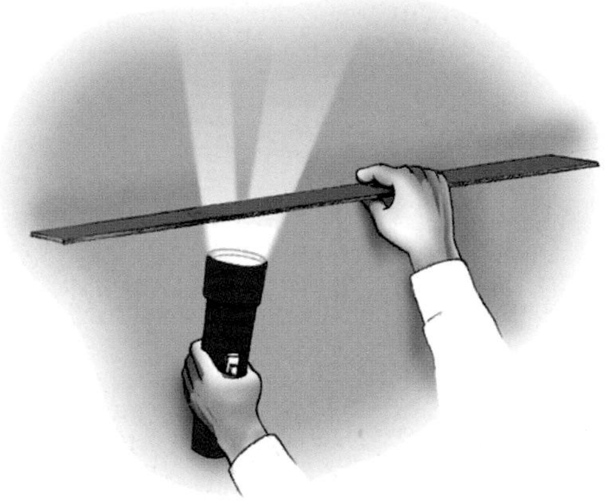

SPRAY STAINS AWAY

Water-stained ceilings really mar the appearance of a room, but textured ceilings are notoriously difficult to paint. If scraping and retexturing are not appealing options, try this first:

Fill a spray bottle with a solution of 6 parts water to 4 parts bleach. Cover the floor and furnishings with old sheets or tarps. Spray the stain thoroughly, but do not saturate the area. It's much better to reapply the solution several times than to get the ceiling so wet that the texture separates or drips off the ceiling.

If the stain is still visible after several applications of bleach, it probably will not respond to additional applications. But, all is not yet lost. Buy some stain-killing primer, and try the spray method again. Be sure to protect the surrounding area: if the mist drifts onto furniture and flooring, it will permanently stain them.

Spray the primer in a circular pattern and keep moving out until you're about a foot from the original spot. If you feather out the painted edges, the primer should blend right in with the ceiling.

If you're adding a door, window or light fixture, plan carefully before cutting into walls or ceilings.

Turn off power to nearby circuits, or the entire house. If water-supply pipes run through the area, close the main supply valve.

Drill small holes and look for wires, pipes and insulation so that you can work around them.

Use only double-insulated tools and grounded outlets when cutting or drilling into walls.

Save the Ceiling

If a leak or plumbing disaster has sent water cascading into the space above a drywall ceiling, you can save the ceiling with some well-placed holes.

The first step is to close the water-supply valve or find and stop the leak. The next step is to remove the standing water from above the ceiling.

Cover the surrounding area with tarps, and position a bucket to catch drips. Working in a circle out from the center of the water-damaged area, use an ice pick or awl to make as many holes as seem necessary. Don't use a corded power tool for this—electricity and water just don't mix. Let the ceiling dry completely; then, fill and repair the holes.

Curtain Call

Next time you're building new exterior walls or framing existing ones, add blocking to each side of the window openings to provide solid backing for attaching curtains, valances and other window treatments.

Cut each block from a 2 × 10 or 2 × 12, and nail it between studs just below the top plate at each end of the header. Be sure the face of the block is flush with the inside edge of the wall studs. This same technique can also be used to provide fastening support for shelving brackets, towel racks, shower grab bars and many other wall-mounted accessories.

No Harm Done

Pulling baseboard molding off any wall without damaging the wall or splitting the molding is a challenge.

To minimize the risk, first insert two stiff-bladed putty knives between the wall and the molding. Then drive a thin pry bar between the two knives. Pull back on the bar, and slip a wood shim into the gap behind the molding. Remove the pry bar and putty knives, move down a couple of feet and repeat the process. Keep going until the molding breaks free from the wall.

If you plan to reinstall the molding, number each section as you remove it.

When nailing up moldings and other thin material, bore a pilot hole first to help prevent splits, especially when nailing near the ends of boards.

If you don't have a small drill bit, insert a finishing nail into your drill chuck—it will bore perfect-size pilot holes.

To keep from bending the nail, avoid putting too much pressure on the drill as you're working.

Hanging Fixtures on a Ceramic Tile Wall

Many people would like to have a grab bar near the tub or another towel bar near the sink but don't feel confident drilling into a ceramic tile wall. There's no need to hesitate—it's not as difficult as it might seem.

Start by placing masking tape over the spot where you want to drill the hole. Bore a hole for a masonry anchor, using a carbide masonry bit that matches the diameter of the anchor and a 3/8" variable-speed drill. Use low drill speed to ensure that the bit does not skip on the tile.

Use a hammer to gently tap a plastic or lead masonry anchor plug into the hole; then, use a screw to attach the fixture.

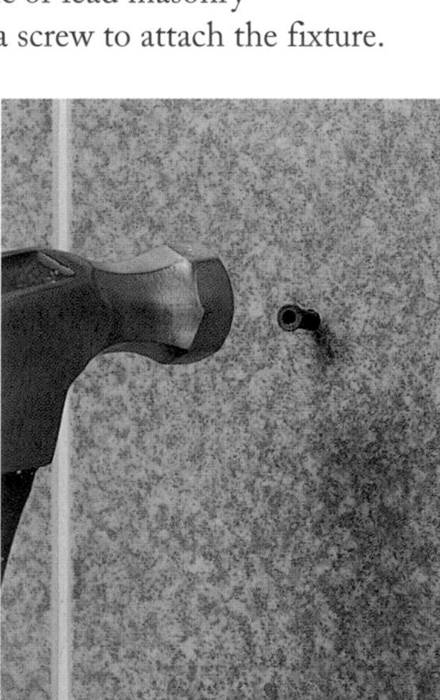

If you don't have a stud finder, you can locate studs by running an electric razor along the wall. The tone of the razor's buzz will change when you pass over a stud.

When you patch small holes in colored walls, the white of the spackle can stick out like a sore thumb. To mask your repairs, mix water-based paint with spackle and apply it with a fine-point paintbrush.

When purchasing wallpaper, make sure all rolls have the same lot number. This number, stamped on the label, indicates when the paper was printed. The consistency of the dye and patterns can vary from lot to lot.

Sizing Up a Room

The following formulas will help determine how much wallpaper to buy for a room:

- Measure the room's perimeter (Example: 20'+20'+15'+15' = 70').
- Multiply the perimeter footage by the ceiling height (Example: 70' × 8' ceiling height = 560 sq. ft.).
- Calculate the area of the windows and doors (Example: 2 standard windows = 30 sq. ft.; 1 standard door = 21 sq. ft.).
- Subtract the total measurement of the windows and doors from the square footage (Example: 560 - 51 = 509 sq. ft.).
- Divide this number by 25, the standard square footage of a single roll of wallpaper, to get the total number of rolls needed (Example: 509 ÷ 25 = approximately 21 rolls).

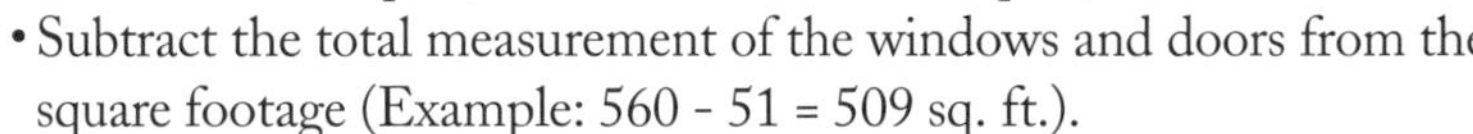

A Gentle Approach

Stripping wallpaper can be a very unpleasant task. Steamers are unwieldy and chemical strippers are messy. Next time you want to remove wallpaper, try this simple plan:

First, use a zipper tool to cut into the surface of the paper. Next, mix one capful of liquid fabric softener to one gallon of hot water. Roll this solution onto the wall with a paint roller and let it soak for 20 to 25 minutes. Grab a corner and pull—the paper surrenders without a fight.

Patching Wallpaper

A stain that won't wash away or a minor tear that can't be mended doesn't mean you have to replace an entire section of wallpaper. It's possible to patch a small area in such a way that it's hardly noticeable. Try this:

Using removable tape, place a matching piece of wallpaper over the damaged portion of the wall. Align pattern exactly with existing wallpaper.

Cut through both layers of wallpaper with a sharp knife. Remove the patch, then apply water to the area of the damaged wallpaper.

Peel the damaged section away from the wall. Apply adhesive to the back of the patch and position it so that the cut edges match exactly.

Exercise caution when using a wallpaper steamer. Steam is hotter than boiling water, and the condensation that often drips from the steam plate is very hot as well.

Be aware that steam burns happen quickly. Protect yourself with long sleeves, heavy pants and shoes, thick gloves and goggles.

Assessing the Damage

How you repair vinyl flooring depends on what kind of flooring you have and how it's damaged. With vinyl tile, the best approach is simply to replace marred tiles. With sheet vinyl, repairing damage requires fusing the surface or patching in new material.

Small cuts and scratches can be fused permanently and nearly invisibly with liquid seam sealer, a clear compound that's available wherever vinyl flooring is sold. To begin, dip a soft cloth in lacquer thinner and clean the area. When the area is dry, squeeze a thin bead of sealer into the cut or scratch.

For tears or burns, you'll have to cut out the damaged area and glue in a replacement patch; this type of work requires an extra piece of identical flooring and a technique called double-cutting (see tip below). Installers often leave a few scrap pieces behind for just such an emergency. If you don't have scraps—and if the style of flooring isn't too old—you might find an identical piece at a flooring dealer. You can also lift a piece of vinyl from inside a closet, under the refrigerator or from some other inconspicuous location.

Patching Sheet Vinyl

To repair flooring using the double-cutting technique, start by taping the replacement patch over the damaged area. Be sure to position the patch so that its pattern aligns exactly with the pattern in the area. Place a straightedge (a steel rule or framing square works well) on top of the patch, centered on one of the pattern lines. Then use a utility knife to cut along the straightedge through both the patch and the flooring. For best results, use a new blade and hold the knife in a vertical position. Make the remaining cuts around the patch in the same way, cutting along the pattern lines.

Next, remove the patch and peel up the damaged section. If your floor is perimeter-bonded, the piece will come up easily because it isn't glued down. If it's fully adhered, scrape up the piece with a putty knife or scraper. Then spread mastic onto the plywood subfloor with a notched trowel. On perimeter-bonded floors, lift up the flooring around the cutout and spread mastic under the edges. Then press the patch into place, cover it with wax paper and weigh it down with a few heavy books. Wait at least 24 hours for the mastic to dry. Apply liquid seam sealer to all the joints around the patch. The repair will be nearly undetectable.

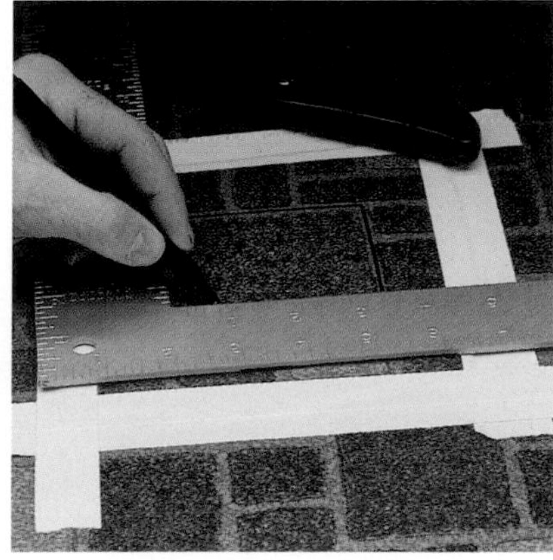

QUICK TIPS

A gouge in a vinyl floor is much easier to repair than most people think.

Shred a scrap of the vinyl with a food grater. Add clear acrylic glue or shellac to the shreds until the mixture forms a paste.

Work this paste into the gouge until it is flush with the surface.

Don't place a padded area rug directly on top of a vinyl floor, particularly in a sunny area. Carpet padding often contains petroleum products that sometimes leave indelible stains on vinyl.

Undercover Work

If you're considering replacing a floor covering, the first step is to determine the number and type of coverings already on the floor. Too many layers of floor covering and underlayments can stress floor joists and ultimately cause a new floor to fail.

An easy way to expose the anatomy of your existing floor is to remove floor vents or registers. Pry up the top layers of flooring to determine how many layers exist and exactly what materials are currently underfoot.

High thresholds are another clue that several layers of flooring have already been installed on top of one another. If you discover several layers, remove them before installing new floor coverings.

Recoating a Vinyl Floor

Even the best vinyl floors eventually begin to show signs of wear. In the kitchen, high-traffic areas wear first, including the areas in front of the sink or stove or around a seating area. Signs of wear include dullness, scratches and dirt that won't come off with normal cleaning.

You can restore shine to the floor by stripping and then recoating it with an acrylic polish. Working in small sections, use a commercial floor stripper to remove the old finish. Use a nylon pad and a buffer to easily remove ground-in dirt. Mop the whole floor and rinse it twice. When the floor is dry, fill small nicks or gouges with latex filler.

Recoat the floor with an acrylic polish. In high traffic areas or areas that are very worn, you'll need two coats. Let the first coat dry overnight; then, apply the second coat.

To make the finish last longer, reduce the amount of wear and tear the floor is subjected to: sweep often, place throw rugs in all doorways and put floor protectors on chair and table legs.

SAFETY FIRST

Resilient flooring manufactured before 1986 sometimes contained asbestos, which can cause severe lung problems if inhaled repeatedly. If you suspect your flooring may contain asbestos, do not attempt to remove it yourself. Consult a certified asbestos-abatement contractor.

Cut to the Quick

Putting down a new floor? You may have to trim the door casings so the new floor fits beneath. Here's how professional remodelers do it:

Place a tile or floorboard upside down in front of the casing as a thickness gauge. Then lay a handsaw on top of the flooring material and trim off the bottom of the casing. Turning the flooring upside down keeps the saw teeth from scratching it.

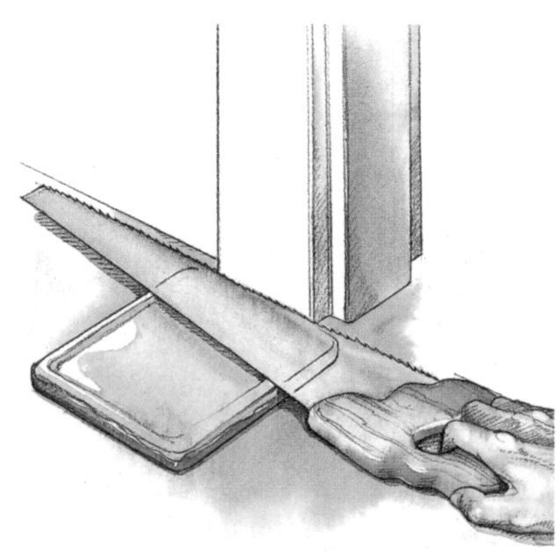

Eliminating Floor Squeaks

Floor squeaks—random, elusive and annoying—are one of the most common complaints among homeowners.

Understanding what causes the squeak is the first step in fixing it. Squeaks occur when two pieces of loose flooring rub together or when the subfloor slides up and down on a nail. This kind of movement is possible because even "dry" lumber loses moisture in its first few years in a house. As wood dries, it shrinks, mostly across the grain—enough to cause gaps between a joist and the subfloor. When someone steps on such a spot, the subfloor slides on the nail, causing a squeak.

When you're able to attack the problem from below, you can use special hardware that pulls the subfloor tight against the joist. But if the squeak is in a second-story floor, using that hardware would mean cutting open the first-level ceiling.

In this case, you're limited to locating the joists with a stud finder and driving new nails or screws. Many hardware or flooring stores carry a tool designed to help you drive a screw from above and then break the head off just below the surface of carpeted floors.

For a hardwood floor, no special device is available or necessary. To secure the squeaky floor, predrill the board and use a ring-shank nail to hold the subfloor down. Drive the nail through the floor and subfloor and at least one inch into the joist. Hide the nail hole by filling it with matching wood filler.

You can also counterbore a flat-head wood screw. The hole for the screw shank should be at least one size too large—if you're using a #8 screw, for example, make a shank hole sized for a #10. The extra space allows the wood to move as it expands and contracts with changes in moisture. Fill the counterbore with a matching wood plug.

Squeaks near the surface may be caused by one floorboard rubbing against another. Try dance-floor wax, available from amusement companies. Work the powdered wax into the gaps between the boards. This wax won't stop any of the wood's movement, but it often stops the noise.

PROBLEM
Hardwood Flooring
Plywood Subfloor
Gap Due to Shrinkage
Joist
Nail Stays Put
Floor Moves Against Nail
SOLUTION
Ring-Shanked Nail
Flat-Head Wood Screw
Oversized Bore

How to Make a Slip-Notch

With the variety of tools and materials available today, more and more homeowners are laying their own hardwood floors. Many people are even adding patterns and borders to their flooring projects.

Those patterns and borders pose a special problem. When you change the direction of flooring strips to vary the pattern or introduce a border, you may lose the tongue-and-groove matchups that hold the flooring strips together. To compensate, you'll need to cut new grooves in the board edges and then make splines from 1/8"-thick plywood.

To join two boards, apply glue in the new grooves, slip in the spline and then edge-join the two mating boards as shown in the illustration at right.

In a border made up of many small pieces in the corner, it's best to glue the pieces together first and then lay them as a unit.

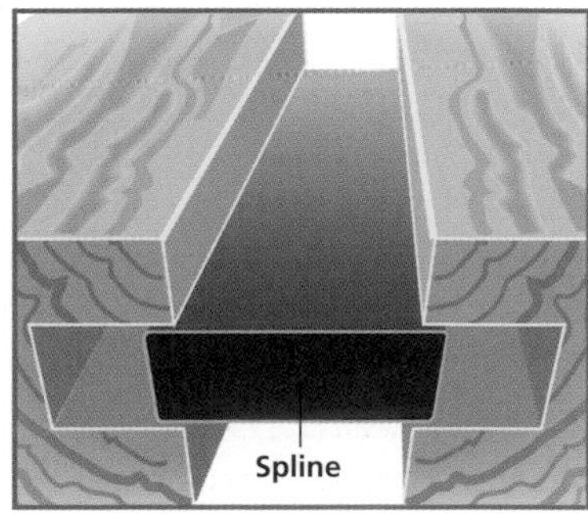

Human skin contains natural oils, so walking barefoot leaves traces of oil that can attract dirt to your carpets. To keep carpets fresh, wear socks, slippers or clean shoes indoors.

Firm Foundation

When comparing carpets, examine the backing or foundation. A tighter grid pattern usually indicates dense-pile carpet that will be more durable and soil-resistant than a carpet that has a looser grid pattern.

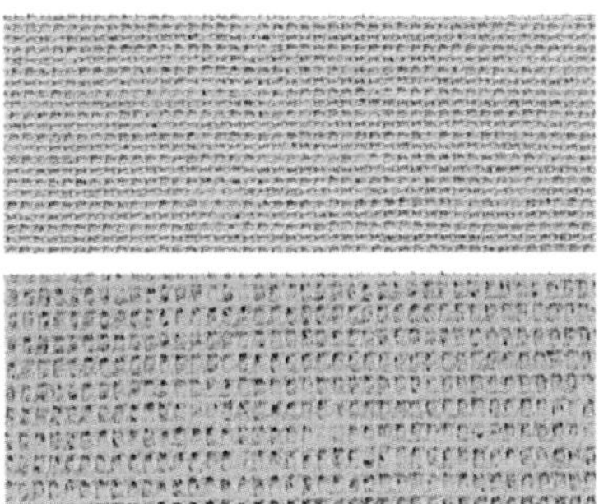

Selecting Carpet

When selecting carpet for your home, you need to consider more than just color and pattern. The material used in the carpet can affect its durability.

In high-traffic areas, such as hallways, choosing a top quality fiber will result in longer wear. The construction of the carpet can affect both its durability and appearance. Even the width of the roll can influence your decision. If you're carpeting a 14-foot-wide room, for example, you may want to choose a 15-foot-wide carpet to eliminate the need for seaming.

Perfect-Match Carpet Patch

You don't have to try to camouflage burns or stains in your carpeting with strategically placed furniture. Replacing small areas is fairly simple.

To begin, place a "cookie cutter" tool over the damaged area, press down and twist until you have cut through the carpet but not the padding. Next, cut a replacement patch from a leftover carpet swatch or from an inconspicuous place, such as inside a closet.

Insert double-face carpet tape under the carpet. Position the tape so that it will stick to both the existing carpet and the patch.

Press the patch into place, making sure the nap or pattern matches the existing carpet. Seal the seam with seam adhesive to prevent unraveling.

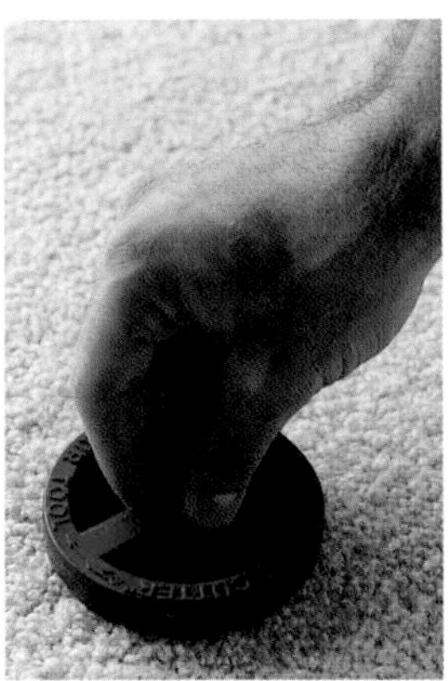

Fiber Type Characteristics	
Nylon	Easy to clean, very durable, good stain resistance; colors sometimes fade in direct sunlight
Polyester	Excellent stain resistance, very soft in thick cut-pile constructions; colors don't fade in sunlight
Olefin	Virtually stain- and fadeproof, resists moisture and static; not as resilient as nylon or as soft as polyester
Acrylic	Resembles wool in softness and look; good moisture resistance; less durable than other synthetics
Wool	Luxurious look and feel, good durability and warmth; more costly and less stain-resistant than synthetics

Coming Clean on Asphalt

Walk across an asphalt driveway on a hot, sunny day, and you'll end up with asphalt on the soles of your shoes. Often you don't see it until you go inside and track it all over the vinyl floor in the kitchen. Fortunately, you can remove most asphalt stains without destroying the flooring.

To remove such stains, first wet a white rag with mineral spirits or household bleach. Place the rag on the stain; then lay a piece of plastic (a bag will do) over the rag to slow evaporation. Leave the rag there for an hour or two. You should then be able to wipe up the stain.

Note: Before putting any solvent on a vinyl floor, get a recommendation from the manufacturer or a retailer. Always test solvents in an out-of-the-way spot first.

Carpet Cleanup

Keeping wall-to-wall carpeting and area rugs clean is an ongoing battle, but this tip can help.

Ordinary glass cleaner removes most stubborn stains from all types of carpeting. Spray the stained area liberally and allow it to soak in for 6-10 minutes, then blot the area with a paper towel. If necessary, repeat the treatment. For extra-tough stains, use a small scrap piece of carpeting as a brush to scrub the area.

Shockingly Simple

Tired of being zapped? Try this trick to defeat static electricity. Pour five parts water and one part liquid fabric softener into an empty pump-spray bottle. Apply a light mist of the solution onto the carpeting as you back out of the room. Try not to miss any areas and pay particular attention to the most frequently walked paths through the room.

Wait about five minutes before returning. Static shocks will be far less frequent.

WALL CLEANER RECIPE

To make a great wall cleaner, add ½ cup ammonia, ¼ cup white vinegar, and ¼ cup baking soda to 1 gallon of warm water. Use this solution to wash walls from the bottom up.

Try using old sports socks as mitts for washing wood moldings and trims. When washing rough plaster walls, sponges leave small fragments behind and rags can leave lint and threads. Use light-colored nylon socks instead.

QUICK TIPS

To remove coffee or fruit juice stains from vinyl flooring, mix one part glycerine to three parts water. Soak a cloth in this mixture and place it over the stain for several hours. Wash and rinse the area thoroughly.

If you spill nail polish on resilient flooring, don't try to clean it with nail polish remover—it can eat into the floor. Try a little scouring powder or steel wool.

Rubbing alcohol removes ink from many surfaces. To clean ink from walls or floors, dip a cotton swab in the alcohol and carefully dab the spot (don't rub), trying to lift as much ink as possible.

Removing Spot's Spots

Anyone who has a pet knows that accidents sometimes happen. Quick cleanup avoids more serious problems, but even conscientious pet owners can find their hardwood floors stained.

A dose of wood bleach followed by a new finish can fix a urine-stained wood floor.

If the floor has been saturated for a long time, the only solution may be to cut out and replace the affected sections.

Appliances

The fast pace of today's lifestyle is made possible, in part, by modern appliances. They bring simplicity, speed and convenience to our lives.

Over just the past few years, the number of single-parent families in the United States has increased by more than 20 percent. And in more than half of two-parent families, both parents worked outside the home, according to the U.S. Bureau of Labor Statistics. The work of maintaining a home and family hasn't changed very much over the years, but the time available to do the work has decreased radically.

Appliances play a major part in helping families survive today's whirlwind of activity. Refrigerators deliver chilled water and ice cubes to anyone tall enough to reach the center of the door. Freezers hold precooked dinners that can be microwaved in minutes as each family member finds time to eat. Timing devices on ovens allow tonight's cook to start dinner while commuting. Even laundry has been simplified. It's rarely necessary to hand-wash clothing—washers and dryers have special cycles for nearly every washable fabric.

We depend on the convenience our appliances offer, so it's important to know how to use and maintain them so that they work as well and as long as possible.

Domestic Appliance Manufacturers

Amana Refrigeration:
Amana: (800) 843-0304
www.amana.com

Frigidaire Home Products:
Frigidaire: (800) 944-9044
www.frigidaire.com
Gibson: (800) 458-1445
Tappan: (800) 685-6005
White-Westinghouse:
(800) 685-6005

General Electric Appliances:
Hotpoint
RCA Appliance
(800) 626-2000
www.ge.com/appliances

Maytag:
Admiral: (800) 688-9920
Jenn-Air: (800) 688-1100
www.jennair.com
Magic Chef: (800) 688-1120
Maytag: (800) 688-9900
www.maytag.com

Whirlpool Corp.:
Estate (Sam's Club)
(800) 253-1301
www.estateappliances.com
Kitchen Aid: (800) 422-1230
www.kitchenaid.com
Roper: (800) 447-6737
www.roperappliances.com
Whirlpool: (800) 253-1301
www.whirlpool.com
Kenmore (Sears):
(800) 927-7957

dishwashers

I'LL TAKE DOOR #2

If you've remodeled your kitchen and want to change the color of your dishwasher, don't go shopping until you've done a little investigation.

You may have one or more colored replacement panels hidden in your dishwasher. Some door panels are a different color on the back side, and some dishwashers come with an extra panel hidden behind the door. This can give you as many as four color choices.

If your dishwasher does not have extra panels or if none of them matches your new color scheme, take the panel to an auto-body shop and have it repainted.

Be sure to take some samples from your new decor to use as a color guide.

High and Dry

When a dishwasher seems to be working but the dishes aren't getting clean enough, it's time to check out your dishwasher detergent.

When powdered dishwasher detergent absorbs moisture, it loses some of its cleaning ability. Store detergent in an airtight container in a cool, dry place. And don't buy the giant economy size unless you will use it quickly. Dishwasher detergent begins to lose its effectiveness within two weeks of being opened.

If a dishwasher or other electrical appliance develops a leak and is surrounded by standing water, don't step into the water to fix it. Instead, go to the service panel and turn off the circuit.

After the electricity is off, close the water-supply shutoff valve for the appliance or the main shutoff valve located near the water meter.

Efficient Dishwashing

No one likes to scratch dried food off of dishes that have just come out of the dishwasher. Here are some strategies to help get your dishes clean the first time.

- Don't block spray arms or detergent cups with dishes. Leave space between items so the water can circulate.
- Clean the drains regularly.
- Level the dishwasher and make sure it's stable.

Sounding Off

Do you put off starting the dishwasher because you don't want to listen to the noise? Here are a few simple ways to reduce the amount of noise a dishwasher generates.

If your kitchen is on a concrete slab rather than on a wood floor, set the dishwasher on a piece of indoor-outdoor carpet to absorb sound.

Make sure the water and waste lines don't rest against the dishwasher—they can act as conduits for noise and vibration.

If you're installing a new unit, position it between cabinets rather than at the end of a row. Leave the smallest gap possible without letting the dishwasher touch the adjoining cabinets.

While You Were Away...

Any time you don't use hot water for two weeks or longer, hydrogen gas can build up in your water heater and hot-water pipes. Introducing hydrogen gas into an appliance with a heating element—a dishwasher, for example—could cause an explosion.

If you've been away from home for a while, open the hot water taps throughout the house and let the water run for several minutes before using the dishwasher or any appliance connected to hot water.

Open several windows, and don't smoke or light any flame while the water is running.

Too Cool to Cool

If your winter plans include a long absence from home, your refrigerator needs attention before you leave home.

If you expect the indoor air temperature to fall below 60°F while you're away, the refrigerator needs to be emptied and cleaned. Below 60°F, the compressor does not run often enough to keep frost-free freezers cold, and below 40°F, it does not run at all.

The odor of spoiled food can permeate a refrigerator so completely that it has to be discarded, so don't take chances. Remove all the food and unplug the unit. Clean and dry both the refrigerator and freezer compartments. If the unit has a water dispenser, turn off the water and drain the tank as directed by the manufacturer.

Finally, block the door open so that air can circulate.

Odor Eaters

If the smell of spoiled food has overpowered your refrigerator or freezer, try these ideas.

Remove all contents and wash the walls and door with dish detergent and warm water. Rinse with a solution of $\frac{1}{4}$ cup of baking soda dissolved in half a gallon of warm water. Block the door open, and position a fan to blow fresh air into the refrigerator overnight.

Fill shallow dishes or pans with activated charcoal, and place several on each shelf. Run the empty refrigerator on low for a few days to give the charcoal time to absorb the odors.

Place a shallow saucer filled with imitation vanilla on each shelf. Run the empty refrigerator on low for a few days.

Loosely wad up sections of newspaper, and sprinkle them with water. Place these bundles in the refrigerator, close the door, and let it run undisturbed for five or six days.

Good Circulation

Although most people's first instinct is to adjust the thermostat if the refrigerator isn't keeping food cold enough, temperature isn't always the problem. Sometimes the refrigerator is just too full.

Cold air must circulate freely within a refrigerator in order to keep food cold. So, throw away foods that are past their prime, and resist the urge to cram containers into every available space. Food will stay colder and fresher with a little room to breathe.

Freezer Protection

Few household incidents are more annoying than opening the freezer to find it awash in mushy, smelly, spoiled food. Here are some ideas that will help you avoid encountering this expensive mess in the future.

Plug the freezer into a grounded outlet that has its own circuit. This will prevent overloads from other appliances from shutting off the freezer's circuit.

Level a chest freezer so the door closes tightly. Position an upright freezer so it's slightly tilted toward the back, creating a natural tendency for the door to close completely.

If you're on an extended vacation, ask a friend to check the freezer periodically.

SAFETY FIRST

Since 1958, the Federal Refrigerator Safety Act has required that refrigerators have inside door releases. Yet, children continue to die in unused refrigerators and freezers.

If you must store an unused refrigerator or freezer in your home, follow one of these recommendations from the Consumer Product Safety Commission.

- **Remove the door**
- **Chain and padlock the door closed.**
- **Use wooden blocks to prevent the door from closing completely.**
- **Remove or disable the door latch.**

Patience Pays

You can improve your oven's energy efficiency in one simple step: avoid opening the oven door while food is baking.

Every time you open the door, the cooking temperature falls about 50°F. That's expensive and may throw off recommended cooking times.

A Burning Issue

A properly calibrated oven evenly distributes heat at a specified temperature. If your oven begins to burn food regularly, investigate before calling a repair person.

Most ovens have a heat deflector to direct heat out of an element hole in the cooktop. If this deflector gets encrusted, it won't allow heat to escape through the vent.

Remove the burners or elements and reflector pans to locate the deflector. Then clean it, the surrounding area and the vent hole. Your oven may now be back to normal.

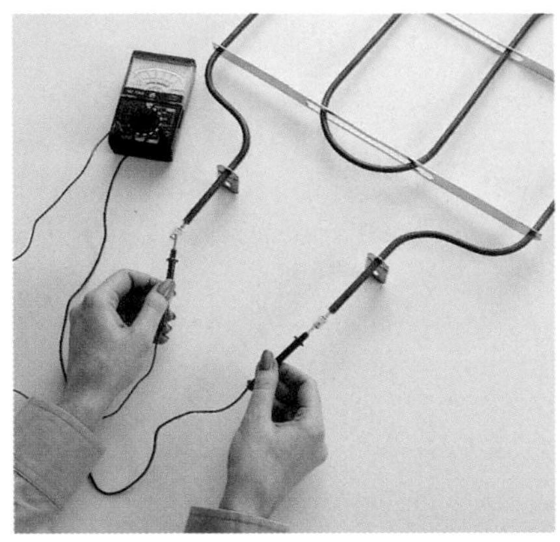

Elemental, Dr. Watson

If your oven isn't heating, there could be a short in the heating element. Replacing an element is a simple matter—there's no need to pay for a service call.

To check the heating element, you'll need the wiring diagram that came with your oven and a volt-ohm-millimeter (VOM).

To prepare the VOM, use a screwdriver or knife to adjust the needle to the infinity mark. Next, put the leads into the jacks and hold the probes together with a rubber band. Turn the ohms adjustment control knob until the needle rests at zero.

Remove the element from the oven. Place one of the VOM probes on each of the element's prongs. Compare the reading to the resistance values described in the oven's wiring diagram.

The value need not match exactly, but a large discrepancy indicates a short in the element. You can buy a new element from any large appliance dealer. Best of all, it's plug-and-play—just plug the new element in and you've fixed the oven and saved yourself a major repair bill.

Shortcut Cooking

Everyone knows that a microwave oven is the fastest way to reheat leftovers and defrost frozen foods. But did you also realize that it's the cheapest, most energy efficient way to cook virtually any meal?

A study commissioned by Northeast Utilities, the power company serving New England, showed that a microwave oven uses 75 percent less energy than a conventional electric or gas oven. It also found that most people could cook up to 80 percent of their meals in a microwave.

Hot Topics

As a result of the renewed interest in gardening these days, many people are rediscovering the art of preserving and canning fruits and vegetables. While there are many sources of instruction available, most overlook an important problem associated with using oversized pots used in canning.

Oversized pots can block airflow around burners, trapping too much heat in a small area. During a prolonged canning session, temperatures can build to 1200°F, which may burn out the elements or cause the cooktop's enamel to craze.

To avoid this problem, allow the cooktop to cool between batches and alternate burners from batch to batch. And, never turn on two burners under one pot.

On the Level

When a washer or dryer isn't level, the bearings, belts, motor and transmission are subjected to excessive wear and tear that may lead to premature breakdowns. Fortunately, this problem is easy to correct.

First, place a spirit level on the appliance to check it from side to side. If adjustment is necessary, use a wrench to thread the front legs up or down until the unit is level. Next, check the level from front to back. If adjustment is necessary, determine whether your unit has self-adjusting rear legs. If so, carefully tilt it forward, then let it down slowly. If the unit's still not level, or if the height difference between the front and rear is greater than the back legs can compensate for, lower or raise both front legs and repeat the process.

Some back legs must be raised and lowered with a wrench. Keep checking the level until the unit is level from side to side and front to back. The machine shouldn't rock at all: press down on opposite corners to make sure it's firmly planted.

SAFETY FIRST

Dryer lint is highly combustible and can cause a fire if left unchecked too long. Excess lint also reduces a dryer's efficiency, so it makes sense to keep your dryer as lint-free as possible.

Clean the lint trap after each load of laundry. If your dryer has an upward venting hose, check the vent connection for lint accumulations. At least twice a year, move the dryer slightly forward and disconnect the vent from the back of the dryer. Clean out the lint from the hose and fitting; then, reconnect the vent.

Long-Legged Trap

Discharge water from a washing machine often is laced with lint, hair, shredded facial tissues and other soggy debris. That's not a problem if the washer drains directly into a large 4"-diameter sewer line. But if it drains into a utility sink, the debris could clog the drainpipe.

Trap the lint before it enters the drain by fastening a nylon stocking over the end of the washer discharge hose. Empty the stocking every couple of weeks, and replace it if it tears.

COOL LAUNDRY

According to the U.S. Department of Energy, 80 percent to 85 percent of the energy consumed for washing clothes is used for heating the water. The agency recommends two ways to reduce the amount of energy used for laundry: use cooler water, and use less of it.

Switching the temperature setting from hot to warm can cut the energy required for a load of laundry in half. Unless you're dealing with oily stains, warm or even cold water will clean just as well as hot. Using a detergent designed for use in cold water will help.

To use less water, wash full loads only and make sure the water level matches the size of the load.

Easy Oven Cleaning

Oven cleaning doesn't need to be time consuming, messy or expensive. Here's a simple, effective method.

Set the oven on 250°F for five minutes, then turn it off. Set a small glass dish filled with ammonia on the oven's top shelf. Place a large pan on the bottom shelf and fill it with boiling water. Let the closed oven sit overnight. In the morning, even baked-on grease should wash right off with soap and water.

Note: Do not use this method on continuous-clean ovens.

SAFETY FIRST

Do not attempt to clean reflector pans, broiler pans or oven racks in a self-cleaning oven unless the manufacturer specifically recommends it.

These items can be damaged by the extreme heat of the cleaning cycle. More important, they could burst into flames if they're heavily coated with grease.

If a grease fire occurs, douse the flames with baking soda or salt to cut off the oxygen supply.

Never attempt to put out a grease fire with water.

Continuously Clean

The inside of a continuous-clean oven is covered with a chemical coating that lowers the temperature at which heat dissolves splatters and spills. The process starts working at around 350°F, but it is more active at higher temperatures.

To keep the cleaning action in effect, protect the surface of your continuous-clean oven.

- Do not scratch or scrub the coating.
- Prevent major spills that could destroy the coating's oxidizing action.
- Once a month, run the empty oven for several hours at 475°F.

Zap Your Microwave Clean

Spills that have been zapped repeatedly in the microwave can take on the consistency of concrete. The best advice is to wipe up spills as soon as they happen, but that doesn't help much when you're trying to scrape last week's spaghetti sauce off the microwave door.

To clean a messy microwave, combine 4 tablespoons of baking powder and 2 cups of water. Boil the mixture in the microwave for five or six minutes. Remove the container, and wash the interior with soap and water.

You can use a similar procedure to remove persistent odors from a microwave. Fill a large glass measuring cup with a mixture of one part lemon juice to three parts water. Boil the mixture in the microwave for three to five minutes. Let the steam cool, and wipe the oven dry.

SLIP AND SLIDE

Over the years, oven racks sometimes get balky, refusing to slide in and out with their former ease.

To make racks slide smoothly, wash their edges and the guides with a soap-filled steel wool pad. After they're dry, rub a drop of vegetable oil on the edges.

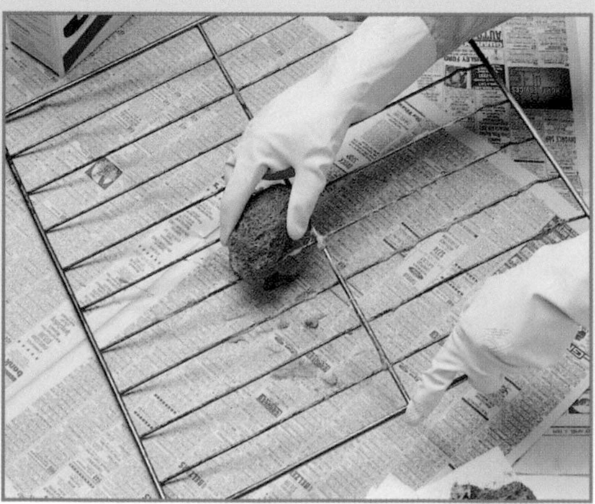

Clean Refrigerators Last Longer

When a refrigerator's coils are dirty, the compressor has to work overtime to keep its cool. Cleaning the coils periodically will reduce the cost of running the refrigerator and make it last longer, too.

With every change of seasons, pull off the front grille and use a wand attachment to vacuum out dust and pet hair.

Three or four times a year, unplug the refrigerator, pull it out and clean the rear-mounted coils with a stiff brush. If the coils are greasy, wash them with soap and water.

Scouring powder can scratch the surface of most appliances. Try using a little moistened baking soda instead.

After cleaning the refrigerator, rinse the walls and shelves with vinegar. It leaves an acidic residue that discourages mold and mildew.

To get rid of hard-water deposits, empty the dishwasher and start it. As soon as it fills, add a cup of vinegar to the water, and let the dishwasher run through a complete cycle.

To remove rust stains, follow the same procedure, but add commercial rust remover to the water.

White and Bright

Home fashions go through cycles similar to fashions in clothing. Although other colors go through phases of popularity, white seems to be a perennial favorite. But keeping appliances white can prove to be a challenge.

To remove yellowing, combine 1/2 cup bleach, 1/4 cup baking soda and 4 cups of warm water. Wipe this solution onto yellowed areas and let it sit for 10 to 15 minutes. Rinse and repeat if necessary.

SAFETY FIRST

If your washing machine's power cord cannot reach a receptacle, do not use an extension cord. If water were to touch the connection between an extension cord and a power cord, you could be seriously injured or electrocuted.

Move the receptacle or install a longer cord on the washing machine.

Keep It Clean

A burst water-supply hose spells disaster, so inspect your washing machine's hoses every month. Replace them if you see bulges or other signs of deterioration.

At least once a month, clean the screens that filter the washer's water supply. On some washers, you can unscrew the hoses and lift out the screens. On other models, you'll need a pair of needlenose pliers or a long screwdriver to remove the screens from the washer's inlet ports. Once you've removed the screens, soak them in vinegar to remove mineral deposits, and scrub them with a small brush.

Down the Drain

To keep your refrigerator smelling sweet, clean the drain tube and drain pan regularly.

The opening for the drain tube usually is found on the refrigerator floor under the storage drawers, or at the top of the back wall. Use a turkey baster to force hot, soapy water into the drain opening and through the tube into the drain pan.

The drain pan is found under the refrigerator, right behind the front grille. Remove the pan and wash it with hot water and baking soda.

AWG

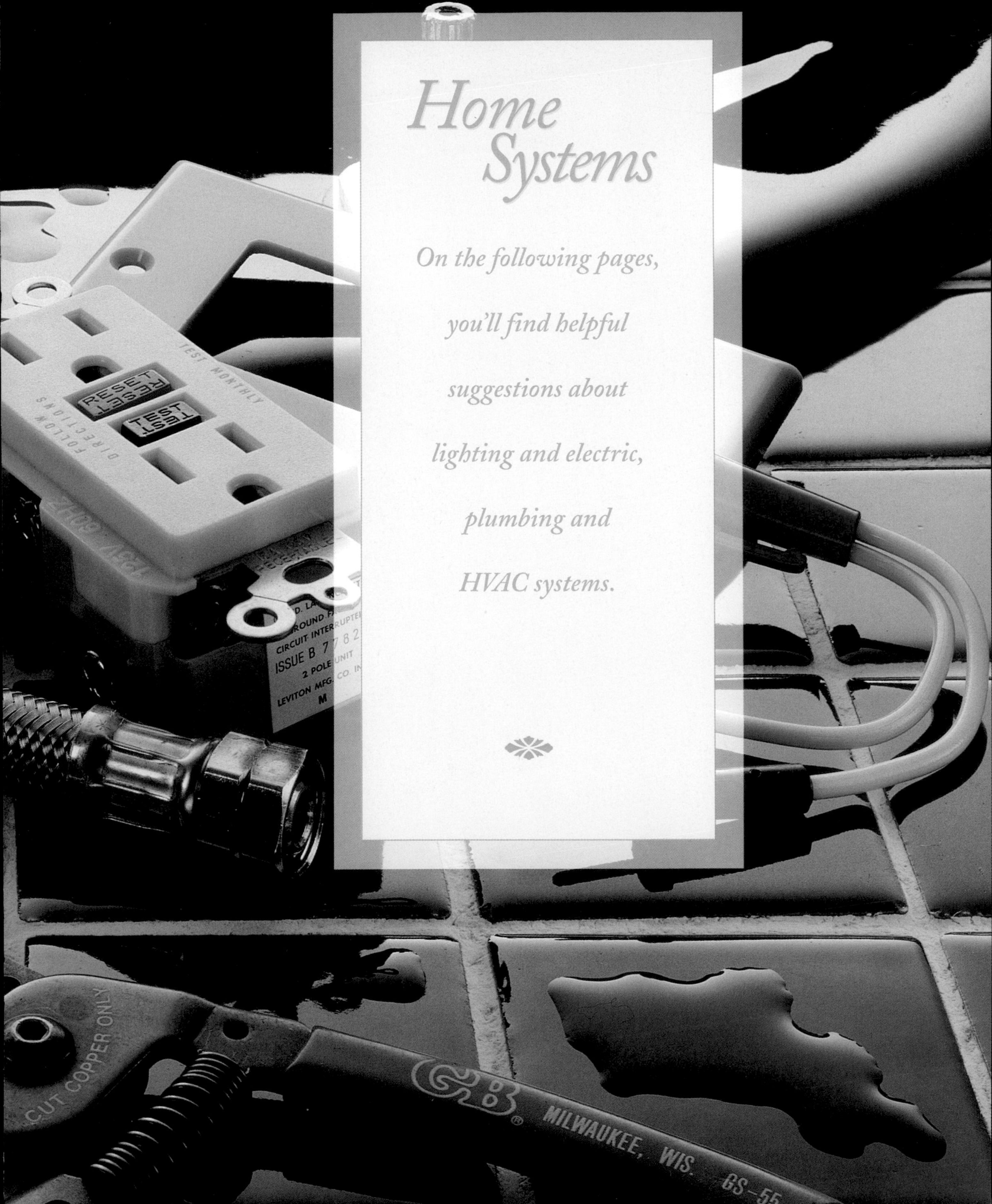

Home Systems

On the following pages, you'll find helpful suggestions about lighting and electric, plumbing and HVAC systems.

AUTO-
WIRE
STRIPPER
INSUL
CRIMPER
NON INSUL

Lighting & Electrical

Your lighting and electrical systems provide many conveniences often taken for granted. You rely on these systems for comfort and security.

Quick Reference

Lighting
pages 42–45

Safety
page 46

Wiring
pages 47–51

Blown fuses or tripped circuits, shorted connections and worn-out light switches are the sort of electrical problems that today's homeowners face, particularly in older houses. Although calling an electrician is the easiest solution, it isn't always necessary and can be expensive.

Making electrical repairs is not difficult, even though many people are hesitant about working with electricity. If you follow some simple safety procedures and use basic common sense, electrical projects are safe, easy and rewarding.

Your home's lighting is another area where you can make repairs and improvements yourself. Upgrading a lighting fixture or adding additional lighting are relatively simple tasks that quickly change the look and feel of a room.

Helpful Terms

Amperage (or amps): Measurement of the rate or volume at which electrical power flows

Box: Device used to contain wiring connections

Cable: Two or more wires that are grouped together and protected by a covering or sheath

Circuit: Continuous loop of electrical current flowing along wires or cables

Circuit breaker: Safety device, found in newer wiring systems, that interrupts an electrical circuit in the event of an overload or short circuit

Continuity: An uninterrupted electrical pathway through a circuit or electrical fixture

Fuse: Safety device, found in older wiring systems, that interrupts an electrical circuit during an overload or short circuit

Hot wire: Any wire that carries voltage; usually covered with black or red insulation

Grounding wire: Circuit wire used to conduct current to the ground in the event of a short circuit; often bare copper wire or covered with green insulation

Neutral wire: Wire that returns current at zero voltage to the source of electrical power; usually covered with white or light gray insulation

Overload: A demand for more current than the circuit wires or electrical device were designed to carry; usually causes a fuse to blow or a circuit breaker to trip

Service panel: Metal box, usually near the site where electrical power enters the house, where electrical current is split into individual circuits protected by circuit breakers or fuses

Short circuit: Accidental and improper contact between two current-carrying wires, or between a current-carrying wire and a grounding conductor

Voltage (or volts): Measurement of electricity in terms of pressure

lighting

Lighting serves a number of purposes, from accenting architectural features to illuminating areas for working, reading and relaxing. Understanding the intended function of different fixtures can help you make appropriate choices when you add or replace lighting fixtures.

The lighting fixtures shown below are the most common household-lighting options. Lighting styles should complement a home's architectural style and the way a room is typically used.

Pendants: Used for general or task lighting. These lamps have either a globe or a shade to prevent glare and are popular choices for lighting over informal dining and parlor game tables; they work well with dimmer switches. Several can be installed in a row to illuminate counters or work areas without cluttering them with portable lamps. These lights can use incandescent, tungsten-halogen or compact fluorescent bulbs.

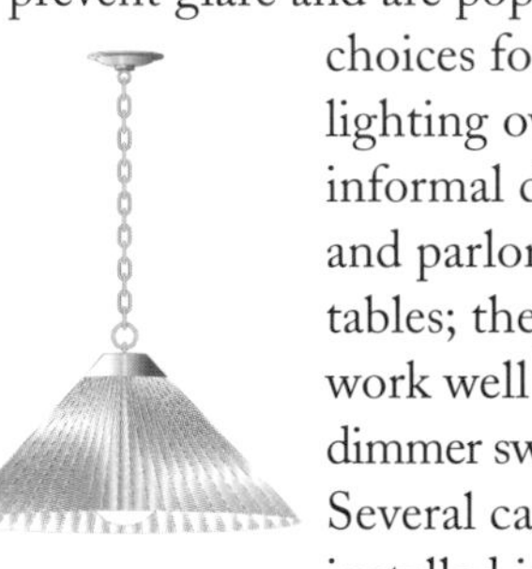

Ceiling fixtures: Used to provide general lighting for an entire room or large areas, such as hallways and foyers. Fixtures are available for use with either fluorescent or incandescent bulbs.

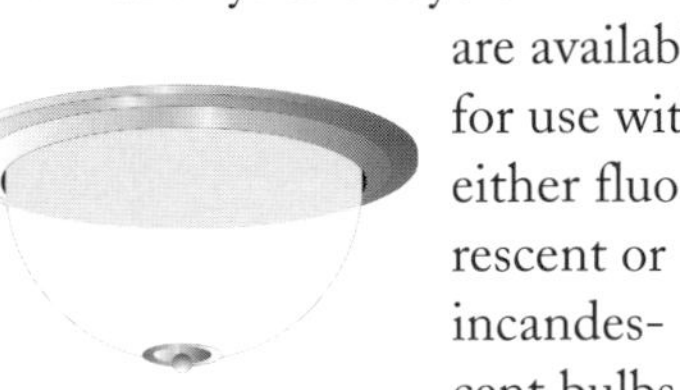

Chandeliers: Stylish fixtures that illuminate and dress up dining rooms, bedrooms, living rooms. Models are available for use with incandescent or tungsten-halogen bulbs. Some models direct light down rather than out and can also be used for task lighting.

Wall mounted: A variety of fixtures are available for accent, task or general lighting. Styles range from swing-arm shaded lamps to decorative sconces and are made for use with incandescent, tungsten-halogen and compact fluorescent bulbs.

Portable lamps: Can be used for general, task or accent lighting, depending on their size and positioning in a room. Available in floor, torchère and tabletop styles, these lamps are made for use with tungsten, halogen, incandescent or compact fluorescent bulbs.

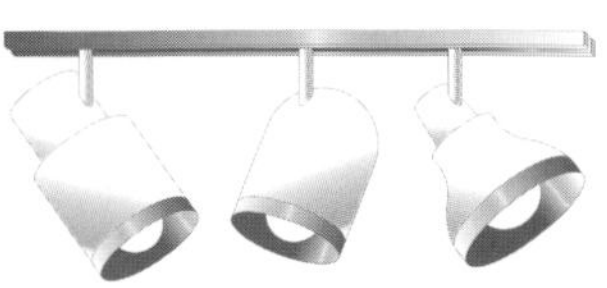

Track: Flexible and efficient lighting used for task, accent or general lighting. Fixtures can be positioned at any point on the track and can be rotated to "aim" a beam of light in any direction. Available in standard or low-voltage models for use with incandescent, tungsten-halogen or compact fluorescent bulbs.

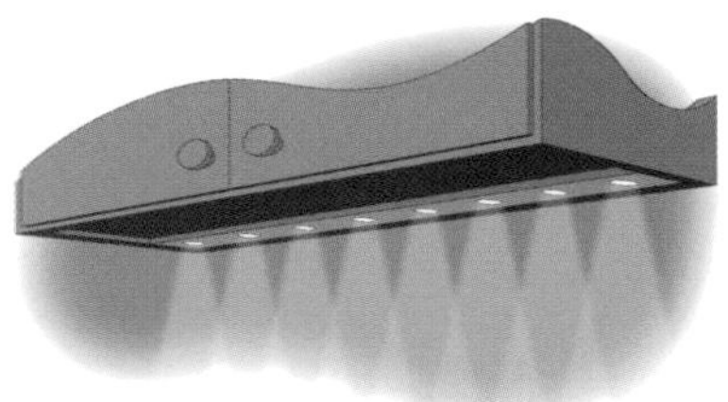

Undercabinet/Undershelf: Generally used for task lighting. Especially useful for eliminating shadows and illuminating kitchen counters and desktops.

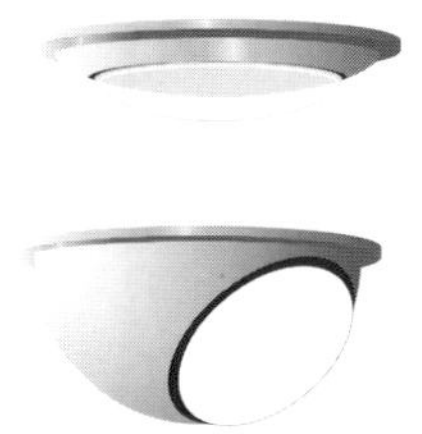

Recessed lighting: Unobtrusive fixtures, often called "can lights," used for general, task or accent lighting. A popular choice for use with low ceilings and soffit areas, both inside and outdoors. Fixtures are available for use with incandescent, tungsten-halogen and compact fluorescent bulbs.

Halogen Lamp Safety

Torchère-style halogen lamps put out a lot of light and are inexpensive—but, it turns out, can also be dangerous. The Consumer Product Safety Commission warns that the lamps burn hot enough to pose a serious fire hazard. A 500W halogen torchère can reach 1,200°F, compared with 260°F for a 75W incandescent bulb. (Many fabrics ignite at around 400°F.) As a result, Underwriters Laboratories no longer certifies torchères with 500W bulbs. UL also introduced a strict test in which a swatch of highly flammable cheesecloth is draped over the top of a lamp for seven hours. If the cloth ignites or develops holes, the lamp fails the test.

When buying a torchère, look for a UL certification as well as for two labels that warn of the heat hazard and advise keeping the lamp away from curtains and other combustible materials. Select a model that has a glass shield or wire guard over the bulb and a heat-sensitive switch.

If you already own a halogen torchère—there are more than 40 million of them in the U.S.—UL suggests you replace the 500W bulb with a 300W version, the lowest wattage that works in most 500W lamps. UL also recommends that you turn off lamps equipped with bulbs rated higher than 100W every time you leave the room.

WHAT WATT?

Most Americans choose bulbs by wattage. In reality, wattage doesn't indicate light output but rather the amount of electricity required to operate the bulb. Choosing by wattage works well if you're buying familiar incandescent bulbs, but compact fluorescent bulbs use much less wattage to produce the same amount of light.

As a result, it's more useful to use light output, measured in lumens, to compare bulbs. Here's an example: Although a 15W or 16W fluorescent light would seem to be a lot less powerful than a 60W incandescent bulb, they're equivalent. Both produce approximately 900 lumens. A 75W incandescent bulb produces about 1,100 lumens, while a 100W incandescent bulb delivers approximately 1,750 lumens.

Following the National Energy Policy Act guidelines, all lightbulb packaging produced after April 25, 1995 must list the amount of power a bulb uses (watts), as well as the amount of light it produces (lumens). Until you become accustomed to choosing lightbulbs by lumens, use the following guide to select fluorescent equivalents for incandescent bulbs (the wattage of compact fluorescents varies slightly by manufacturer).

- 13W to 16W fluorescent equals a 60W incandescent
- 20W fluorescent equals a 75W incandescent
- 23W to 28W fluorescent equals a 100W incandescent
- 39W fluorescent equals a 150W incandescent

QUICK TIPS

To make installation faster and keep you from straining your neck, assemble recessed lighting fixtures on the floor before you begin to install them.

To easily remove and install bulbs in light fixtures that are out of reach, make an extender out of a broomstick and the bulb clip found inside some lamp shades. Wrap the clip with electrical tape; then tape it securely to the end of a broomstick.

If you'd like to use energy-efficient compact fluorescent bulbs instead of incandescent bulbs, but can't find a fluorescent bulb that fits within the harp (the metal loop that supports the shade), try using a harp adapter with the fixture. These adapters can usually accommodate the larger-size fluorescent bulbs.

Replacing a Starter

If your fluorescent lamp fixture is flickering, the problem could be found in the starter, a small twist-in device in the fixture. Starters are inexpensive and easy to replace.

To remove a starter, push it in, turn it counterclockwise a quarter turn, then pull it out. Take the old starter with you for reference when shopping for a replacement. Purchase a replacement that matches the wattage rating of the original starter.

To install the new starter, push it in and turn it clockwise until you hear it click into place.

Buying Fluorescent Tubes

Replacing the tube in a fluorescent light fixture used to be as simple as making sure the new bulb was the same length as the old one. However, fluorescent tubes are now available in a large variety of colors ranging from cool to warm.

Here's a quick way to get the quality of light you want—check the temperature rating for the tube. The temperature rating of fluorescent tubes is measured in "degrees kelvin." The higher the kelvin rating, the cooler the light will appear. Harsh fluorescent lights, generally found in offices and schools, typically have ratings of 4000°K or higher. Warmer fluorescent lights require tubes with a rating near 3000°K.

Also check for a Color Rendering Index (CRI) when replacing fluorescent tubes. The CRI for natural sunlight is 100. Standard warm fluorescent tubes generally have a CRI of 50. However, more expensive fluorescent tubes with a higher CRI rating produce light that appears to be more natural. The higher the CRI rating, the warmer the light.

SAFETY FIRST

Instead of using your bare hands to remove a shattered lightbulb, use half of a raw potato. Unplug the lamp, and press the flat, raw area of the potato into the bulb. Twist to remove the bulb.

. . . .

Prevent dangerous overheating and light fixture failures by using lightbulbs that are within the wattage ratings printed on the fixture.

FLUORESCENT LIGHT TROUBLESHOOTING

PROBLEM:	EFFECTIVE REPAIRS:
Tube lights partially or flickers:	• Rotate tube to seat it properly in sockets • Replace tube if discolored or if pins are damaged • Replace the starter • Replace ballast or fixture
Tube does not light:	• Rotate tube to seat it properly in sockets • Check wall switch; repair or replace as needed • Replace tube and starter • Replace sockets if chipped or if tube doesn't work • Replace ballast or the entire fixture
Black substance leaking from ballast:	• Replace ballast or the entire fixture
Fixture hums:	• Tighten ballast nuts or screws • Replace ballast or the entire fixture

A Real Fan

Ceiling fans equipped with light fixtures are excellent choices for general lighting. In addition to illuminating the room, they can make a room more pleasant and provide year-round savings on heating and cooling bills. There are a variety of ceiling fans available with domes for evenly lighting the room or downlights for providing focused lighting.

In addition to choosing the right lighting feature, you need to select a fan with the appropriate blade span. For rooms up to 15' × 20', you'll need to purchase a fan with a blade span of at least 42". For larger rooms, choose a model with a minimum blade span of 52". Install more than one ceiling fan in rooms that are long or extremely large.

If you are replacing an overhead fixture with a ceiling fan, anchor the fan to a ceiling joist or to a support brace installed between joists. Wall-mounted controls and a dimmer switch will give it more flexibility and keep you from struggling with cords, especially in rooms with high ceilings.

Setting the direction of the blades correctly helps make your home cooler in the summer and warmer in the winter. In the summer, set the direction so that the hot air in the room is pulled upward. Reverse the direction of the fan in the winter so that warm air is pushed down. Adjusting your fan this way will also help you lower your utility bills. You will save between 4 and 8 percent of your cooling expenses for every degree you raise the thermostat in summer and from 1 to 2 percent on heating costs for every degree you lower the thermostat in winter.

Positioning Track Lighting

Track lighting is an attractive, flexible lighting alternative. You can adjust the lights to accent a specific object, such as a painting, provide task lighting over a desk or wash a wall with general lighting.

The key to working with track lights is to position the track correctly. A common mistake is to place track lighting in the center of a room, which results in glare and shadowing. The best method is to install the track two to three feet away from a wall. Then position the lights at 60-degree angles to illuminate specific objects or the wall. Aim the lights toward the objects to be illuminated so the lights won't shine directly in your eyes.

SAFETY FIRST

Fluorescent tubes contain a small amount of hazardous mercury. Do not dispose of old fluorescent tubes by breaking them. Check with your local environmental control agency or health department for disposal guidelines.

SAFETY FIRST

Most household electrical repairs are simple, but caution and good judgment are essential when working with electricity. Common sense can prevent accidents.

Always turn off power to the area or device you are repairing. At the main service panel, remove the fuse or shut off the electrical breaker that controls the circuit you are servicing. Check to make sure the power is off by testing for current with a neon circuit tester. Restore power only when the repair or replacement project is complete.

Follow the safety tips shown on these pages. Don't attempt an electrical project beyond your skill or confidence level. Never attempt to repair the service entrance head—the wires that deliver electricity to your home. They are always live unless turned off by your utility provider.

Simple Safety Guidelines

Shut off power to the proper circuit at the fuse box or main service panel before beginning work.

Identify the circuits within your home by making a map of your electrical circuits. Refer to this map when you need to turn circuits on and off for electrical repairs (see page 47).

Close the service panel door and post a warning sign to prevent others from turning on the power while you are working on electrical projects.

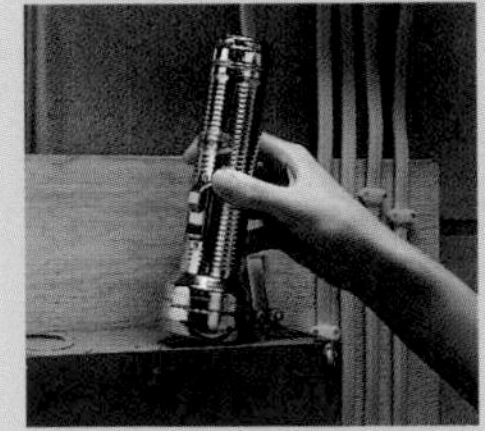

Keep a flashlight near your main service panel. Check the batteries regularly.

Use a neon circuit tester to check for power at the receptacle or fixture before beginning to work (see page 49).

Use only UL-listed electrical parts or devices. These devices have been tested for safety by Underwriters Laboratories.

Wear rubber-soled shoes while working on electrical projects. On a damp floor, stand on a rubber mat or dry wooden boards.

Use a fiberglass or wood ladder when making routine household repairs near the service entrance head to avoid possible electric shock.

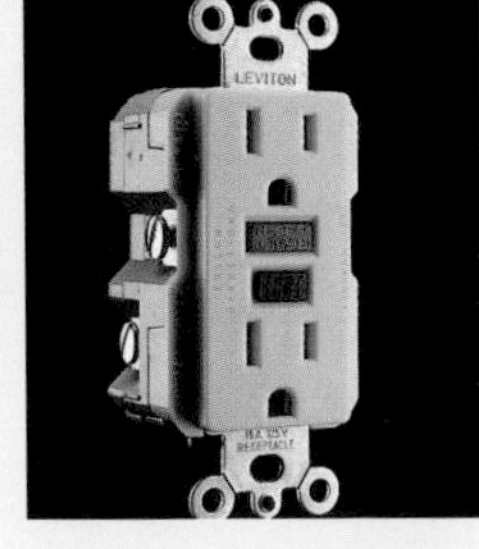

Use GFCI receptacles (ground-fault circuit-interrupters) in "wet" rooms (both kitchen and laundry), basement workshops, garages and other locations specified by your local electrical code (see page 51).

Knowledge Is Power

In almost every case, the first step in electrical repair is shutting off the power to the circuit being repaired. Making a map of your home's electrical circuits allows you to turn off the right circuit without guesswork.

Shut off power to one circuit. Make a list of the outlets, appliances and lights that don't operate when this circuit is off. Repeat with each circuit.

When you've identified each circuit, make a rough sketch of each floor of your house. Label the outlets, switches and appliances served by each circuit. Tape a copy of this drawing and the list of circuits to the door of your service panel.

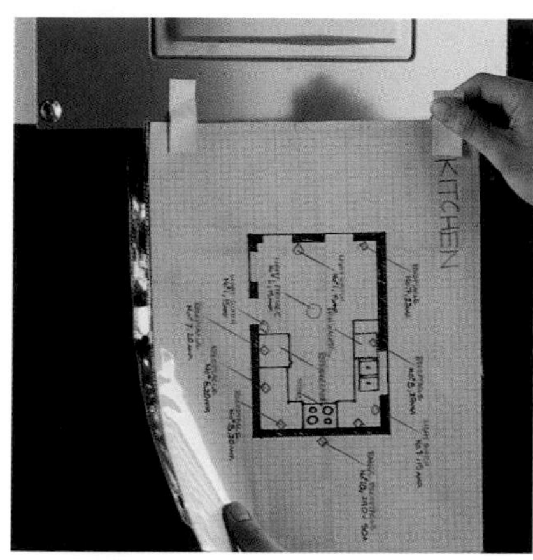

CODE SECRET

An electrical code book is enough to intimidate many homeowners. Although much of it is complex, the code can be a useful reference.

For example, to meet current code, every room must have an electrical outlet at least every 12 feet along the perimeter and within 6 feet of any doorway. Because every UL-listed lamp has a cord at least 6 feet long, you should never need an extension cord between a lamp and an outlet.

Individual wires are color coded to identify their function. In some circuit installations, the white wire serves as a hot wire that carries voltage. If so, this white wire may be labeled with black tape or paint to identify it as a hot wire.

Wire color	Function
White	Neutral wire carrying current at zero voltage
Black	Hot wire carrying current at full voltage
Red	Hot wire carrying current at full voltage
White, Black	Hot wire carrying current at full voltage
Green	Grounding wire
Bare Copper	Grounding wire

Wire sizes are categorized by the American Wire Gauge system. This gauge system allows you to determine whether your circuit wires are adequate for the size of your fuses or circuit breakers and helps you select wiring when adding circuits.

Wire gauge	Capacity & use
AWG #6	60 amps, 240 volts; central air conditioner, electric furnace
AWG #8	40 amps, 240 volts; electric range, central air conditioner
AWG #10	30 amps, 240 volts; window air conditioner, clothes dryer
AWG #12	20 amps, 120 volts; light fixtures, receptacles, microwave oven
AWG #14	15 amps, 120 volts; light fixtures, receptacles
#16	Light-duty extension cords
AWG #18 to 22	Thermostats, doorbells, security systems

Aluminum Wire

If your home was built or had circuits added between 1965 and 1973, it may have aluminum wiring, which was installed in more than a million houses during that time. Copper prices skyrocketed in the decades after World War II, and aluminum was thought to be a reasonable substitute. Unfortunately, aluminum wiring eventually proved to be a potential fire hazard. According to federal statistics, aluminum wiring is 55 times more likely to overheat than copper wiring.

The major problem with aluminum wiring is that it's a less efficient conductor of electricity than copper. This deficiency results in expansion and contraction that can loosen connections on receptacles, switches and light fixtures. Loose connections create increased resistance that can overheat wires and start fires.

Aluminum wire is easy to identify. It is white and its sheathing is marked "AL" or "Aluminum." Copper-clad aluminum has a thin outer skin of copper, but if you cut through it, you'll see a whitish core of aluminum.

If your home has aluminum wiring, the only safe alternatives are to completely replace it with copper wiring or to add copper "pigtail" wires between aluminum wiring and all receptacles, switches, lighting fixtures and appliances.

According to the U.S. Consumer Product Safety Commission, these pigtail connections must be made with special COPALUM connectors and a crimping tool licensed by the AMP Corporation.

These upgrades must be performed by a licensed electrician who is trained to install COPALUM connectors. For information on finding a certified electrician with this training, contact the AMP Corporation at (800) 522-6752.

TOOL BOX

One of the most basic wiring skills is making complete, secure connections. The advent of twist connectors has simplified this task.

First, choose the correct size wire nut for the size and number of wires you're connecting. Then strip about 1/2" of insulation from each wire. Hold the wires parallel and screw the twist connector onto the wires so the twist connector's metal threads grip the bare ends of the wires.

Make sure the twist connector completely covers the bare wires, and tug gently on each wire to make sure it's secure.

Replacing a Receptacle

The problems created by a worn-out receptacle range from merely annoying to dangerous. And, because receptacles are easy to replace, there's no reason to delay.

Turn the power off at the service panel; then test both top and bottom receptacles for power using a neon circuit tester. Remove the coverplate, then the mounting screws, and pull the receptacle from the box. Confirm that the power is off by testing both sets of screw terminals with a circuit tester. The tester should not glow.

Label each wire to indicate its location on the receptacle screw terminals; then disconnect all wires and remove the receptacle.

Select a receptacle rated for the amperage and voltage of the circuit. Reconnect the wires as directed by the labels. Replace the coverplate and turn on the power. Test the receptacle for power.

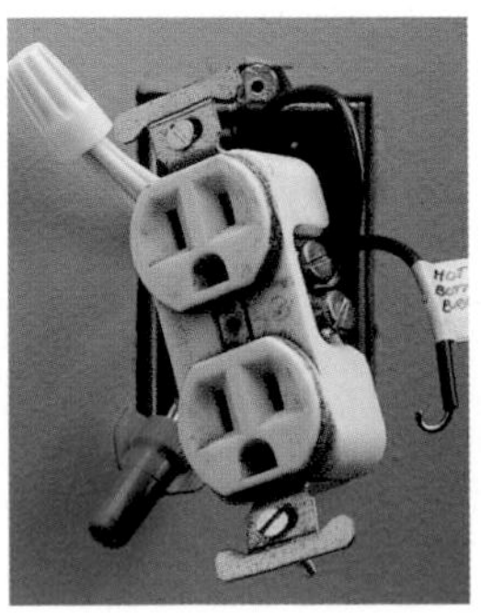

Testing a Switch

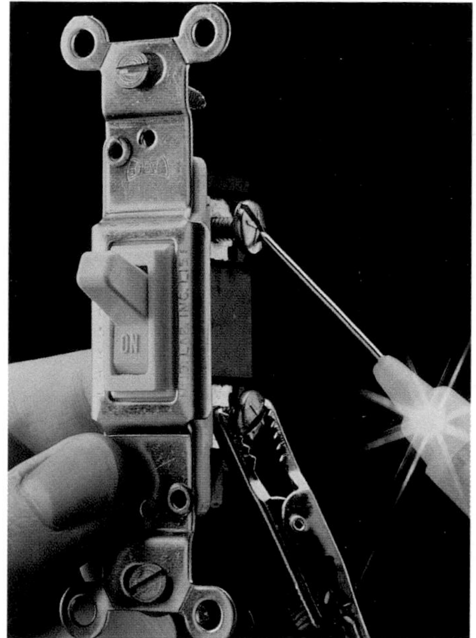

At one time or another, almost every homeowner has tolerated a broken light switch. But there's really no need to live with this petty aggravation—repairing or replacing a switch is simple and safe.

Begin by turning off the power to the circuit. Next, remove the coverplate, then disconnect and gently pull the switch out from the box. Test for power by touching one probe of a circuit tester to the metal box or the grounding wire and the other to each screw terminal in turn. The tester should not glow. If it does, check the circuit—it must be off before you go any further. When you're sure the circuit is off, disconnect the circuit wires from the switch.

To test the switch, attach the clip of a continuity tester to one of the screw terminals, and touch the probe to the other.

If the tester glows only when the lever is ON, the switch is good and the problem lies elsewhere in the circuit.

TOOL BOX

Always "test" a continuity tester before you use it. Touch the tester clip to the metal probe. The tester should glow. If not, the battery or lightbulb is dead and either they or the tester must be replaced.

When you store the tester, attach the alligator clip to the plastic insulation. That way the clip cannot accidentally come into contact with the probe and wear out the battery.

Replacing a Switch

If you know that a switch is defective, you can easily replace it. Turn off the power to the switch at the main service panel. Remove the coverplate and the mounting screws, then pull the switch from the box. Be careful not to touch any bare wires or screw terminals until the switch has been tested for power with a circuit tester. When you're sure the power is off, move on to the next step.

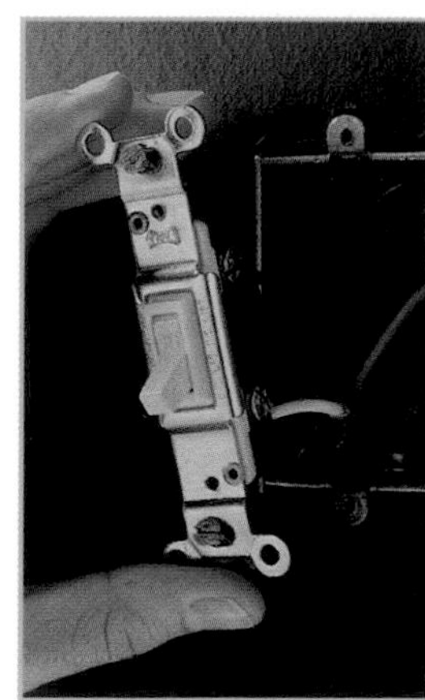

Tag the white (neutral) wire with black tape to indicate that it's hot; then disconnect the wires.

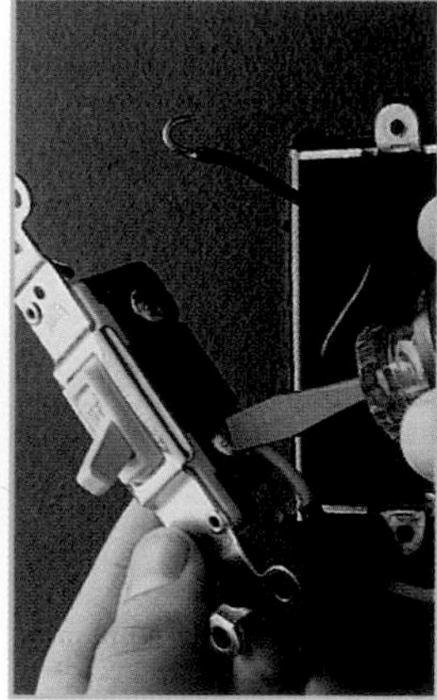

Attach the wires to the new switch. If the new switch has a green ground screw, connect it to the ground wire in the box.

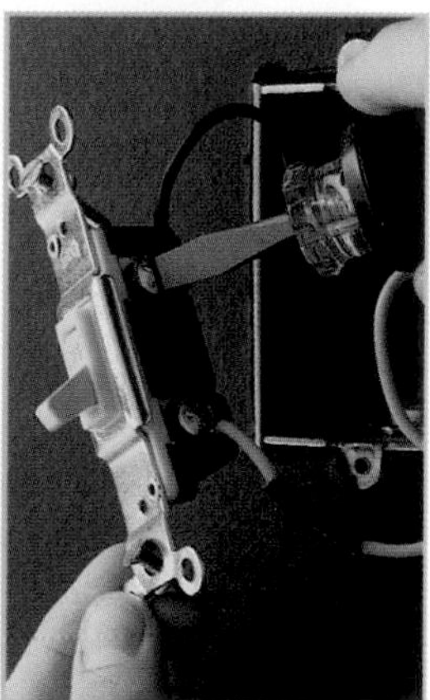

When all the connections are secure, push the switch back into the box, carefully tucking in all wires. Tighten the mounting screws and attach the coverplate.

NEAT AND TIDY

Looping wires tightly around screw terminals is crucial when wiring electrical outlets and switches. But if you're not an experienced electrician, trying to get the ends of the wire to stay in place around the screws while you tighten them can be frustrating. Here's how the professionals make neat connections quickly and easily.

Strip about two inches of insulation from the end of the wire. Wrap the bare wire clockwise around the screw and allow the extra length to extend past the terminal. Tighten the screw; then bend the excess wire back and forth so it breaks off flush with the screwhead.

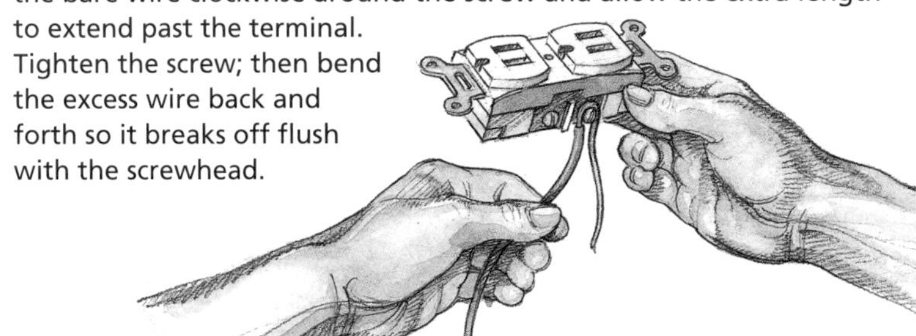

Who's on First?

Have you ever disconnected a receptacle or switch only to realize you're not sure where the wires go on the new device?

Avoid that problem by labeling the wires with small tabs of masking tape before you disconnect them. Use the labels as a guide when attaching the wires to the new receptacle or switch.

Here's another good idea: When you're working on a complicated device, take a Polaroid picture or make a short videotape before you take it apart. Use the photo or video as a guide when you're ready to reassemble the device.

Common Electrical Problems and Solutions

When an electrical problem occurs in your home, visualize the circuit's path and look for interruptions. Anything that interferes with its circular flow can cause a short circuit. Here are some common electrical problems and solutions. Always turn off power to the circuit before working on any electrical wiring or device.

PROBLEMS	SOLUTIONS
Bare wire extends past a screw terminal. Exposed wire can cause a short circuit if it touches the metal box or another wire.	Clip the wire and reconnect it to the screw terminal using the technique described above left.
Wires are connected with electrical tape, which can deteriorate over time. This leaves bare wires exposed inside the electrical box and often leads to short circuits.	Replace electrical tape with twist connectors. If necessary, clip away a small portion of the exposed wire so the bare wire is completely covered by the connector.
Dust and dirt in an electrical box can cause a hazardous short circuit or fire.	Pull out the receptacle and vacuum the electrical box. Check boxes for dust and dirt every time you do routine repairs.
Scratches and nicks in bare wires interfere with the flow of current and cause wires to overheat.	Clip away the damaged portion of wire, then restrip about 3/4" of insulation and reconnect the wire to the screw terminal.

Strike Insurance

Most of the more expensive electronics and appliances in your home—computers, microwave ovens, stereos, TVs, VCRs, answering machines, etc.—contain computer chips that require constant voltage to operate correctly. It only takes one lightning strike to cause permanent damage to your home's electrical system and appliances, or to cause a fire. If your home isn't properly prepared, voltage from lightning can quickly travel through your electric system, overloading any electronic appliances that are plugged into the system and possibly setting the entire electrical system on fire. Protecting your home from lightning damage is a relatively inexpensive way to ensure the safety of your home and belongings.

The simplest way to protect home electronics is to unplug them during thunderstorms, but this is not always possible.

To ensure that your electronics and appliances are protected, have an electrician install new outlets that contain surge protectors.

Another precaution worth taking is outfitting your electrical panel with a secondary lightning arrester. This secondary arrester captures surges on the "hot" power lines that bring electricity into your home and directs the voltage from lightning surges straight into your home's grounding system.

If you choose to install a secondary arrester, have a qualified electrician install it. Improper installation of a secondary arrester can cause significant damage to your electrical system.

Ground-Fault Protection Can Save a Life

Many people mistakenly believe that the circuit breakers or fuses in their service panel will protect them from a potentially fatal shock. While fuses and circuit breakers are designed to protect the wires on the circuit from overheating, they don't necessarily protect you from shock.

Most fatal electrical shocks in the household occur when appliances come in contact with water and when children play with electrical outlets. The danger from these accidents can be significantly reduced by installing inexpensive devices called ground-fault circuit-interrupters (GFCIs).

GFCIs, when properly installed and maintained, immediately shut off power to the outlet when a power surge is detected. The device monitors the current flowing through the receptacle. When it detects an imbalance between the hot and neutral wires servicing the receptacle, it turns the power off within 1/4 of a second—fast enough to prevent injury to healthy people.

NEC electrical code requires that GFCIs be installed on all receptacles in bathrooms, garages, basements and many other locations where water can be present, such as near a kitchen sink. Older homes benefit greatly from having their receptacles updated with GFCIs, especially in homes with young children.

The TEST and RESET buttons on a GFCI should be tested monthly. Test by pressing the TEST button. If it's working properly, the RESET button will pop out, shutting off the power to the outlet.

QUICK TIPS

Before dismounting a chandelier, label the lights that aren't working properly. This will help you focus only on the bulbs that aren't working and solve the problem more quickly.

Since chandeliers are usually heavy, it's a good idea to work with a helper when removing one. Support the fixture to prevent its weight from pulling against the wires as you take it down.

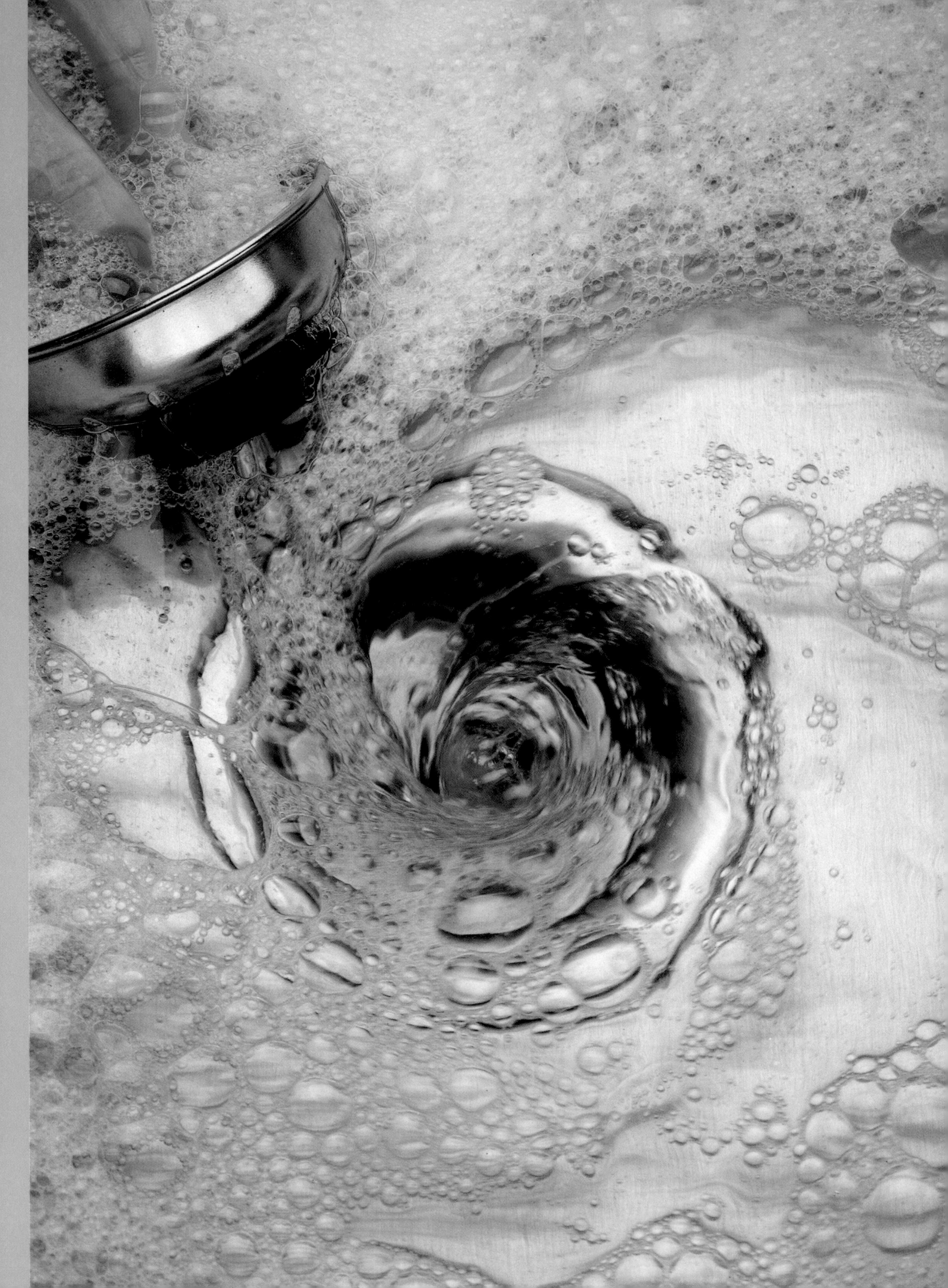

Plumbing

The plumbing system delivers fresh water and disposes of waste water—tasks crucial to your family's health and comfort.

QUICK REFERENCE

Most people don't give their plumbing system a thought until a drain gets clogged, a pipe leaks or a toilet overflows. Although it's easy to take your plumbing system for granted, it's not a good idea.

By understanding the system's basics, practicing preventive maintenance and recognizing early signs of trouble, you can repair minor problems and avoid major ones. Even if you already appreciate and maintain your plumbing system, there are always new ideas and better, faster or cheaper ways to accomplish the same old tasks.

Helpful Terms

Ballcock: The valve inside the toilet tank, often outfitted with a round float, that regulates the amount of water in the tank

Cartridge: A component inside newer-model faucets that contains all mechanical parts controlling the flow of water from the tap

Draincock: A valve at the bottom of a hot-water heater that can be opened to drain the water inside the water heater

Flapper valve: Valve that controls the flow of water from the tank into the bowl; referred to as the "flush valve" in older toilets that use flush balls

Float: The plastic or copper ball inside the tank of a toilet that controls the fill valve

Flush ball: In older toilets, this rubber sphere seals the opening to the flush valve and controls the flow of water from the tank into the bowl

Stem: The piece on which the handle is mounted on a compression faucet; a neoprene washer is attached to the stem; together these parts control the flow of the hot and cold water

Trap: The curved pipe under a sink or bathtub that connects the drain with the drain line; the trap uses collected water to seal the drain line from sewer gases

Power Plunging

Often called a plumber's friend, the plunger is a homeowner's first choice for clearing sinks, toilets and bathtubs. Here's a trick that makes it possible to clear a clogged kitchen sink even though it's connected to a dishwasher:

Before plunging, tighten a C-clamp down onto the dishwasher hose. This helps direct all of the plunger's power down the drainpipe and directly to the clog. Don't forget to remove the clamp once you've cleared the clog.

Using a Hand Auger

If you find yourself faced with a drain clog that a plunger can't cure, you probably need to enlist the help of a hand auger. Push the cable into the drain until you reach resistance. Set the auger lock so that at least 12" of cable extends from the opening. Crank the auger handle in a clockwise direction to move the cable past this bend in the drain line. Release the lock, pull out 12" more of cable, tighten the lock and continue cranking until you meet resistance, which indicates a clog or obstruction. To bore through clogs, apply steady pressure and crank clockwise. To retrieve an obstruction, crank counterclockwise. If you can't bore through or retrieve anything, reconnect the trap bend and try to clear the nearest branch drain line or main waste and vent stack.

All Stopped Up

Pop-up stoppers in bathroom sinks eventually stop sealing, which lets your basin of warm water drain away before you're finished with it. There's no need to live with this nuisance—the fix takes only a couple of minutes.

Locate the horizontal rod that projects out the back of the drainpipe. Make sure the rod passes through a hole in the clevis strap and is held in place by a spring clip. If the rod has slipped out of the clevis strap, pinch the clip to compress it; then slide the rod through the clip and into one of the middle holes in the strap. Test and readjust to another hole if necessary.

To improve the seal, hand-loosen the screw at the upper end of the clevis strap, push the strap up about 1/2" on the vertical lift rod and retighten the screw. If the lift rod won't stay up, try retightening the knurled round fitting that holds the rod to the drainpipe.

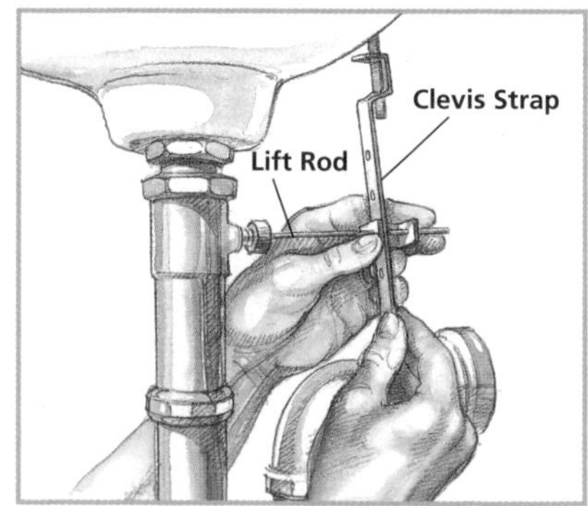

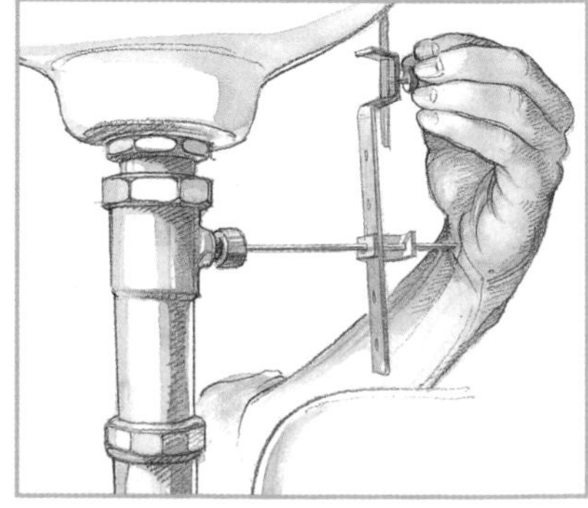

All Soaped Up with No Place to Go

Your home's plumbing system is more interconnected than you may realize. For instance, if the lowest draining fixture in the house (usually a toilet or shower drain) bubbles or overflows when the washing machine drains, it's a signal of trouble somewhere in the system.

This bubbling may indicate a break in the sewer pipe outside the house or a plug in the main drain. Follow up, with a plumber if necessary, until you find and fix the problem. If you have a septic system, the bubbling may be an indication that the septic tank needs to be pumped.

Spouting Off

Sometimes it's nearly impossible to unscrew a threaded tub spout by hand, especially if it's been in place for years. A thick wooden dowel should provide the leverage you need.

To remove the spout, insert the dowel into the spout opening and turn it counterclockwise. If you plan to reuse this fixture, wrap the dowel with a soft cloth so it doesn't scratch the finish.

Before using a pipe wrench or slip-joint pliers on a tub faucet or showerhead, wrap the fixture with a washcloth to keep the tool's teeth from permanently scratching the finish.

Clearing Clogged Showerheads and Faucets

If your showerhead or faucets send forth an uneven, partial stream of water, odds are the spray holes are clogged with mineral deposits or sediment.

To bring back the flow to a showerhead, start by removing the head. In most cases, you can simply twist it off by hand. If the head is too tight, wrap it with a cloth and loosen it with pliers while using a second set of pliers to hold the stem (the pipe coming out of the wall). Now disassemble the parts of the showerhead.

If you're repairing a clogged faucet, start by unscrewing and separating the parts from the spout.

Place the disassembled parts in a pan of warm distilled vinegar or a commercial lime-dissolving solution. If you are fixing more than one showerhead or faucet, use a separate pan for each to ensure easy reassembly. Let the parts soak overnight to loosen deposits and sediment. Then unclog any blocked holes with a sewing needle or thin wire.

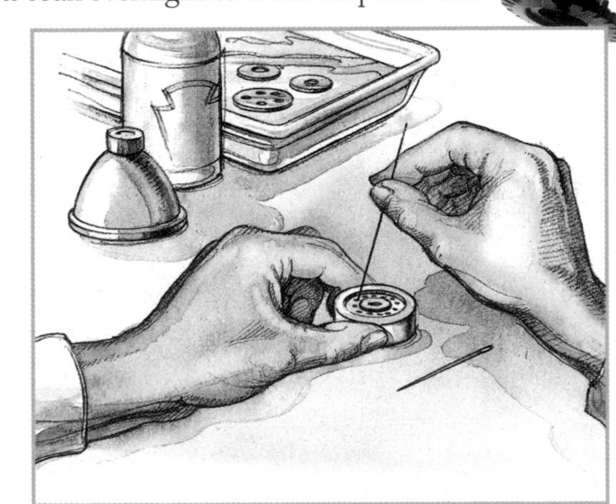

Rinse the parts thoroughly in clean water, and reassemble the fixture. Run the fixture for a minute to flush out any remaining traces of the vinegar or lime dissolver.

No Sweat

A sweaty toilet tank is unattractive and messy. More important, dripping moisture can rot the surrounding flooring. The most effective solution to this condensation is to install an antisweat valve on the water supply line. This valve blends a little hot water with the incoming cold, warming the tank just enough to avoid condensation.

You can also line the inside of your toilet tank with foam insulation, which prevents cold water from chilling the tank walls. Kits that consist of precut panels are available from home centers and plumbing-supply outlets. Unfortunately, liners won't work with most low-flush toilets because they reduce the tank capacity too much for an efficient flush.

Colorful Clues

To find the source of a toilet leak, put a few drops of food coloring into the tank.

- If colored water finds its way into the bowl, the flapper valve inside the tank is faulty.
- If it drips down the outside, the seal between the tank and bowl needs to be replaced.
- If colored water puddles on the floor after each flush, the wax seal beneath the toilet is cracked and must be replaced.

No Deposit Required

If a toilet fills slowly or doesn't flush adequately, hard-water deposits may be restricting the water flow between the tank and bowl. If that's the problem, you have to get rid of the deposits so the toilet can flush properly.

First, bail all the water out of the bowl. Next, take the lid off the tank and pour a quart of high-acid-content cleaner down the overflow tube. Turn on the vent fan and open a window for ventilation. Wait at least an hour.

Wrap a cloth around the end of a straightened wire hanger and swab out each hole beneath the rim of the bowl. The cleaner is caustic, so wear rubber gloves and safety goggles.

If any holes are completely plugged, use the bare end of the hanger to poke through the hardened clog. Flush the toilet. If the flow isn't substantially improved, repeat the process.

Old Bolt Removal

Although the fasteners on newer toilet seats typically are made of plastic, most old toilet seats are held in place with metal bolts that tend to corrode in place over time. They often are impossible to remove with a wrench. So the only option is to cut the seat off with a hacksaw.

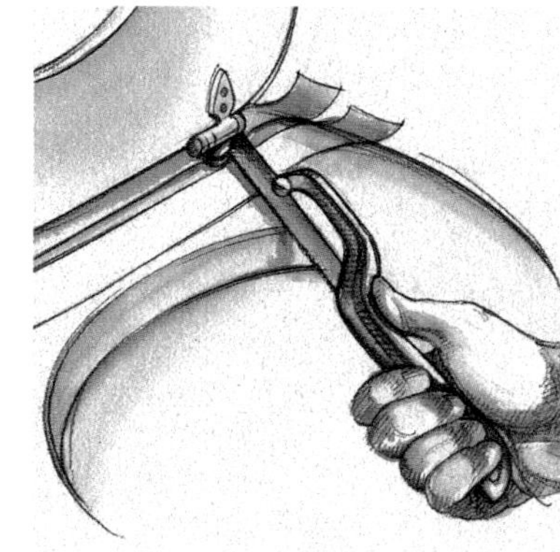

First, protect the top of the toilet with strips of duct tape or thin cardboard. Then, using a close-quarter hacksaw as shown here, cut through the bolts. If you don't have this type of saw, remove the blade from a standard hacksaw and use it to cut through the stubborn bolts.

Fast Fix for Leaky Toilets

If your toilet periodically runs for no apparent reason, the culprit could be a small leak where the tank ball or flapper fits into the overflow valve seat. Mineral deposits and sediment can collect on the valve seat and prevent the ball or flapper from forming a watertight seal.

Before you buy replacement parts, try this: Raise the ball or flapper out of the way and scour the brass valve seat with fine steel wool. If your toilet has a plastic valve seat, use a plastic scouring pad. Scrub the ball or flapper clean, too. Odds are, you'll have fixed the problem.

Cause and Effect

Sewer gas isn't just unpleasant, it's flammable and can make you sick. If you smell sewer gas near a toilet, investigate the cause and solve it as quickly as possible. Here are some possible causes and their solutions.

The water level in the bowl is too low, allowing sewer gas to enter. Regularly flush toilets that are not used to ensure that the bowl isn't evaporated dry. Examine the bowl thoroughly for cracks that may be causing a slow leak. If the bowl is cracked, replace the toilet.

The wax ring is damaged or deteriorated. If you can rock the toilet back and forth, replace the wax ring and be sure the toilet is seated securely.

Bacteria from the sewer has traveled to the house side of the toilet trap and is living inside the rim of the bowl. Open the tank and pour bleach or other disinfectant into the overflow pipe of the flush valve. Flush the toilet several times. The disinfectant will flow through the rim of the bowl, eliminating the bacteria.

The roof vent is clogged. Check the vent, and remove obvious obstructions. Run a snake down through the vent to clear the pipe.

It's All Over Now

Though most toilet problems can be resolved fairly easily, there are some that can not. In the following situations, replacing the toilet is your only recourse.

Cracked tank or bowl. Even if the crack doesn't seem to be leaking, turn off the water immediately and replace the toilet as soon as possible.

Object stuck in the toilet. Combs, toys and even toothbrushes can become lodged in toilets, especially with a young child's help. If you are unable to retrieve the object, replace the toilet.

COMMON TOILET PROBLEMS

PROBLEMS	SOLUTIONS
Toilet handle sticks or is hard to push	• Adjust lift wires • Clean and adjust handle
Handle is loose	• Adjust handle • Reattach lift chain or lift wires to lever
Toilet will not flush at all	• Make sure water is turned on • Adjust lift chain or lift wires
Toilet does not flush completely	• Adjust lift chain • Adjust water level in tank
Toilet overflows or flushes sluggishly	• Clear clogged toilet • Clear clogged main waste-and-vent stack
Toilet runs continuously	• Adjust lift wires or lift chain • Replace leaky float ball • Adjust water level in tank • Clean and adjust flush valve • Replace flush valve • Repair or replace ballcock
Water on floor around toilet	• Tighten tank bolts and water connections • Insulate tank to prevent condensation • Replace wax ring • Replace cracked tank or bowl

Find, Fix and Prevent Plumbing Leaks

Each year common household plumbing leaks cause millions of dollars in property damage and waste countless gallons of water. Ironically, most of these expensive leaks can be repaired with inexpensive gaskets and seals. Often, the most difficult part of the job is pinpointing the source of the leak. Use the table below to find and fix plumbing leaks around your home.

Diagnosing and Repairing Common Household Leaks

LOCATION OF LEAK	SYMPTOM	LIKELY CAUSE	CORRECTION
• Toilet, internal	Sound of running water	Faulty fill-valve diaphragm	Clean diaphragm; if brass, replace
• Toilet, internal	Periodic filling	Badly adjusted float Worn flapper	Bend float arm or adjust linkage Replace flapper and dress seat
• Toilet, external	Water beneath tank	Loose or corroded tank-bolt washers	Tighten/replace tank-bolt nuts
• Tub drain	Tub won't hold water	Badly adjusted linkage	Adjust linkage
• Shower drain	Water on ceiling below	Broken drain seal	Remove hair screen; tamp packing
• Tub/shower	Water beneath unit after use	Faulty grout, caulk	Regrout/caulk surround seams and faucet trim
• Faucet spout	Water at base when on	Worn spout seal	Replace spout O-rings
• Faucet handles	Water under handles	Worn stem packing	Repack stem or replace cartridge
• Faucet valve	Faucet drips from spout	Worn seals/cartridge	Replace seals/cartridge
• Faucet hose spray	Nozzle drips or hose leaks	Calcification/wear	Clean or replace
• Sink drain	Water on cabinet floor	Corroded trap	Replace with plastic trap
• Water heater	Constant water on floor	Rusted tank	Replace heater immediately
• Water heater	Occasional water on floor	Pressure release valve or thermostat	Replace valve or thermostat
• Clothes washer	Occasional water on floor	Air-hammer shock	Install air chambers in laundry
• Clothes washer	Water on floor	Defective hose	Replace hoses
• Garbage disposal	Periodic water in cabinet	Broken drain seal	Reputty drain flange
• Garbage disposal	Drips from disposer base	Worn drum/body	Replace disposal
• General pipe leaks	Seep or spray of water from pipe	Corrosion or frozen-pipe damage	Solder hole, replace section or use patch kit

Eliminating Water Hammer

If you hear a loud banging sound in the walls when you turn off a faucet and the noise seems to be coming from the plumbing, the problem you are experiencing is known as hydraulic shock, or "water hammer."

When a faucet is turned off quickly, it causes a spike in the water pressure and a shock wave subsequently rolls through the pipe. When the wave hits a dead end, like a closed faucet, it reverberates and makes a pounding noise.

The problem can sometimes be solved by simply turning off the faucet more slowly. The sure cure, however, is to install a water-hammer arrester in the line, very close to the problem faucet.

The arrester acts like a tiny shock absorber to dampen vibration and muffle the pounding sound. Normally, an arrester is installed on both the hot line and cold lines. Water-hammer arresters are available at plumbing supply dealers.

Basement Backup

Sewage backing up into your basement through a floor drain, utility sink, shower drain or toilet when it rains heavily is one of the most unpleasant scenarios you can face.

To resolve this problem, you should install a valve in your sewer line beneath the basement floor. Several types of valves will work. The most convenient is a check valve, which contains a large flapper that automatically prevents flow in the wrong direction. Unfortunately, it can collect debris, which will prevent it from closing tightly.

The alternative is a manual shutoff valve. If you install one, however, you'll have to dash down to the basement to close it whenever a severe storm hits. And while the valve is closed, you can't use any of the drains in your house.

Another solution is to install a manual valve as a backup to the check valve, or to add manual valves to each basement drain. This way you can still use the upstairs plumbing during a storm. Check on pricing with a local plumber before you make a decision.

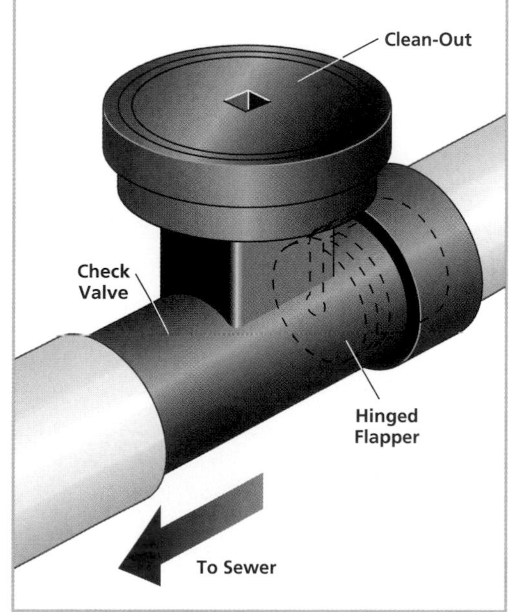

WARM PIPES

Extremely cold weather can be disastrous for water pipes that run along outside walls or unheated spaces, such as the attic or basement.

To keep these pipes from freezing, place insulation between the pipes and the unheated space. Don't insulate between pipes and the living area, though. Seal around pipes and vents that pass through wall framing, using an expandable polyurethane foam sealant. Use silicone caulk to seal cracks on the outside of any wall cavity that contains pipes.

If possible, pipes for sinks and lavatories should come up through the floor rather than in from the exterior walls.

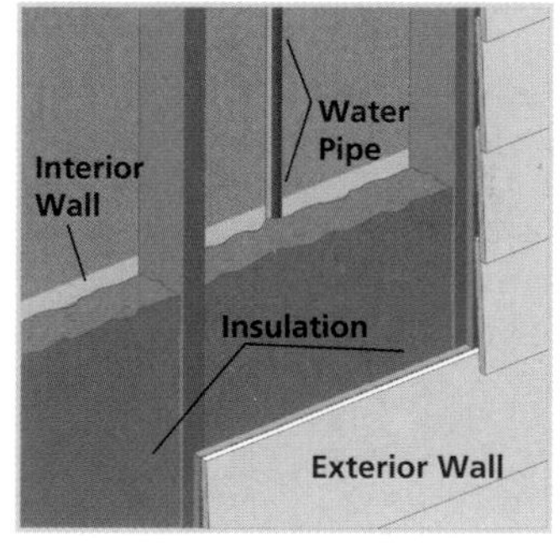

Quiet Please

Improperly installed water pipes can raise a racket by banging against floor joists. To quiet them, cushion pipes by wrapping them in rubber blankets cut from old inner tubes or garden hoses. Wrap the material completely around the pipes and secure it to the joists with nail-on metal pipe strapping. Install these silencing blankets every 4 feet or so.

Hot-Water Delivery

In very long runs of hot-water pipe, the water may cool before it reaches the fixtures. The solution is to run an extra line back to the water heater and install a bronze recirculation pump.

Begin by cutting a T-fitting into the end of the hot-water line at the bathroom. Run a ½" copper pipe back to the water heater. Install a recirculation pump, check valve and an aquastat (water thermostat).

Cut a T-fitting into the cold-water pipe that supplies water to the heater, and install a second check valve in the cold water line that leads to the heater. Once the line and pump are installed, set the aquastat to 110°F so it starts the pump whenever water temperature at the bathroom falls below that level, providing a steady supply of hot water on demand.

Healthier Water Heater

Inside most water heaters there's a long magnesium bar known as an anode rod. The metal piece protects the tank from rust by corroding before the tank does. Once the bar disintegrates, however, the tank begins to corrode. You can at least double the life of your heater by replacing the rod before it dissolves completely—every four years or so, depending on your water quality.

First, shut off the cold-water supply line to the heater. Then turn off the gas line or circuit breaker. Attach a garden hose to the draincock and carefully drain off several gallons of water. To remove the old rod, loosen its hexagonal fitting on top of the heater with a long-handled ratchet wrench, then lift out the rod.

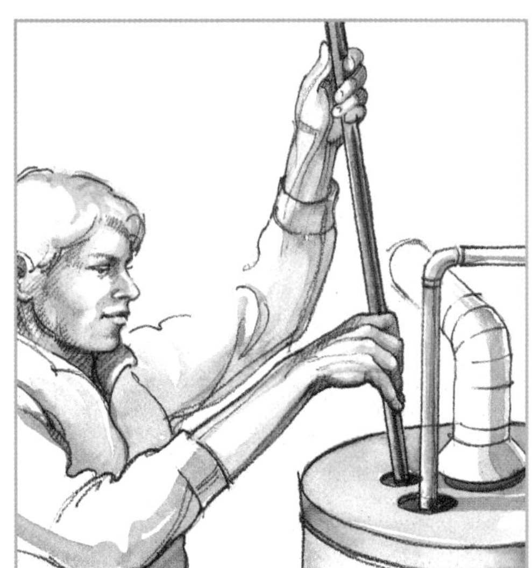

Before installing the new rod, wrap its threads with Teflon tape for better sealing. Then insert the rod into the tank and tighten it with the wrench.

Note: You can purchase bendable anode rods that are more easily maneuvered into tanks where there is little headroom.

Steam Bubbles
Anode Rod
Scale or Sediment
Curved Dip Tube
Fullport Ball Drain Valve

Daily Gurgles

Many homeowners have been startled by ominous thumps and gurgles coming from a water heater, but there's a simple explanation for this phenomenon. The sounds are produced by bubbles of steam in the water heater, and the solution is quick and easy.

The problem begins with an accumulation of sediment or hard-water scale in the bottom of the tank. When the burner comes on, the heated water can't rise because of this layer of scale and sediment, and the trapped water gets hot enough to form bubbles of steam. As the bubbles rise and escape, they condense back into water. The sound you hear is produced by collapsing bubbles.

In areas with very hard water, scale accumulates quickly unless the water is softened. You can flush out scale and sediment if the tank is fitted with a drain valve. Drain a few gallons of water from the tank every few weeks to keep the scale from building up again.

If you're replacing your water heater, look for a model with a dip tube that curves at the bottom. The curved tube swirls the incoming water around the tank bottom, helping to reduce sediment buildup.

Plumbing repairs often bring you into contact with waste water and other sources of bacteria that can cause infectious diseases.

Immediately after completing plumbing repairs, especially when working on toilets, wash your hands thoroughly with hot water and antibacterial soap.

Go Fish

If a small metal object—a pin, piece of flatware or paper clip—falls down a drain, it's time to go fishing. Tie a magnet to a piece of thick string and drop it down the drain. If you're lucky, you'll "catch" the object.

Soak It All In

To remove lime buildup from a toilet bowl, close the fill valve and flush the toilet until the bowl is empty. Soak white paper towels in distilled white vinegar and place them over the deposits. Let them soak for several hours. Scrub with a plastic brush. Repeat, if necessary.

Down the Drain

To keep the drains in your house running freely, treat them weekly. Combine 1 cup of baking soda, 1 cup of salt and 1/4 cup of cream of tartar. Pour 1/4 cup of this mixture into each drain, followed by 2 cups of boiling water.

Expansion Possibilities

Fill the tub with water before you apply caulk between the tub and the wall. By applying caulk when the tub is weighted down with water, you eliminate the possibility of cracking the caulk the first time you fill the tub for a bath.

Too Scratchy

Replace your toilet brush as soon as the bristles begin to wear down. If the bristles are too short, the metal braid can leave marks or scratches on the bowl. Marks caused by the high-carbon content of the braided frame of the brush can be removed with scouring powder. Scratches, however, cannot be removed, and they make it impossible to keep the bowl clean.

An Alternative Solution

Commercial drain cleaners are caustic, poisonous and usually unnecessary. To clear a clogged drain, try a cup of baking soda followed by a pint of vinegar. In fifteen minutes, pour two or three cups of boiling water into the drain, and the clog should be cleared.

If you do use a commercial drain cleaner, put a large plastic funnel into the drain opening and pour the chemicals directly into the drain. The funnel keeps the chemicals from damaging the fixture's surface or chrome.

Low-Pressure Solution

Mineral deposits in your piping can cause low water pressure. To remove some sediment, close the main shutoff valve. Go to the faucet that is farthest away from the water supply, remove the aerator from the faucet, and open the tap.

Now, reopen the main valve. The force of water pressure should carry some of the mineral deposits through the lines and out the open tap.

Rubbing alcohol removes mildew and stains from silicone caulking around tubs and in showers.

Fight soap scum by applying a light coat of mineral oil to glass shower doors.

To keep bathroom surfaces free of soap scum and mildew, coat them with paste wax. Do not wax tubs or shower floors.

Try using liquid dishwasher detergent and an old toothbrush to clean grout.

Automobile rubbing compound removes spots from stainless steel sinks. It also leaves a thin film of wax that fights future spots.

Filtre
1000
Outperforms all other 3 month, 1" (2.5 cm) filters at removing AIRBORNE ALLERGENS including Pet Dander, Mold and Bacteria AND MICRO PARTICLES including Smoke, Viruses and Dust.
• Also traps most large particles including Pollen and Lint
• No antimicrobial added: Filtrete™ filtering material will not support the growth of bacteria, mold, mildew or fungi in normal use
• 3 months of filtering performance
Filtre antiallergène pour particules microscopiques et l'air ambiant
Filtro reductor de alérgenos y micropartículas
16x25x1

HVAC

Your heating, ventilation and air-conditioning systems are perhaps the greatest contributing factors to the comfort of your home.

A well-designed, well-maintained HVAC system is reliable, efficient and safe. It creates and maintains a consistent, comfortable climate within your home, regardless of outside weather conditions.

Weather extremes place unusual demands on an HVAC system and, as a result, problems or breakdowns often occur during the coldest or warmest times of the year. Periodic inspection and preventive maintenance help you avoid the inconvenience and expense of unexpected problems. These measures also make your system more energy efficient and less expensive to operate. Experts estimate that preventive maintenance can reduce your energy bills by an average of 10-25 percent. And finally, preventive maintenance makes your HVAC system safer by reducing the risk of carbon monoxide poisoning.

This chapter suggests ways to upgrade and maintain your HVAC system, as well as ideas that will improve the air quality in your home.

Helpful Terms

CFM rating: The CFM (cubic feet per minute rating) for ventilation fans is the measurement of how quickly and how much air a fan moves; this information is usually disclosed on a fan's housing

Carbon monoxide: Odorless, colorless, tasteless gas produced by defective or improperly vented fuel-burning appliances; deadly in large quantities

Duct system: The formed-sheet-metal pathway that distributes air from a heating or cooling plant throughout the house

Duct damper: Louvers inside duct systems that can be adjusted to increase or decrease the flow of air through a specific duct

Radon: Naturally occurring radioactive gas that becomes dangerous when highly concentrated in a well-sealed house; a leading cause of lung cancer

Zoned central air: A central A/C system that is divided into two or more zones with separate thermostats that operate independently of each other

Balancing Heating and A/C Systems for Even Distribution

In a balanced heating-and-cooling system, warm or cool air is supplied according to the needs of each room. If your system doesn't deliver enough heated or cooled air to rooms that are far away from the source, you can adjust the systems to distribute air more efficiently.

To make the balancing process easier, map your duct system just as you would map the circuits to your electrical system, noting which ducts lead to each room. Make labels from masking tape and apply the labels to the appropriate ducts.

You will need to adjust your damper settings once in the winter and once in the summer to properly balance the system. Balancing your system on days with typical temperatures gives the best results. Follow the steps outlined below to make the adjustments:

Check the joints between the ducts. Leaks from loose or missing duct tape are common. When checking for leaks, don't forget the crawl space, if you have one. Seal any cracks or loose seams to minimize air leakage.

Purchase one table-type thermometer for each room in your house. Place each thermometer with a separate duct and register.

Adjust dampers in the ducts and at each register and grille. For rooms that are typically the warmest—usually smaller rooms or those nearest the furnace or central air unit, partially close the duct dampers by turning the wing nut clockwise.

Place one table thermometer at desk height in each room. Check the settings several times during the day. Close or open dampers until temperatures are roughly the same in every room.

Once the room temperatures are balanced, mark the settings on the dampers with a felt-tipped marker. Use different colors for the winter and summer settings.

Duct tape fails for a number reasons, including applying it to dirty surfaces and using the wrong kind of tape. If you're going to use tape, start by cleaning the surface with a nonflammable residue-free cleaner, such as isopropyl (rubbing) alcohol. For rectangular metal ducts, use a cloth-backed tape made specifically for furnace ducts. If your ducts are made of fiberglass, a metallic duct tape is the best choice.

Mastic Instead

When it comes to sealing ducts, there are two camps—those who use duct tape and those who use mastic. While duct tape is a tried-and-true solution, mastic has advantages. Some contractors consider duct tape to be a temporary solution—arguing that it eventually rots, harbors mold and mildew and eventually comes undone. These mastic advocates claim that mastic is a better, more permanent solution.

If you decide to use mastic, take care to select a product that is appropriate for the job. Because your furnace conducts heat, the product you choose must perform consistently when heated and without posing a fire hazard. Experts recommend that you purchase a water-based mastic with a flame-spread rating of 25 or less and a smoke-developed rating of 50 or less.

Because most hardware and home centers don't carry duct mastic, you may need to purchase it from a heating-equipment distributor or heating contractor.

Duct mastic comes in 1-gallon buckets. To seal your ducts with mastic, use a trowel or paintbrush. Wear heavy rubber gloves that will resist tearing.

Fill the joint or crack with the mastic, and apply an even coating with a ½" overlap. The product will cure quickly, forming a durable seal.

To save energy and use your air conditioner more efficiently, turn it off when you leave the house for an extended period of time. Recooling the house when you return requires less energy than maintaining the temperature while you're away.

Muffling the Cooler

If your central air-conditioning unit dispenses a lot of noise with its cold air, there are several ways to block the sound.

If you can hear the unit from inside the house, chances are it's been positioned too close to a window. Have the unit moved away from the window but still close enough to use the existing hookup. Or, install a storm window to block some of the sound.

If noise is a problem outdoors, deflect it upward by building a 6-ft.-high privacy fence with boards on both sides. The boards should be staggered so you can't see through the fence but air can still flow. Check the owner's manual for the minimum clearance between the fence and the central-air unit.

If you're shopping for a new central-air unit, look for one with a scroll compressor, the quietest type available. And when comparing noise level ratings of one unit to another, make sure the decibel data is taken at the same distance from the source.

Rezoning the A/C

In homes with central air, it's common for one or two rooms—or even an entire story—to be warmer than the rest of the house. The ideal solution is to convert the central A/C to a two-zone system that delivers more cool air to the warmest area.

Turning a one-zone system into a two-zone setup involves adding dampers within the ductwork, extra thermostat-control wiring and, sometimes, new A/C equipment.

Another option is installing a window air conditioner in the overly warm room. If you run this unit during the hottest hours of the day, the main system won't have to chill the whole house just to make the hot spot comfortable. If the added window unit is a high-efficiency model, it can actually save electricity during peak cooling periods.

KEEPING COOL

Keeping cool in the summertime is a real challenge in some climates. Air conditioning makes your home more comfortable, but there can be a significant price tag attached to that comfort. To lower cooling costs, limit the amount of sunlight your house absorbs.

Choose a light color for your exterior paint or siding. Dark colors absorb 70 to 90 percent of the radiant energy that strikes them, while light-colored surfaces reflect radiant energy (heat) away from the house.

Install a radiant barrier on the underside of your roof. While there is some difference of opinion over their effectiveness, the Department of Energy continues to state that radiant barriers can reduce heat gains through ceilings by about 25 percent. In some areas of the country, utility companies offer financial incentives for installing radiant barriers, so check with your local utility company as well as insulation contractors.

Apply reflective window coatings or films on windows. Approximately 40 percent of heat gain is transferred by windows. *Sun-control films* can reflect as much as 80 percent of the incoming sunlight. They also reduce the transmission of light. *Combination films* let more heat in, but also transmit more light. They are a good choice for homes in areas that include both hot and cold seasons.

Shade your home with landscaping, awnings, shutters and solar screens. The point is to block the sunlight before it reaches the house. Combinations of trees, shrubs and exterior shading devices can reduce indoor temperatures as much as 20 degrees on extremely sunny days.

If your air conditioner is not cooling effectively and oily water appears in the drip pan, call a service technician. The oily water indicates that the unit is leaking Freon—a toxic refrigerant that can cause severe burns.

Fixing a Dripping Bathroom Fan

If your bathroom is located beneath an uninsulated attic, you may notice water dripping from the grille of the ceiling fan in the winter.

The dripping water is caused by moist bathroom air condensing on the cold walls of the fan's ducting. A lateral duct run through an uninsulated area should be installed with a slight slope away from the fan when possible. This permits any water that collects in the duct to drip outside. Fan ducts can also be insulated, which keeps them warm and prevents condensation from forming.

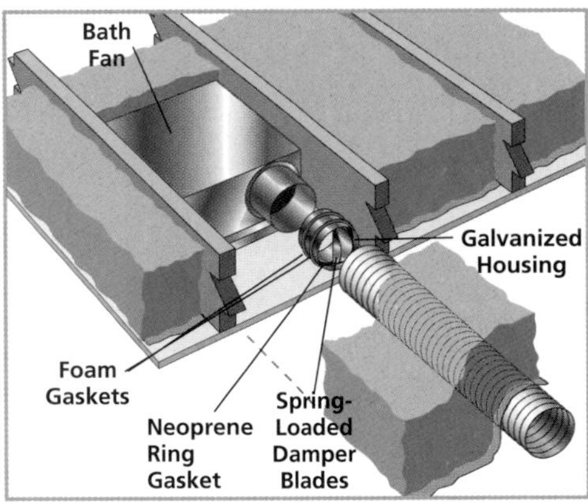

To stop the dripping, try starting the fan a few minutes before you take a shower. This will warm up the duct before the moist air enters it. Continue running the fan for at least 15 to 20 minutes after showering to empty the duct of any residual moisture. If your fan is operated by a simple on/off switch, swap it for a timer switch. If that doesn't work, you may also have to wrap the duct with insulation or replace it with insulated ducting.

Another common bathroom fan problem is heated air escaping from the bathroom fan after it has been turned off. This problem is caused by a faulty damper inside the fan.

Most fans have a duct damper to block airflow when the fan is turned off. It consists of a pair of spring-loaded butterfly plates located inside the fan's duct outlet. To check these, separate the duct and fan housing. Look for debris around the plates, which may be preventing the butterfly plates from closing.

The dampers should open only when the fan is running. Check the damper spring, which may have become disconnected or broken. If the plates are worn out or broken, you'll need to replace them with a retrofit damper.

Troubleshooting Basement Moisture

In order to resolve a moisture problem in a basement, you have to determine the source of the moisture. Here's a low-tech, yet effective, way to find where the moisture is coming from: Cut a few 12" × 12" squares of aluminum foil or thick plastic, and tape them on the walls and floor. Wait several hours; then check for condensation on the outside of the foil or plastic. If the surface is wet, moisture is in the air—a problem you can often solve with a dehumidifier.

If the underside of the foil or plastic is wet, moisture is passing through the wall or floor from the soil. An interior coating can provide some relief, but you should also attack the source.

For starters, avoid heavy watering of your foundation plantings. Check and make sure that all gutter downspouts are directed away from the house, and make sure that foundation grading carries water away from the house.

MOISTURE BUSTERS

There are numerous steps you can take to reduce moisture accumulation in the basement. Try these easy, practical measures:

- Seal the outside basement door
- Caulk gaps around plumbing pipe entrances
- Vent your dryer exhaust outside
- Keep the upstairs basement door closed
- Close and seal all basement windows
- Cover walls with 6-mil polyethylene
- Apply a sealant to the concrete slab floor
- Run a dehumidifier

Choosing Smoke Detectors

It's common knowledge that smoke detectors are a home-security essential. It's less widely known that specialized detectors are designed for specific areas of the house.

In kitchens, detectors with silencing features prevent the false alarms that might otherwise be triggered by cooking smoke.

In hallways and stairways, units with safety lights illuminate escape routes in an emergency.

In garages, heat detectors that sound only when the air temperature reaches 135°F are more efficient than smoke detectors, which can be set off by a car's exhaust fumes.

Carbon Monoxide—The Silent Killer

Carbon monoxide (CO) is known as the silent killer because it's odorless, colorless and tasteless. It's produced in the home when fuel is burned by a furnace or water heater. If the appliance is defective or not venting properly, CO can collect in the house and pose a health risk. Approximately 250 people die each year in the United States from CO poisoning.

One of the best ways to protect your family is with a CO detector. They're available at most home centers and hardware stores for about $30 to $60.

Another way to stay safe is to perform regular inspections of your home's heating system. The safety specialists at Underwriters Laboratories suggest that you look for these signs of potential CO danger:

- Condensation on the windows and walls of the furnace room.
- Streaks of black soot around the furnace's service door.
- Accumulating rust on fireplace flue pipes.
- Soot falling and building up in the fireplace.
- Poor draft in the chimney, a sign that it may be blocked.
- Water seeping from the base of a chimney, vent or flue pipe.
- Damaged or discolored bricks at the top of a chimney.

You should also have your heating system inspected once a year by a qualified technician. UL has published on informative booklet titled *Questions and Answers about Carbon Monoxide and CO Detectors*. To obtain a free copy, write to: Underwriters Laboratories, Literature Dept., 333 Pfingsten Road, Northbrook, IL 60062.

Radon Alert

Radon is a naturally occurring radioactive gas. It is present everywhere, and inside a tightly sealed house it can be highly concentrated and deadly. According to the Environmental Health Center (a division of the National Safety Council), exposure to elevated radon levels is a leading cause of lung cancer, second only to cigarette smoking.

Testing your house for radon is the only way to detect the presence of this gas. Contact the Environmental Protection Agency or your state health department to receive a recommendation for a qualified radon testing service or radon-control contractor.

SAFETY FIRST

Change the batteries in your smoke detectors twice a year. A convenient way to remember is to change them in the fall, when you set the clocks back, and in the spring, when you set them ahead.

TEST YOUR AQ (AIR QUALITY)

Your mother was right—fresh air is good for your health. But many of us aren't letting enough fresh air into our homes. The supersealed homes built in the 1970s and 1980s do not admit as much fresh air as older, more drafty, houses. As a result, the poor air quality plays host to a myriad of health risks, including allergy-causing molds and mildews, radon gas and carbon monoxide exposure.

The following checklist is designed to help you determine the quality of the air in your house. If you answer "yes" to more than 10 of these questions, you'll need to take steps to improve your air quality.

- ❑ Are cars parked in an adjoining enclosed garage? (Count one "yes" for each car.)
- ❑ Does the air in your house seem stale?
- ❑ Do you have polyurethane, ureaformaldehyde or asbestos insulation?
- ❑ Do you use rooms located below ground level?
- ❑ Is there rust or corrosion on your heating vents?
- ❑ Does anyone living in the house smoke?
- ❑ Is there moisture or mildew on your windows or walls?
- ❑ Do furry pets live in the house?
- ❑ Does anyone regularly spend more than 12 hours at one time in the house?
- ❑ Do you have houseplants?
- ❑ Do you use products in pressurized aerosol canisters, such as deodorant or hairspray?
- ❑ Do any residents have chronic health problems such as asthma, bronchitis, allergies or hypersensitivity pneumonitis?
- ❑ Are there unusual odors?
- ❑ Does dust quickly accumulate on your furniture?
- ❑ Are there dirt or dust stains on your walls, draperies or furniture?
- ❑ Did you recently winterize your home?
- ❑ Are there any residents younger than 4 or older than 60?
- ❑ Does your house regularly feel unusually warm or cold?
- ❑ Do you use insecticides, such as flea bombs, inside?
- ❑ Do you practice any of the following hobbies inside: jewelry making, woodworking, model building or pottery?
- ❑ Do you use any unvented gas appliances?
- ❑ Do the flames on the heater or stove burn yellow rather than blue?

Breathe Easier

If you have two minutes and a couple of dollars to spare, you can quickly improve the air quality in your home.

Simply replace the filter for your central air-conditioning or forced-air heating system. The degree of improvement you get will depend on the filter you select.

A standard $1.99 fiberglass filter protects against dirt, dust and lint. Upgrading to a $10 filter provides even more protection against these pollutants, while a pleated $25 filter delivers even better protection and also blocks some pollen.

SAFETY FIRST

Always turn the electricity to a furnace or air-conditioning unit off before performing any maintenance to the blower fans.

Never adjust the "high limit" switch (located on the fan control switch panel) inside a forced-air furnace. The high limit switch automatically shuts the furnace down if it becomes too hot.

Air Cleaner Standards

Chances are, if you live with a smoker you probably own at least one air cleaner. But is it effective?

An easy way to rate an air cleaner is by determining the appropriate clean-air delivery rate (CADR) for the room in which you're using the machine. CADR is the amount of clean air delivered by an air cleaner; this measurement should be included either on the air cleaner or in the manufacturer's literature.

Below are the optimal CADR ratings for common-size rooms:

ROOM SIZES (SQ. FT.)	CADR
80	50
120	80
144	100
192	120
224	145
320	200
360	230
400	250
480	300

Maintaining Central Air-Conditioning Systems

Central air-conditioning units require some basic maintenance. Replacing the furnace filter monthly, even during cooling season, will ensure that your system operates with an adequate airflow.

Other important maintenance steps include keeping the cabinet louvers, coils and aluminum fins clean and debris-free. To clean these parts, remove the cabinet cover. With a garden hose or shop vac, clear away any dirt or leaves that have accumulated on the cover. Also, hose or vacuum the dirt from the coils and fins. Check the cover periodically and remove any debris that collects, especially after a thunderstorm.

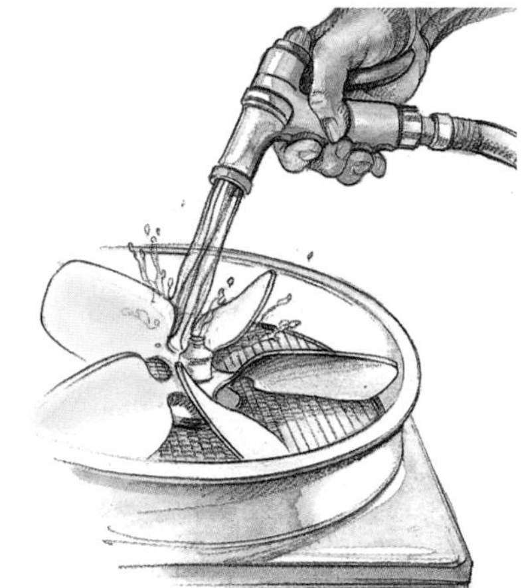

Clean Machine

Gas-burning furnaces will function efficiently for years, provided they receive proper maintenance. In addition to changing the filters, you should clean the air shutters twice a year. In the fall before heating season and in the spring afterward, use the soft brush attachment on your vacuum cleaner to vacuum the air shutters. The vacuum will remove the dirt and dust that have accumulated to keep the pilot light working efficiently.

Do the Math

Like many homeowners, you may experience the unfortunate problem of having an air-conditioning system that cannot effectively cool the entire house. And an inefficient system can really drive up your utility bills in the summer.

Before upgrading your A/C system, determine what size unit is best for your home.

A/C units come in a variety of sizes, measured in "tons." A ton is a measurement equivalent to 12,000 Btu (British thermal units). Home air-conditioning systems are available in sizes from 1 to 7 tons.

To determine what size unit you need, hire a contractor to calculate the amount of "heat gain" your home experiences in the summer. Heat gain, which is measured in Btu, is the amount of heat that is in your home and the rate at which this heat is produced. With the help of specialized tables, contractors calculate a specific measurement of the heat gain for your house. The tables take into account factors such as insulation type, insulated and uninsulated square footage, number and size of windows and directional location of windows and doors.

Once you have an accurate heat gain reading, you'll know how many tons are appropriate for your home's new A/C system.

Maximize Winter Energy Savings

- Close doors and heating ducts in unoccupied rooms.
- When your fireplaces are not in use, close the dampers.
- Change furnace filters monthly.
- Vacuum heat registers weekly.
- In the winter, set the thermostat to 68°F when you're home and to 58°F when you're away or sleeping.

QUICK TIPS

To keep your thermostat functioning accurately, periodically remove the cover and slide a business card between the contacts. The paper will remove any dirt or dust that could affect the connection.

Extinguishing the pilot light in your furnace at the end of heating season will not only save energy but prevent rust. That's because water vapor, released by the burning pilot light, condenses on the surface of the heat exchanger and promotes rust.

Central air-conditioning units run more efficiently when they are cool. The best way to ensure that the unit stays cool is to shade the outdoor compressor. Try using an overhead lattice panel or awning, or planting shrubs.

Painting

This chapter covers all phases of interior and exterior painting, from buying to cleanup.

3"
76.2 mm

Interior Painting

Freshly painted walls create a backdrop for a beautiful room. Preparation is the key to attractive, long-lasting paint jobs.

Quick Reference

A fresh coat of paint is a quick way to add a fresh sense of polish and style to any room. That may be one of the reasons that architectural paint sales in the United States amount to over $6 billion annually. Another way to look at the numbers: Americans purchase approximately 3 gallons of paint per capita each year.

You don't have to hire professionals to get a great paint job. By preparing surfaces properly, selecting the right paint and materials and using professional techniques, you can achieve a smooth, long-lasting finish. Armed with the ideas in this chapter, you can protect yourself from toxic paint fumes, avoid painting windows shut, purchase the right amount of paint and select exactly the color you want.

Helpful Terms

Acrylic: A synthetic resin-based paint; synonymous with "latex"

Alkyd: An oil synthesized from organic sources, such as plant fiber, hydrocarbons and petroleum-based chemicals; indicates an oil-base paint

Binder: A liquid in latex or alkyds that forms a solid film after solvents evaporate

Drying agent: A compound added to paint either to extend or retard drying time

Enamel: Paint that forms a hard, glossy surface; often used on woodwork and trim

Glaze: Mixture of paint, water and paint conditioner; mainly used for decorative painting techniques; forms a translucent top coat when dry

Latex paint conditioner: Product that increases the drying time and extends the wet-edge time of paint; originally developed for use in paint sprayers with latex paint, it is an essential part of making glazes for faux finishes

Open time: The amount of time a paint remains wet or workable after it is applied to a surface

Pigment: An element, such as iron oxide or titanium dioxide, that imparts color or coverage qualities to the dried paint

Primer: A product used before painting to seal porous surfaces so the paint spreads smoothly with even penetration; also used to ensure good paint adhesion

Wet edge: A painting technique that involves painting from wet areas into dry, blending the paint to minimize lap marks

Imagine That

Trying to visualize how a color will look on your walls? Here are some helpful suggestions:

Buy a pint of the color you are considering. Paint a 2 × 3-ft. piece of canvas; then tape the canvas on the wall. Move it to several different places in the room during this testing phase.

Check the sample at several different times of day. Notice how the color changes under varying lighting situations. If a room is most often used at a specific time of day, check the color at that time.

When you've decided on a color, keep a small piece of the canvas to use as a guide when shopping for other items for the room.

SAFETY FIRST

Protect yourself against toxic vapors, such as those from oil-based paints and solvents, and against toxic particles, such as asbestos or sawdust from treated lumber, with a dual-cartridge respirator. Correct use of a respirator can prevent lung irritation and disease. Choose an OSHA-approved respirator and use the proper filters in the respirator cartridges. Replace the filters frequently, according to manufacturer's directions.

Surface Impressions

Selecting paint isn't as simple as you might think. In addition to the spectrum of colors, there are sheens, or finishes, to consider.

There are four basic paint sheens: gloss, semigloss, eggshell (satin) and flat. Flat and eggshell paints are less reflective, which means they hide minor surface imperfections. Gloss and semigloss paints are more durable and generally easier to clean. The chart below will help you select the most appropriate type of paint finish for each room of the house.

INTERIOR PAINT SELECTION GUIDE

FLAT	EGGSHELL/SATIN	SEMIGLOSS
Ceilings	Ceilings	Kitchen
Hallways	Hallways	Bathroom Cabinets and Doors
Bedroom	Bedroom	
Living Room	Windows and Trim	
	Living Room	**GLOSS**
	Cabinets and Doors	Windows and Trim
	Bathroom	Kitchen
	Kitchen Windows	Cabinets and Doors
	Trim	Bathroom

Penny-Wise Paint

Buying less expensive paint may seem like an easy way to cut the cost of painting a room. But before you buy paint, compare the coverage rates and compute the approximate cost to complete the whole project with different paints. A cheaper price per gallon does not always translate to a less expensive job. The chart below illustrates an example where cheaper paint is actually more expensive in the long run.

COMPARING COST AND DURABILITY

CONSIDERATIONS	PAINT QUALITY	
	Low	High
Average cost per gallon	$6.99	$17.99
Average coverage per gallon (1 coat)	250 sq. ft.	400 sq. ft.
Amount needed to paint 1,200 sq. ft.	4.8 gals.	3 gals.
Cost to paint 1,200 sq. ft.	$33.55	$53.97
Estimated life of paint	4 yrs.	8 yrs.
Average cost per year	$8.39	$6.75
Cost over 8 years	$67.10 (2 coats)	$53.97 (1 coat)

Brushing Up on Brushes

Buying paintbrushes can be confusing. You have to pick the right type, size and shape for the specific job you're working on.

Here's a simple guideline to follow when choosing brushes: water-based paints require water-tolerant brushes, while oil- and alkyd-based paints need natural-bristle brushes.

Water-tolerant brushes are made with synthetic filaments. Most professionals prefer synthetic brushes with nylon filaments, but water-tolerant brushes can also be made with polyester filaments.

Synthetic brushes come in three basic shapes: solid, cross-sectional and hollow. The solid shape is the easiest to clean and lasts the longest. However, the cross-sectional filament is an economical choice. Many professionals say that you should avoid the hollow-shape brushes.

Natural-bristle brushes are a good choice if the paint you're using is not water tolerant. Any brush labeled as natural, China, hog or boar has bristles made from pig's hair. Like human hair, natural bristles react to water by puffing up and becoming unruly. However, these brushes hold their shape well when used with oil-based paints. Natural-bristle brushes can tolerate harsh solvents that literally melt synthetic brushes.

Both synthetic and natural brushes are available with tips that are ragged, or flagged. The flagged tips help the brushes carry more paint and deliver it evenly onto a surface.

However, many new reduced-solvent paints are heavier and resist flowing when applied with flag-tipped brushes. For this reason, some synthetic brush tips are sanded and tapered to make the paint flow more easily.

Synthetic and natural brushes also come with two different trim styles.

Wall brushes (above, top) are generally thick brushes designed to carry lots of paint and distribute it widely. They range from 3 to 5" in width.

Wall trim brushes are usually square and used for creating broad strokes over a large area.

Trim brushes (above, middle) are for painting doors, cabinets and "cutting" ceilings and walls. They range from 2 to 3" wide.

Chisel trim brushes have a fine, diagonally cut point and are used primarily for detailed work.

Sash brushes (above, bottom) are used primarily for painting windows, molding and baseboards. They come with an angled or square shape and generally run from 1½ to 2½" wide.

Getting Ready

To achieve a high-quality, long-lasting paint finish that adheres well to the surface, it's important to prepare the surface properly.

The preparation steps vary, depending on the type of surface you are painting. Often it is necessary to apply a primer to the surface before painting it.

PREPARING SURFACES FOR PAINTING		
SURFACE TO BE PAINTED	**PREPARATION STEPS**	**PRIMER TYPE**
Unfinished wood	• Sand surface • Wipe with damp cloth to remove grit • Apply primer	Fast-drying oil-based or latex primers
Previously painted wood	• Wash surface and rinse with clear water; allow to dry • Sand surface lightly, removing any loose paint chips • Wipe with damp cloth to remove grit • Apply primer to any areas of bare wood	Fast-drying oil-based or latex primer, only on areas of bare wood
Previously varnished wood	• Wash surface and rinse with clear water; allow to dry • Sand surface to degloss • Wipe with damp cloth to remove grit • Apply primer	Fast-drying oil-based or latex primer
Unfinished wallboard	• Dust with hand broom or vacuum with soft brush attachment • Apply primer	Flat latex primer
Previously painted wallboard	• Clean surface to remove any grease and dirt • Rinse with clear water; allow to dry • Apply primer, if necessary	Flat latex primer, only if painting over dark, strong colors
Unpainted plaster	• Sand surfaces as necessary • Dust with hand broom, or vacuum with soft brush attachment • Apply primer	Polyvinyl acrylic primer
Previously painted plaster	• Wash surface and rinse with clear water; allow to dry thoroughly • Fill any cracks with spackling compound • Sand surface to degloss • Apply primer, if necessary	Polyvinyl acrylic primer, only if painting over dark, strong colors

Prepping Concrete Surfaces

Preparation is the key to a good paint job, particularly when the surface to be painted is a concrete floor, such as in a laundry room or shop.

First, sweep and scrape off the dirt from the floor. Then clean off any grease, oil and other contaminants, using solvents or a cleaning solution. Remove all traces of soap from the laundry room floor.

Next, etch the concrete with a muriatic acid solution. Before you begin the etching process, get the proper safety gear; the acid is strong enough to burn skin and eyes. You'll need chemical-resistant rubber gloves, splashproof goggles and rubber footwear. If you can't ventilate the work area, wear a dual-cartridge respirator.

Mix a solution of one part muriatic acid to three parts water in a plastic or enameled-metal pail. Add the acid to the water, not the water to the acid. Apply the solution at a rate of one gallon per 100 sq. ft. and scrub the floor with a stiff-bristle brush. Leave the solution on the floor until it stops bubbling. Rinse it thoroughly with clear water; then wipe it down with a damp sponge mop to eliminate puddles. If the floor isn't dry after four hours, repeat the rinsing procedure.

After it has thoroughly dried, vacuum the floor to remove the powder residue. Then paint the floor with an alkyd or urethane-latex floor and deck enamel.

Next time you're painting windows, try something new. Rather than masking off the glass with tape, try a liquid masking product.

This acrylic latex product is specially formulated to prime and seal wood trim and to mask off the glazing quickly and efficiently. Paint the thick, white paste onto the trim, lapping over onto the glass.

When the masking is dry, it forms a clear, thin sheet that sticks solidly to the wood but peels away from the glass quite easily, leaving a clean, unpainted surface.

Cut Paint Prep Time

Professionals trim prep time by using glazing putty instead of wood filler or spackle to fill nail holes and make minor repairs on wood trim. Usually used to hold glass in windowpanes, the pliable putty is ready to use right out of the container. It won't shrink and it can be applied so it doesn't require sanding. For best results, use putty that doesn't contain linseed oil.

High-Ladder Act

One challenge you'll face when painting the walls and ceiling of a staircase leading from a first-floor foyer up to a second-story hallway is reaching high spots safely.

A number of expensive, multi-jointed ladders are designed for tricky situations like this. But an extension ladder, sturdy plank and ordinary stepladder will work just as well.

To paint the head wall—the vertical area above a staircase—try the ladder-and-plank arrangements shown in the illustrations. The setup works for tall walls and high ceilings. To adjust your working height, simply move the plank up or down on the ladder rungs. Be sure to use a sound scaffold plank or rent an expandable aluminum one. Be sure the plank is level, and never place it on the very top of the ladder. Move slowly and carefully when working on the scaffolding, and use sawhorses or rope to block off the staircase to traffic.

Boxing Paint

Even though custom colors are mixed according to specific formulas, color can vary slightly from one can to another. If your painting project requires more than one gallon of paint, you could end up with a noticeable variance.

To avoid this problem, mix, or *box*, the paint. Pour all the paint into a large pail. Stir the paint thoroughly with a wooden stick or power drill attachment.

It's in the Bag

Next time you're using latex paint, save time by covering the paint tray with a plastic grocery bag. Turn the bag inside out, slip it over the tray and pour in some paint. When you're done, pour any leftover paint back into the can for storage. Slide the bag off the tray and and set it out of the reach of children and pets. When the paint is completely dry, put the bag into the garbage.

QUICK TIPS

Here's an easy way to remember what color or style to buy when you need to touch up paint or repair wallpaper: Before you replace the switchplate covers when painting or wallpapering a room, write the paint color or the wallpaper name and numbers on a piece of tape. Stick the reminder on the back of a cover and replace it.

Keeping a Wet Edge

Many people cut in along the edges of an entire room before beginning to roll the paint. But, pros will tell you it's better to cut in a small area and then roll it while the edge is still wet.

This technique, called "keeping a wet edge," gives you a smooth finish and avoids the lap marks that can develop when you paint over dry edges.

Professionals always try to roll paint from dry areas back into wet areas, blending the paint to create a continuous layer.

If two people are working on the project, one can cut in with a brush while the other rolls large areas.

Another way to minimize brush marks along the edges is to slide the roller cover slightly off the frame of the roller when rolling near the ceiling line or wall corners. This lets you get closer to the ceiling with the roller, eliminating brush marks.

Window Painting 101

Although it may seem quite simple, there is an art to painting windows. Here are a few tips from the pros:

Whenever possible, remove double-hung windows from their frames for painting. To create an easel, drill holes and insert two nails into the legs of a wooden stepladder, then set the window up easel-style for easy painting. Or, lay the window flat on a bench or sawhorses. Do not paint the sides or bottom of the sash.

Using a tapered sash brush, paint the wood next to the glass. With the narrow edge of the brush, overlap the paint onto the glass to create a weather seal. When you've painted all the way around the window, clean the excess paint off the glass with a putty knife wrapped in a clean cloth. Rewrap the knife often so that you're always wiping with clean fabric. Leave a 1/2" paint overlap from the sash onto the glass.

Paint the rest of the window in the following order: flat portions of the sash, case moldings, sill and apron. Use slow brush strokes and avoid painting the joint between the sash and the frame.

If you must paint windows in place, move the painted windows up and down several times during the drying period to keep them from sticking. Use a putty knife as indicated in the photo below to avoid touching the painted surfaces.

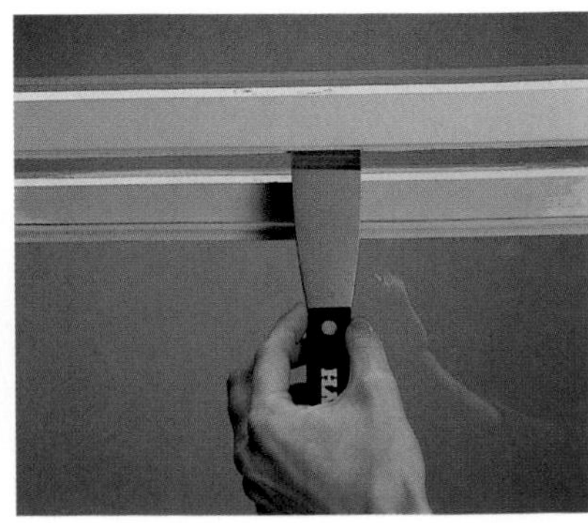

Decorating Techniques

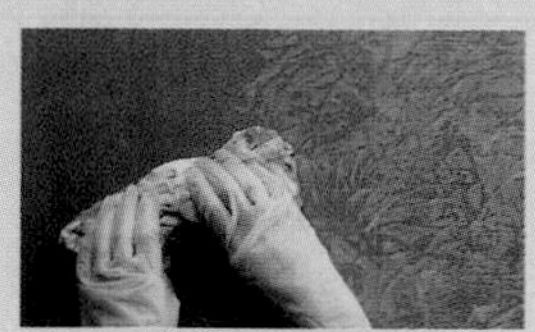

Rag rolling:
Roll a lint-free rag into an irregular shape and fold it to approximately the width of both hands. Then roll the rag through a coat of wet glaze, working upward at varying angles. Refold the rag frequently and change rags as often as necessary to remove glaze in a consistent pattern.

Sea sponge:
Saturate a damp sea sponge with paint or paint glaze. Blot the sponge lightly on a paper towel and press it repeatedly onto the surface, working quickly and at varying angles. Repeat with one or more additional colors if desired.

Rolled corrugated cardboard:
Tape a roll of corrugated cardboard securely together. Use the corrugated end to make designs in coat of wet glaze. Or apply glaze directly to cardboard; blot, and then print designs on the surface.

Color washing:
Apply color-washing glaze to wall in a cross-hatched pattern with a wide paintbrush, beginning in one corner. The more you brush the surface, the softer the appearance will be. Brush over the surface again with a dry brush to further soften the look.

Crumpled paper:
Press crumpled paper into a coat of wet glaze. Or apply glaze directly to paper; press onto the surface, crumpling the paper.

Fan brush:
Press a fan brush into wet glaze, making uniform rows of fan-shaped impressions. Or apply glaze directly to fan brush and print fan-shaped designs on the surface.

Paint Conditioning

Many types of decorative painting require the use of a paint glaze, made by adding paint conditioner to the paint. This conditioner extends the drying time of the paint, giving you time to manipulate the paint in a variety of ways.

To make a basic glaze, mix together one part latex or craft acrylic paint, one part latex paint conditioner and one part water. This coating can be used with decorative techniques such as the ones described above.

Paint fumes are more dangerous than many people realize. The term "adequate ventilation," which often is included in paint product warning labels, means that there should be no more vapor buildup indoors than there would be if you were using the material outside.

If the product label includes the warning "harmful or fatal if swallowed," you should assume that the vapors are dangerous to breathe. Open windows and doors, and use a fan for ventilation when painting indoors.

Use an OSHA approved dual-cartridge mask to filter vapors if you cannot ventilate a work area sufficiently. If you can smell vapors, the ventilation is not adequate.

Exterior Painting

Your home's exterior paint makes a strong first impression. A well-painted house indicates a quality home and a responsible owner.

According to the National Paint and Coatings Association, approximately 500 million gallons of architectural paints are manufactured in the United States each year for do-it-yourselfers and painting contractors. In fact, architectural paints, which include household paints, account for more than half the paint and coatings sold in the United States each year. These numbers reflect a simple truth: a new coat of paint can brighten your home's exterior and quickly improve its appearance.

Whether you're doing the painting yourself or hiring a professional, the information in this chapter can help you save time and money, select the best materials for the job and achieve a superior, long-lasting finish.

Helpful Terms

Alligatoring: Widespread flaking and cracking of painted surfaces

Blistering: Bubbles on painted surfaces; caused by trapped moisture

Color retention: A paint's ability to maintain its original color after prolonged exposure to direct sunlight, indirect light and oxidation

Heat gun: Tool frequently used to loosen paint when stripping a surface; generates extremely high temperatures and must be used with caution

Hiding: A paint's ability to form an opaque film that effectively covers, or hides, previous layers of color or surface stains

Mildewcide: An additive that retards or prevents the growth of mildew, algae and fungus on painted surfaces

Peeling: Paint failure associated with persistent moisture problems; occurs when paint falls away from the surface in flakes

Pigment: An element, such as iron oxide or titanium dioxide, that imparts color or hiding to the dried paint film

Rheology additives: Chemical added to both alkyd and water-base paints that improves flow and leveling

Volatile organic compounds (VOCs): Carbon-base liquid solvents, such as turpentine, alcohol, xylene and various petrochemicals, that evaporate rapidly as paint dries; also often referred to as volatile organic substances (VOSs)

evaluation

Evaluating the painted surfaces of your house will help you identify problems with siding, trim, roofs and moisture barriers. Check sheltered areas first.

Evaluating Old Paint

Initial signs of paint failure in areas that receive little or no direct sunlight are a warning sign that neighboring areas are in danger of similar paint failure.

Blistering describes paint that bubbles on the surface. It is an early sign that more serious problems, like peeling, may be forming.

Blistering can result from poor preparation or hasty application of primer or paint. The blisters are caused by trapped moisture as it forces its way through the surface.

Scrape and touch up localized blistering. For widespread damage, remove paint down to bare wood, then apply new primer and paint.

Localized blistering and peeling indicates that moisture, usually from a leaky roof or gutter system, is trapped under the paint. Check above to find the source of the leak. Also look for leaking pipes inside the wall. Correct moisture problem before you scrape, prime and repaint.

Peeling occurs when paint disengages entirely from the surface, falling away in flakes.

Peeling is often associated with persistent moisture problems, generally from a leak or a failed vapor barrier.

Identify and correct the moisture problem. If the peeling is localized, scrape and sand the damaged areas only; then touch up with new primer and paint. If it's widespread, remove the old paint down to bare wood. Apply new primer and paint.

Clearly defined blistering and peeling occurs when a humid room, like a bathroom, has an insufficient vapor barrier. If you can clearly see a line where an interior wall ends, remove the wall coverings and replace the vapor barrier or use a vapor-retarding paint.

Alligatoring is widespread flaking and cracking of surfaces, typically seen on old paint and surfaces with many built-up layers of paint.

Alligatoring can be caused by excessive layers of paint, inadequate surface preparation or insufficient drying time for a primer.

Repainting will not permanently cover significant alligatoring. Remove the old paint down to bare wood; then prime and repaint.

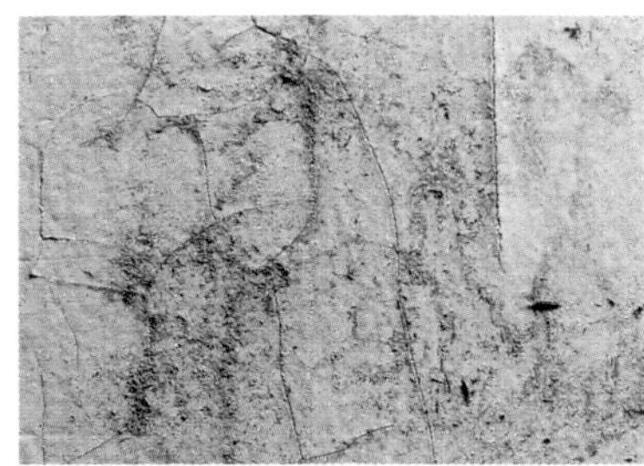

Mildew forms in cracks and in humid areas that receive little direct sunlight. Wash the areas with a 1:1 solution of household chlorine bleach and water, or with trisodium phosphate (TSP) to kill the mildew.

Good Painting Weather

Check the weather before you start painting, and keep an eye on the sky while you work. Damp weather or rain that falls within two hours of application will ruin your paint job.

The best time to paint is on a mild day (between 60° and 85°F) with little or no wind. On windy days, dust and dirt can be blown onto the freshly painted surface.

Always avoid painting an area in direct sunlight. Exposure to hot sunlight dries primers and paints too quickly, trapping moisture below the dried surface. This can result in blistering, peeling and other types of paint failure. Lap marks and brush marks are also more likely to show up if you paint in direct sunlight.

Estimating Paint Needs

Add:
Square footage of walls (length × height)
Square footage of soffit panels
15% allowance for waste

Subtract:
Square footage of doors and windows

Determine:
The coverage rate (350 sq. ft. per gallon is an average rate)
Read the paint label to find this figure

Divide:
The total square footage by the coverage rate to determine the number of gallons you will need for each coat of paint

SAFETY FIRST

For large projects, such as painting a house, relying solely on ladders is inefficient and dangerous. Use scaffolding for projects that require you to work at heights for extended periods of time. If you rent scaffolding, ask for assembly and use instructions.

Insert sturdy blocking under scaffold feet if the ground is soft or uneven. Add more blocking under legs in sloped areas, and use the adjustable leg posts for final leveling. If the scaffold has wheels, lock them securely with the brakes.

Anchor scaffolding by tying it to a secure area, such as a chimney. If no sturdy anchoring spot exists, create one by driving a #10 screw eye into the fascia. When the project is finished, remove the screw eye and fill the hole with caulk.

Test the Surface

If you live in an older home, there are probably several layers of paint covering its exterior. As paint ages, it often loses its elasticity and begins peeling and chipping. Painting over these existing layers could be a costly mistake. Your fresh new coat of paint will be ruined if sections of the old paint deteriorate and fall off the house.

Try this simple test to determine whether or not you can safely paint over old paint layers: with a utility knife, etch a 1" by 1" square grid pattern, using six lines 1/8" apart in each direction, into the paint on several sections of the exterior. Don't scratch too deeply or you will damage the surface. Firmly tape a 2"-long section of masking tape over the center of the grid. Then yank the tape off of the house. If any paint comes off with the tape, you'll need to remove all of the old paint and apply a coat of primer before you begin painting.

TOOL BOX

Removing thick layers of old paint is an unpleasant necessity, but there is a way to make this task less time-consuming—use a heat gun to loosen the paint before scraping.

Aim the heat gun at the surface, and move it constantly. Scrape as soon as the paint releases.

Heat guns generate extreme heat that is focused in small areas. To avoid starting a fire, read and carefully follow the manufacturer's directions and precautions.

Preparation Is the Key

Preparing the surface is a crucial part of the exterior painting process. Generally, the more preparation work you do, the smoother the finish will be and the longer it will last.

For the smoothest finish, sand all the way to bare wood with a power sander. For a less time-consuming (but rougher) finish, scrape off loose paint, then spot-sand the rough edges. Pressure washing alone removes some flaky paint, but will not create a satisfactory finish.

If you decide to sand lap siding, rent a siding sander with a disk the same diameter as the width of the reveal area on your siding. Check with rental store personnel for specific use instructions, and read the manufacturer's directions and precautions.

The Pressure Is On

If you decide to pressure-wash your siding, use the right equipment. For the average house, a pressure washer with 1200 to 2500 psi is appropriate. Less than 1200 psi won't do an adequate job and more than 2500 psi could damage your siding. Nozzle sizes are important, too. Experts recommend using 15- and 25-degree nozzles. You'll also need an extension attachment and a rotating scrub brush for hard-to-reach areas. As you work, direct the water stream at a downward angle, and avoid getting too close to the surface with the sprayer head.

Removing Paint from Metal and Masonry

You'll have an easier time removing old paint from metal and masonry if you use the right tools for each task.

Use a wire brush to remove loose paint and rust from metal hardware, such as railings and ornate trim. Apply metal primer immediately after brushing to prevent new rust from forming.

Scuff-sand metal siding and trim with medium-coarse steel wool or a coarse abrasive pad. Wash the surface before priming and painting.

Use a drill with a wire-wheel attachment to remove loose mortar, mineral deposits or paint from mortar lines in masonry surfaces. Clean broad, flat surfaces with a wire brush. Correct minor damage with masonry-repair products.

Spread tarps over delicate plants and shrubs and on the ground around your house to collect debris and prevent damage from excess paint.

Turn off the power to air-conditioning units and other exterior structures near the house and cover them with tarps as well.

Paint Primer

As you plan an exterior painting project, certain questions may arise. Here are answers to four commonly asked questions:

Do I need to use a primer? A primer should be applied to any unpainted surface. When repainting, apply a primer if the surface (or patches of it) has been stripped or worn down to bare wood.

Which is best, latex or oil-based paint? Latex paints adhere well to most surfaces and resist bleaching and fading better that oil-based coatings. Oil-based paints create thinner coats and leave sharper lines on woodwork and trim.

Can I use latex paint over an oil-based paint? Today's acrylic latex paints provide excellent adhesion to oil-based paints.

Do I have to apply two coats? The best process is to apply one primer coat followed by two top coats of paint. However, if the surface was previously painted and the old paint is still sound, a single coat of new paint will offer protection from the elements.

QUICK TIPS

To paint efficiently, hold the paintbrush at a 45-degree angle when painting broad, flat areas. Apply just enough downward pressure to flex the bristles and "squeeze" the paint out of the brush.

To achieve a smooth finish, load your paintbrush with the correct amount of paint for the area you're painting, and avoid over-brushing.

First Things First

Painting a house is a major undertaking, and, like many big jobs, it needs to be broken down into manageable tasks. Addressing these tasks in a logical sequence makes the process simpler.

Working on one face of the house at a time, prime an area, let it dry, and then paint the primed area. Plan your project so that you can paint within two weeks of priming. If more than two weeks pass between coats, wash the painted surface with soap and water before applying the next coat. If you don't, the next coat may not adhere properly.

Prime and then paint surfaces in the following order:

- Face of the fascia.
- Bottom edges of the soffit panels.
- Any decorative trim near the top of the house.
- Gutters and downspouts, beginning with the back sides and working toward the fronts. (Use metal primer for these areas.)
- Soffit panels and trim. Start by cutting in around the edges of the panels using the narrow edge of the brush; then feather in the broad surfaces of the soffit panels with full loads of paint. Make sure you brush paint into the grooves between panels.
- Bottom edges of lap siding. Use a 4" paintbrush held flat against the wall. Paint the bottom edges of several siding pieces before returning to paint the faces of those boards.
- Broad faces of the siding boards. Working from the top down, paint all the way to the foundation. Shift the ladder or scaffolding and move to the next section. Paint up to the edges of the corner trim and window and door trim. If you're not planning to paint the trim, use a paint shield.
- Foundation. Using anti-chalking masonry primer, cut in around the windows; then paint the broad surfaces, working the paint into any mortar lines.
- Doors and windows (see page 86 for the correct sequence).
- Inside edges of door and window jambs, casings and brick moldings.
- Outside edges of casings and brick molding.
- Faces of doorjambs, casings and brick molding, feathering fresh paint around the edges.
- Wooden door thresholds and porch floors. Use specially formulated enamel floor paint for maximum durability.

Just Right

Most professional painters agree that brushes provide better coverage than rollers or sprayers. According to recent research, the total paint coat (primer and top coats) should equal four to five mils, which is approximately the thickness of a piece of newspaper. To consistently achieve optimum coverage with a brush, try this technique.

Load your paintbrush with a full load of paint. Starting at one end of the surface, make a long, smooth stroke until the paint begins to "feather" out.

As you finish the stroke, lift the brush gradually from the surface so you do not leave a definite ending point. If the paint appears uneven or contains heavy brush marks, smooth it out. Avoid over-brushing.

Reload your brush and make a stroke from the other direction, painting over the feathered end of the first stroke to create a smooth, even surface. If you can see where the two strokes meet, rebrush with a light coat of paint. Feather out the starting point of the second stroke.

All in Good Time

For a smooth surface on doors and windows, use a sash brush and take care not to let the edges dry as you work from one area to another. Paint in the following sequence:

- Beveled edges of raised door panels and the insides of muntins or frames on windows.
- Faces of the door panels.
- Rails (horizontal frame members) on doors.
- Faces of the stiles (vertical frame members).

Board and Batten

On board and batten, or any vertical-panel siding, paint (1) the edges of the battens or top boards first. Paint (2) the faces of the battens before the sides dry; then paint (3) the large, broad surfaces between the battens, feathering in at the edges of the battens. Rollers are good tools for panel siding (use a 5/8"-nap sleeve for rough-textured panels).

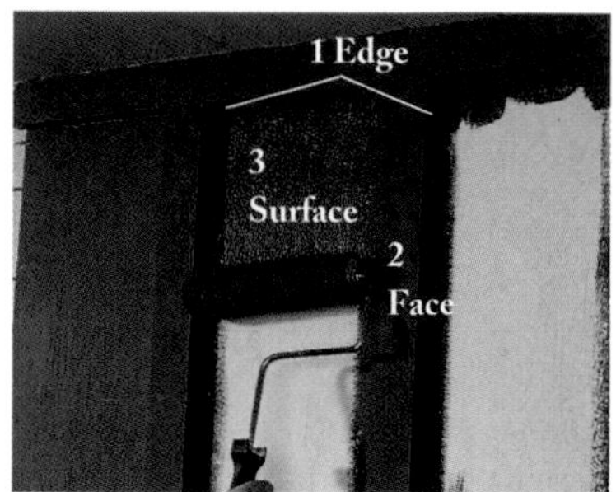

Stucco

Stucco is a popular, easily maintained exterior surface. However, because stucco is porous, it requires special care.

To ensure that the paint is absorbed, use a specially formulated masonry paint. Paint stucco with a roller and a 5/8"-nap sleeve.

Dealing with Leftovers

There are only three things you can do with open cans of paint: save them for later, give them away or throw them out.

Stash it. Don't get rid of every last drop of paint. Save some for touch-ups, especially if you used a custom-mixed color. To keep the paint fresh, place plastic wrap over the can. Then replace the lid tightly, tapping it with a rubber mallet all the way around, and store the can upside down for a tight seal.

Donate it. If the paint is still usable, give it away. Housing organizations, religious groups and schools are obvious candidates. Community theater groups are often thirsty for paint.

Toss it. Throwing liquid paint in the trash is illegal almost everywhere; oil-based paint, for example, is considered a hazardous waste. Call the sanitation department in your area for information on paint collection. Even water-based (latex) paint in liquid form is prohibited in landfills. But most waste collectors will accept solid, dried latex paint—again, call first to check. To dry out latex paint, pour it in a cardboard box and add cat litter, shredded newspaper or any absorbent material. Put the box out of the reach of children and pets, and let it dry. When the paint is completely dry, put the entire box in the trash.

Keep Your Spirits Up

Place used mineral spirits in a sealed container until solid paint sediments settle out. Pour off the clear solvent for later use; then set the residue outdoors in a protected location where children and pets cannot reach it. Let the residue dry completely; then dispose of it in an approved manner.

TOOL BOX

When cleaning a brush in a container of solvent or water, don't stand it up—you'll bend the bristles. Instead, rinse out all the paint, rake the bristles out straight with a brush comb and hang the brush to dry.

When the brush is dry and ready for storage, wrap the bristles in a sheath cut from a brown paper bag. Place a rubber band around the metal ferrule to secure the sheath; then lay the brush flat or hang it up.

SAFETY FIRST

Never use kerosene, mineral spirits or other solvents to wash paint off your skin. These hazardous materials are skin irritants and can be absorbed by the body.

Ordinary vegetable oil will remove oil or oil-based paints and stains from skin, safely and inexpensively.

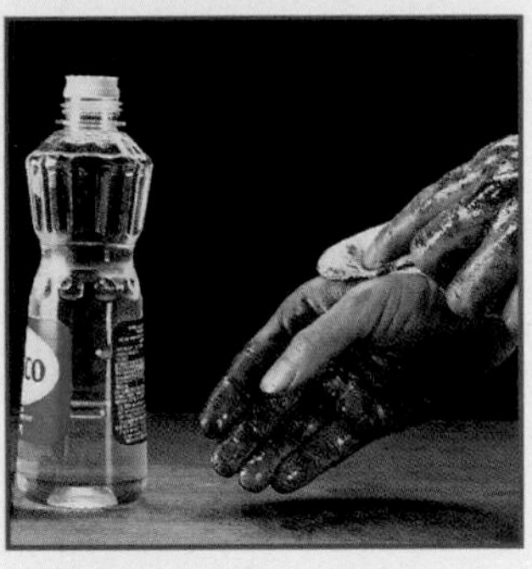

Handling It

Protect your hands by making a paint bucket handle from a length of old garden hose. Slice a spiral cut in the hose; then fit it over the wire bucket handle.

Exteriors

In this chapter you'll find new ideas for maintaining and improving your home's siding, roofing and insulation.

LAMONT®

Roofing

Investing in high-quality materials and performing the necessary roof maintenance are the best ways to protect your home and everything inside.

Your roof is the shell that protects you and your house from the elements. Each year, your roof may face abuse from extreme heat, high winds, hail, heavy rain and snow. Any one of these elements can take its toll, and in most regions our roofs must stand up to a combination of these forces. That is why making regular inspections of your roof is an important responsibility. Preventive maintenance, early detection of roof failures and prompt repairs are the keys to keeping your roof in top shape.

In moderate and cold climates, inspect your roof twice a year. Each spring, check to see how well your home weathered the winter. Look for signs of damage or wear to your roof system. Make repairs immediately to extend the life of your roofing and protect your home from further damage. In the fall, clean your gutters and repair any loose, buckled or missing shingles to prevent damage during the winter months.

If you live in a warmer climate, inspect and, if necessary, repair your roof annually and after severe storms. Keeping your gutters clear is especially important if your region receives a lot of rain.

Helpful Terms

Drip edge: Metal strips protecting the edges of eaves where rainwater flows into the gutters

Fascia: Facing boards that close off the eave area at the roof over hang; attached to the rafter tails or rafter lookouts, the fascia provides a surface to which gutters are attached

Flashing: Formed sheet metal, aluminum or copper that surrounds pipes, chimneys and other elements where they penetrate the roof; also directs the flow of water on a roof

Shakes: Wood roofing shingles, usually made from cedar, that have at least one grain-split side

Sheathing: 1× boards or plywood that covers the rafters and creates a surface for roofing

Valley flashing: The long runs of flashing that drain the area between two intersecting roofs

Pinpointing Leaks

The best place to begin inspecting a leaking roof is inside the attic. Look for discoloration, streaking or rot on the roof sheathing and rafters. To pinpoint the source of the leak, find the highest point of the discoloration. Once you've found the source, measure from that point to the nearest identifiable roof element, such as a vent or chimney. When you go out on the roof, use this measurement to locate the leak.

If the damage is minimal and rot has not set in, simply repair the shingles or flashing. If there is substantial rot, have a professional replace the damaged sheathing and reshingle the roof.

Ice-Dam Breaker

If you live in a cold, snowy region, you already know about the damaging effects of ice dams. Gutters clog up with ice, and water runoff from the roof gets trapped by the ice. Eventually, ice builds up on the roof and forms under the shingles. When the ice under the shingles melts, it can leak into the house.

The only way to avoid ice dams is to improve insulation, vapor barriers and ventilation in the attic. However, there is a simple way to minimize the damage if an ice dam has already formed.

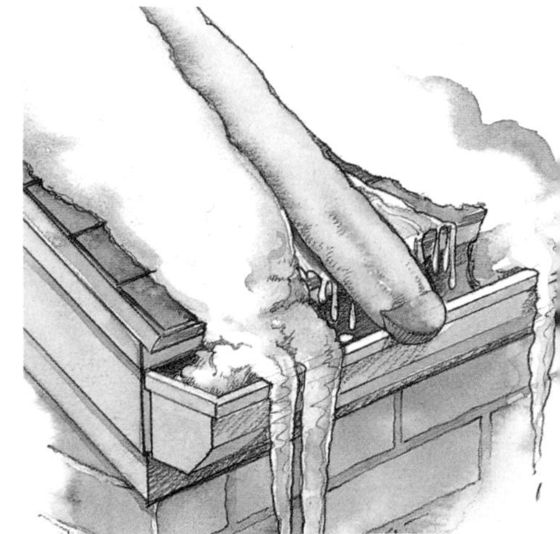

Fill a leg of a discarded pair of panty hose with a calcium chloride ice melter, and tie it closed. Lay the hose onto the roof so it crosses the ice dam and overhangs the gutter. If necessary, use a long-handled garden rake or hoe to push it into position. The calcium chloride will eventually melt through the snow and ice and create a channel for water to flow down into the gutters or off the roof.

COMMON SHINGLE PROBLEMS

Buckled or cupped shingles usually are caused by lingering moisture beneath the shingles. This moisture is created by condensation from poor attic ventilation or by leaky shingles or flashing. You can anchor loose areas with plastic roofing cement.

Damaged and worn shingles become increasingly common as a roof ages. As shingles get older, their protective mineral surface wears down. Depending on your specific situation, repair by tearing out and replacing the old shingles or by covering the old shingles with a layer of new ones.

Use binoculars from ground level instead of climbing a ladder for quick visual inspections of roofs, gutters, chimneys and second-story areas.

When inspecting damaged roof areas, use an awl or thin-bladed screwdriver to probe beneath the surface. Sometimes damaged wooden sheathing looks almost normal on the surface.

Repairing worn, brittle asphalt shingles can be a difficult chore. To make the process faster and easier, heat the shingles with a hair dryer first. The heat softens the shingles and their adhesive backing.

Buckle Down

Slightly damaged or worn roof materials can be patched or repaired, avoiding the expense and work of replacing some or all of your roof. All you need is a good plastic roof cement, available at hardware stores.

Preparation is the key to making efficient repairs. Before applying roofing cement, wipe down the building paper and the underside of the shingle you're repairing and let the area dry completely. Then use roof cement for making the following repairs:

Attaching loose shingles: To reattach a loose shingle, first, prepare the area; then, apply roof cement liberally to seat the shingle in a bed of cement.

Tacking down buckled shingles: Start by cleaning out and preparing the buckled area. Fill the gap with the cement; then, press down on the shingle.

Sealing gaps around flashing: To prevent roof leaks caused by loose flashing, clean out the old roof cement from around the open area. Then apply a fresh coat of roof cement around the flashing joints and edges.

QUICK TIPS

Before you replace a section of asphalt shingles, age the new shingles to more nearly match the old ones.

Wipe the shingles with mineral spirits, and rinse them thoroughly. This process removes some of the granules and lets more of the asphalt show through, simulating the effects of exposure to sun and rain.

REPLACING DAMAGED ASPHALT SHINGLES

Shingles can be damaged in many ways—a tree limb may hit the roof and tear a small area; wind may catch a loose edge and pull shingles off; someone may walk on the roof during extremely hot or cold weather. Whatever the case, it's simple to replace a shingle or two:

Pull out damaged shingles in the repair area, beginning at the top. Be careful not to damage surrounding shingles that are still in good condition. Remove old nails with a flat pry bar.

Install replacement shingles, beginning with the lowest shingle in the repair area. Nail above the tab slots with 7/8" or 1" roofing nails. Install all but the final shingle with nails.

Apply roof cement to the underside of the row above the final shingle, above the seal line. Slip the final shingle into place, and press it into the roof cement. Lift the shingle immediately above the repair area, and nail the replacment shingle in place.

shingles

Relief for Splitting Headaches

Wood shingles usually last longer than asphalt shingles, but if they split they need to be replaced. You can make this repair yourself by following these steps:

Use a hammer and chisel to split the damaged shake or shingle, and remove the pieces. Pry out the pieces by cutting nails in overlapping shingles with a hacksaw blade slipped underneath the shingle. Gently pry up shingles or shakes above the repair area. Cut new shingles or shakes for the lowest course, about 3/8" smaller than the available space.

Nail replacement pieces in place with ring-shank siding nails. Fill in all but the topmost course you are repairing. Apply a coat of roof cement where these shingles will sit, cut them to fit and slip the shingles beneath the course above. Then press down on these topmost shingles to seat them in the roof cement.

QUICK TIPS

New wood shakes and shingles probably won't match the color and weathered appearance of the existing shingles. To quickly age new shakes and shingles, spray them with a solution of one pound baking soda dissolved in one gallon of warm water. Place the shingles in direct sunlight for four or five hours.

Read asphalt shingle warranties carefully. These warranties are often nontransferable. If you buy a newly shingled home, chances are the warranty will lapse once the sale is complete.

SAFETY FIRST

Use extreme caution when working on a wood-shingle roof. Wood shingles that are wet or covered with moss are very slippery.

Do not use a ladder when making extensive, time-consuming roof repairs. Rent scaffolding instead, which provides a safer, more stable surface for working. Get assembly and use instructions from the rental center.

Save a Bundle

Whether you're repairing a section of asphalt shingles or reshingling the entire roof, you'll need to know how many shingles to buy. Even if you're not purchasing the shingles yourself, you can use the following formula to double-check your contractor's estimate.

Shingles are sold in bundles but estimated in squares—the amount needed to cover 100 square feet. The most common type of shingle, called a three-tab or strip shingle, is generally packaged 3 bundles per square. Check with your building center or supplier to determine how other types of shingles are packaged.

To estimate how many bundles you need, calculate the square footage of the roof area that needs to be shingled. Increase that number by 15%, to account for trim allowance. Divide the total by 100, then multiply by the number of bundles per square (3 in this case) to find the number of bundles you'll need to purchase.

For example, if your roof is 750 square feet:

1. 750 + 15% = 862.5
2. 862.5 ÷ 100 = 8.625
3. 8.625 × 3 = 25.875 (round off to 26 bundles)

RECOGNIZING FLASHING PROBLEMS

Early diagnosis of flashing problems can save time and money. Inspect your roof occasionally to spot the following signs of common flashing problems, and make the designated repairs.

Loose flashing is usually caused by external forces like high wind or ice; it should be repaired before damage occurs.

To repair, pull back the flashing enough to clean out any old sealant. Resecure with fresh roof cement and new fasteners.

QUICK TIPS

Use aviation snips to cut rolled flashing material when making patches for small repairs.

Use copper or galvanized steel flashing, rather than aluminum, around chimneys and other masonry structures. Lime from the mortar can cause aluminum to corrode.

In a Flash

When replacing complicated flashing, such as the saddle flashing around chimneys and dormers, save the old flashing to use as a template when cutting the new pieces.

When you put on a new roof, also replace the flashing. Most roof flashing is interwoven with the shingles, and is difficult to replace if it has to be retrofitted to existing roofing.

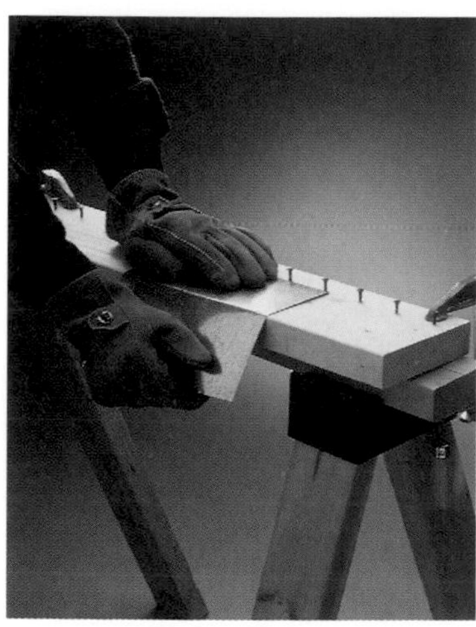

Patching Valley Flashing

Your roof relies on valley flashing to carry water down and off its surface. Deteriorated or damaged valley flashing can quickly lead to leaks. By following the steps below, you can temporarily repair damaged flashing yourself:

Measure the damaged area and cut a patch from flashing material of the same type as the original flashing. The patch should be wide enough to slip under the shingles at each side of the repair area. Break the seal between the valley flashing and the shingles around the damaged area. Scrub the damaged flashing with a wire brush, and wipe clean.

Apply a bed of roof cement to the back of the patch. Cut a slit in the old flashing; slip the top of the patch underneath the old flashing and insert the edges under the shingles on each side. Place the bottom of the patch on top of the old flashing and press it securely into the roof cement. Add cement at the seams and the shingle joints. Feather out the cement to prevent water-damming.

MATCHING ACCESSORIES

Over time, leaf and debris accumulation in gutters can cause significant damage. The excess weight from these blockages can strain gutters, causing overflowing, joint leaks and broken hangers. These problems, in turn, can lead to damage to the fascia, walls and foundation of your home.

Besides cleaning your gutters, the best way to prevent damage is to install mesh gutter guards and downspout strainers. These products help prevent debris from collecting. When selecting gutter guards, purchase a model that matches the width and profile of your gutters to ensure complete coverage.

Gutter accessories designed to protect your foundation from water damage are also available. Add splash blocks beneath downspouts and extensions to carry water away from the house.

Rehanging a Sagging Gutter

A common gutter problem, particularly on older homes, is sagging gutters. Rehanging them is a relatively simple project that you can tackle with only a few tools and a ladder—and some patience.

To rehang the gutter, start by snapping a chalk line along the fascia that follows the original slope of the gutter. The slope of gutters moves toward the downspout and is usually a 1/4" grade per 10 ft.

Next, remove all the gutter hangers in the sagging area and lift the gutter until it is flush with the chalk line, as shown. Once the gutter is in place, reattach the hangers, shifting their location slightly so that you're not using the original hanger holes. Replace the original hangers if they are in poor condition. Space hangers no more than 24" apart and within 12" of each seam.

Patch It Up

Standing water can corrode gutters, leading to holes and eventually collapse. Fixing a corroded section quickly will keep corrosion from spreading. Follow these steps to make repairs:

Wash and dry the corroded area to remove all dirt, grit and grime.

Sand the area to bare metal, and cut a metal patch several inches longer than the damaged section. Use the same metal as your gutters—aluminum, copper or galvanized-steel flashing. These metal squares are available at home centers and lumberyards.

Bend the patch as needed to conform to corners; test its fit, and mark its location with a pencil.

Remove the patch, and spread a thick layer of roofing cement over the entire area with a putty knife or scrap of wood. Embed the patch in the cement, pressing down firmly.

Apply a second coat of cement over the entire patch and beyond it onto the gutter as shown below.

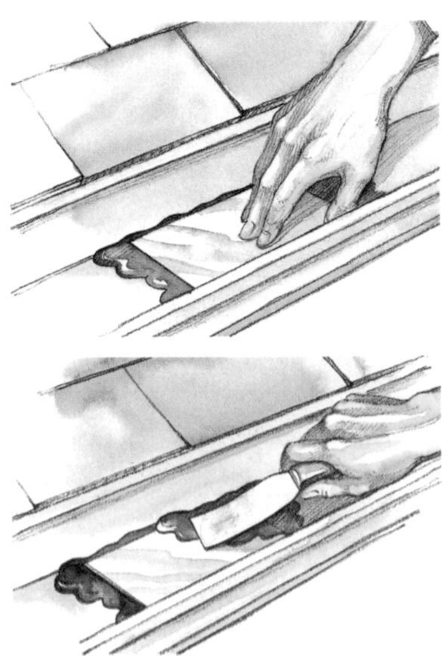

Gutter Talk

The rule of thumb for gutter repair is that if the damaged area is less than two feet long, you can replace only the damaged section. If the damage extends beyond 2 ft., it's time to replace the whole gutter.

To prevent corrosion, select replacement pieces made from the same type of metal (usually aluminum or galvanized steel) as the rest of your gutter system. Trace the profile of your existing gutters and take the drawing with you when you're shopping for replacement pieces. If your gutters are more than 15 years old, they are probably a little larger than gutters made today. Check salvage yards or have a new section custom-bent by a metal fabricator.

Here are a few suggestions that will simplify the removal process. Insert wood spacers into the gutter, near each hanger, as shown in the photo at right. This helps equalize the pressure on the gutter, protecting it from damage when you pry out the gutter spikes. And, before you begin cutting out a damaged section, slip spacers between the gutter and fascia, near each end of the damaged area. These spacers give you room to work so you don't damage the roof while you're cutting into the gutter.

Sealing Leaking Joints

Temperature fluctuations cause metal gutters to expand and contract. This process can be particularly hard on the joints in your gutter system. Over time, you may begin to have problems with leaking joints along the gutter and downspout. To repair this problem and prevent further damage, follow these steps:

Drill out the rivets or remove the screws that secure the joint. Scrub both parts of the joint using a stiff-bristled brush (it's okay to use a wire brush on metal gutters). Clean the area with water, and let dry.

Apply gutter caulk to the joining parts; then, reassemble the joint. Let the caulk dry; then, reinforce the joint with new fasteners and add new hangers if the originals need replacing.

QUICK TIPS

Use a butyl-rubber-based gutter caulk, which flexes without losing its seal, to fill small holes and seal minor leaks in metal or vinyl gutters.

To clear a clogged downspout, try using water pressure. Insert a garden hose in the bottom of the downspout, and cover the opening and the hose with a cloth to keep the water inside the downspout. Have someone turn the hose on full force. You'll know the clog is broken up when water bubbles out the top of the downspout.

Pest Prevention

If bats or birds are roosting in your attic, it's time to inspect your soffit. These are the horizontal panels under the eaves that span the area between the fascia and the outside walls. If you find damaged or missing panels, your best bet is to install a new soffit.

A complete soffit system consists of fabricated fascia covers, soffit panels and support channels that hold the panels in place. Purchasing a system with vented panels allows you to greatly increase attic ventilation—something most older homes could use. Most soffit systems sold at home and building-supply centers are made of aluminum or vinyl. Follow the manufacturer's instructions for installation.

Fascia Lift

Sagging gutters can quickly damage the fascia boards to which they're attached. You may not notice fascia damage until you repair or replace damaged gutters. But you'll have to repair the damaged sections before you can reattach your gutters.

Use the following process:

Remove the gutters, gutter hangers and shingle moldings around the damaged section of fascia.

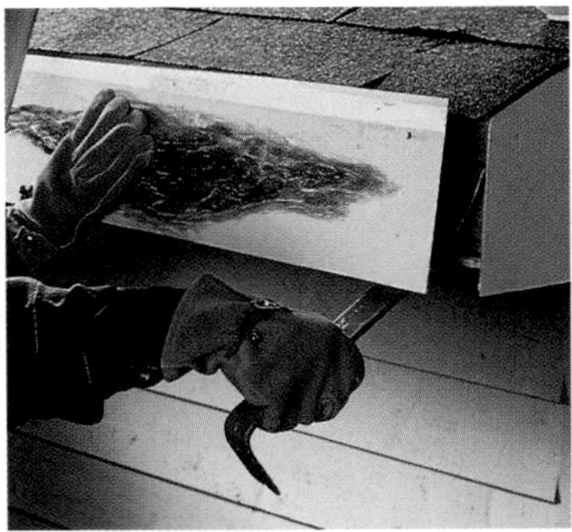

Using a flat pry bar, remove the entire board without cutting it. Also remove any old nails that remain.

With a circular saw, cut off the damaged portion of the fascia from the removed section.

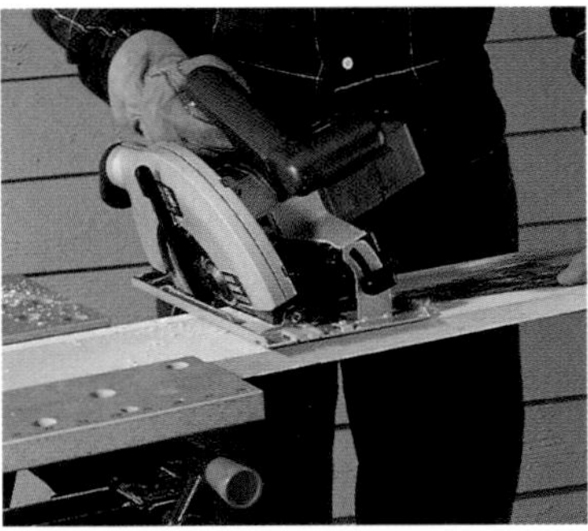

Set your circular saw for mitering, and make the cut at a rafter location. (You can identify rafter locations by the nail holes.)

Reattach the original, undamaged portion of fascia, using 2" galvanized deck screws.

Drive the screws into the rafter lookouts or rafters.

Use the circular saw to cut a patch board to replace the damaged section, mitering the end to match the adjoining piece.

Attach the patch board, using deck screws. Then drill pilot holes; drive ring-shank nails at an angle through the mitered ends of both boards to lock the joint in place.

Reattach the shingle moldings and trim, using 4d galvanized finishing nails. Set nail heads flush with the board. Prime and paint the patch to match the fascia.

Reattach the gutters, when the paint is dry.

SAFETY FIRST

Stay clear of power, cable television and telephone connections into your house when working on the roof or cleaning and repairing gutters.

Insert sturdy wood blocking under ladders or scaffolding feet if the ground is uneven, soft or slippery. The blocking ensures that equipment stays level and stable while you're working.

Stain Fighters

Fiberglass shingles commonly develop dark, mildewlike stains. The stains are caused by an algae called *Gloeocapsa magma* that feeds off the limestone in fiberglass shingles.

The best way to kill the algae is to install 7" copper or zinc strips under the shingles along the top of your roof, as shown. When it rains, the rainwater will carry small amounts of metal residue down the roof. Continuous exposure to copper or zinc will prevent algae growth and stains.

If you are planning to install new fiberglass shingles, look for shingles that contain copper-coated granules.

How Long Should This Take?

If you are planning a roofing repair, fill in the chart below to determine how long the repair should take. This chart is also helpful for evaluating a roofing contractor's estimates and invoices.

TASK	TIME REQUIREMENT	AMOUNT	TOTAL TIME
Tear Off	1 hr./square*	______	______
Install Building Paper	30 min./square*	______	______
Apply Shingles:			
• Flat run	2 hrs./square		
• Ridges, hips	30 min./10 ft.		
• Dormers**	1 hr. each	______	______
Install Flashing:			
• Chimneys	2 hrs. each		
• Vent pipes	30 min. each		
• Valleys	30 min./10 ft.		
• Skylights	2 hrs. each		
• Drip edge	30 min./20 ft.	______	______
TOTAL TIME FOR PROJECT:		______	______

Note: All time estimates are based on one worker. Reduce time by 40% if there is a helper.
* One square = 100 sq. ft.
**Include area of dormer surface in "flat run" estimate.

End of the Line

How can you tell when it's time to replace your asphalt-shingle roof? Sometimes the answer's obvious: if you have a number of leaks, if you can see many missing, loose, split or curled shingles, or you can see several bare patches where the mineral surface has worn away.

Sometimes the answer's not so obvious. Here's a method used by roofing professionals: To check the viability of asphalt shingles, select one or two shingles on the sunniest side of the roof. Bend a corner of each back and forth. If the shingles crumble or break, it's time to replace the roof.

If you use a pressure washer to clean your roof, make sure the spray fan is wide and the psi is low. Hold the nozzle at a distance so the pressurized water does not erode, break or damage shingles.

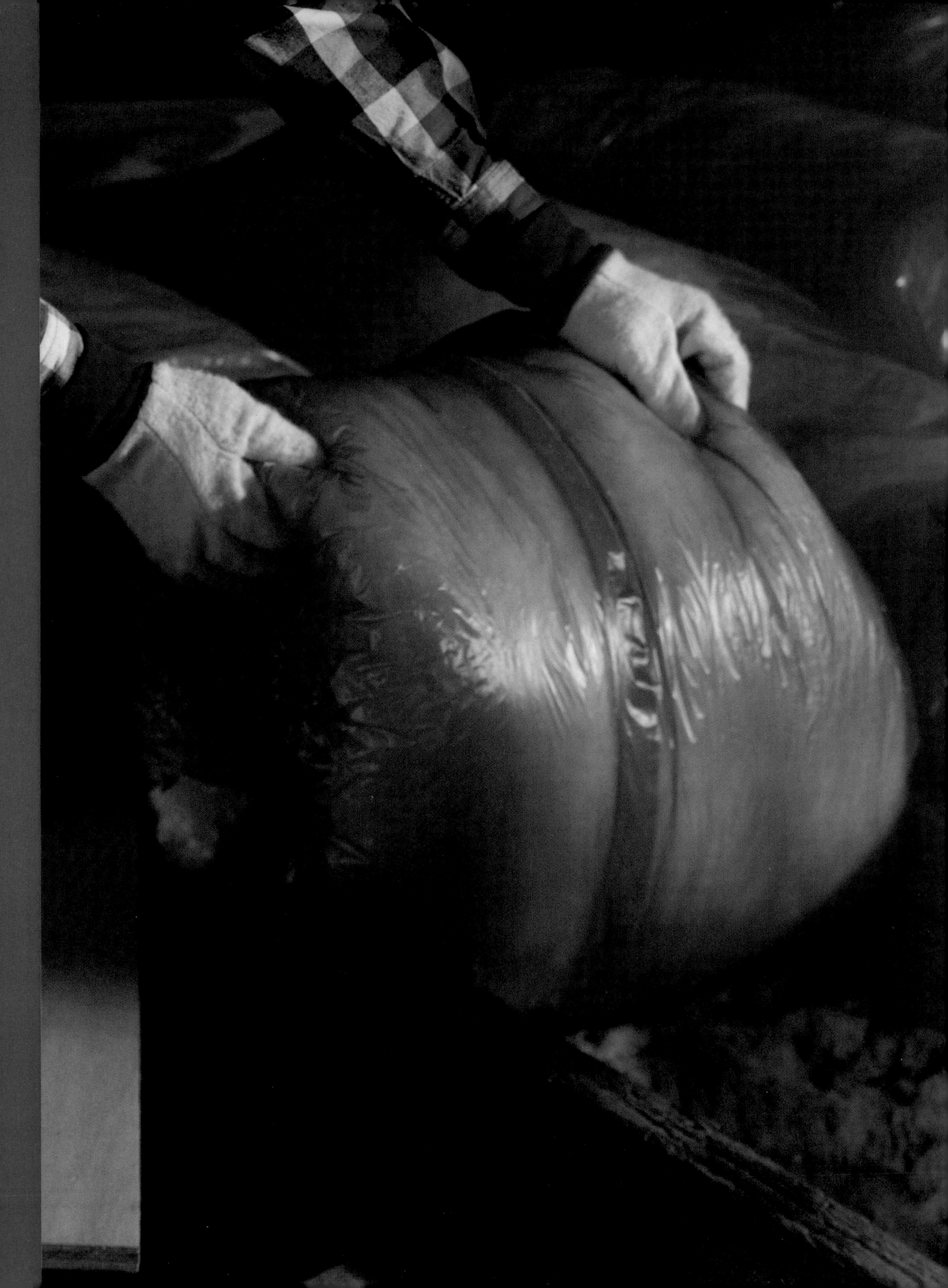

Insulation

Insulation and weatherproofing create a "thermal envelope" that improves your home's energy efficiency. Maintaining that envelope saves money in every season.

Heating and cooling account for 45% of the $115 billion that Americans spend each year on fuel and electricity, according to the U.S. Department of Energy (DOE). The DOE also estimates that average homeowners can save 10% on their energy bills simply by updating their insulation and weatherproofing. The investment required to generate these savings is often minimal. In fact, in some climates, you can pay back the cost for weatherproofing projects with the energy savings from one heating season.

If you live in a climate that includes extreme heat or cold, adequate insulation and weatherproofing are vital. Although the importance of keeping warm air inside your house during cold weather is more obvious, it's equally important to stop the infiltration of hot air during warm weather.

Whether you're concerned for the environment or just want to spend less money on utility bills, the information contained in this chapter should help you recognize and take advantage of energy-saving opportunities all around your house.

Helpful Terms

Attic blanket: Unfaced fiberglass insulation; sold in rolls and flat batts sized to fit standard joist cavities

Attic bypass: Openings into the attic from the house's interior space; examples include recessed light fixtures, exhaust fans and chimneys

Baffles: Plastic or polystyrene barriers attached to rafters; they keep attic insulation from obstructing the air flow under the roof

Rigid insulation: Boards of open or closed-cell foam that can be attached to the inside face of exterior walls, such as in a basement or the exterior face under siding

Vapor barrier: An impermeable membrane used on the inside face of exterior walls; discourages moisture generated in living space from migrating into stud cavities and condensing; can be paint, sealed rigid insulation or (most commonly) 6-mil polyethylene plastic

Tightly Sealed

Air leaking through the cracks and leaks in an average home can account for as much as one-third of the total heat loss in your home. These cracks are roughly the equivalent of having a 2-ft. hole in one wall.

Sealing air leaks with caulking and weather stripping can pay for itself in about one heating season.

Common sources of air leakage are shown in the drawing at right. Check your home for leaks, and seal as many of these areas as is practical.

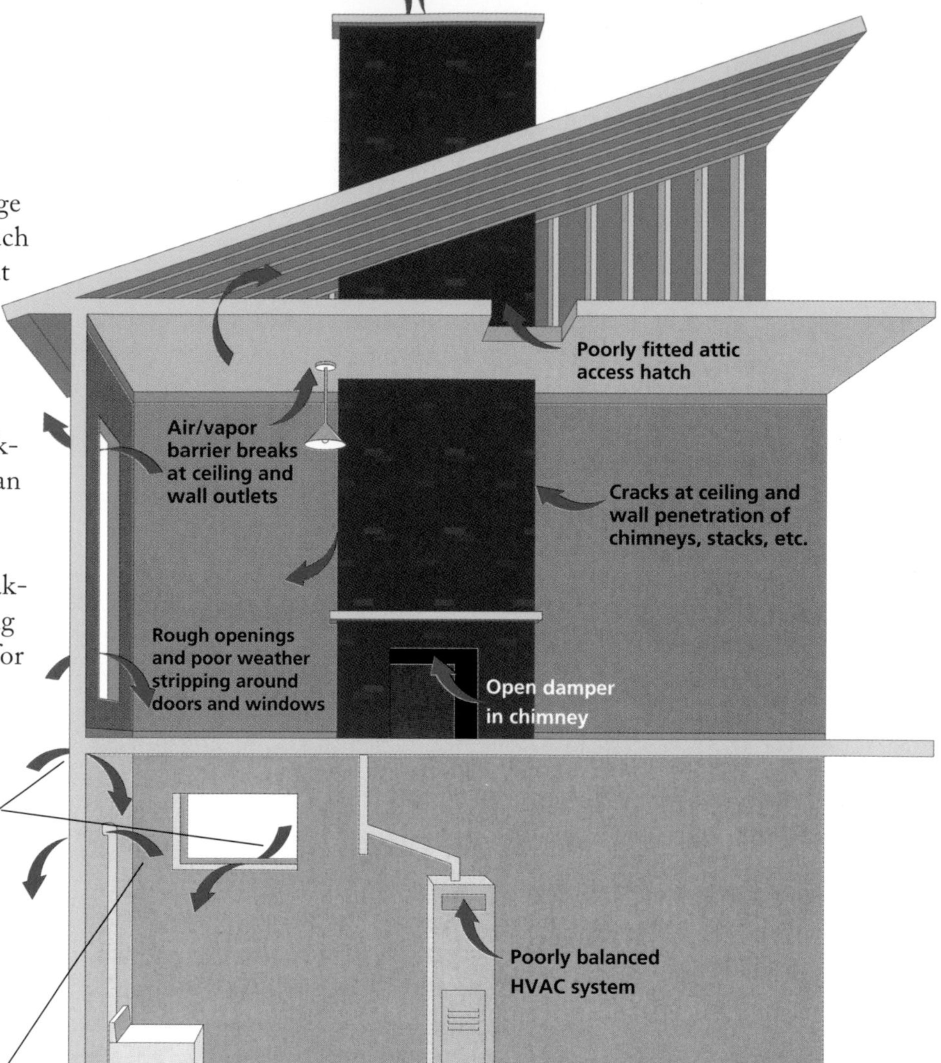

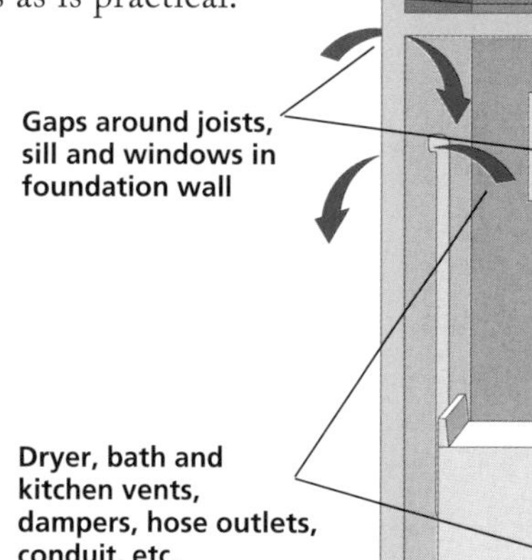

Loss Detection

Some indications that your home is not energy efficient are obvious—general draftiness, frosted windows, ice dams and high energy bills, for example. It may be more difficult to detect inadequate wall insulation or the loss of warm air around a chimney. Here are some ways to detect energy loss in your home:

Determine whether the insulation in unheated attics meets recommended standards. Measure the depth of the insulation between joists. For loose insulation, multiply the number of inches by 3.7 to find the total current R-value. For fiberglass insulation, multiply by 3.1 per inch. Compare the total to recommendations on the chart on page 103.

Measure the temperature in several different parts of a room. A difference of more than one or two degrees from one area to another may mean that the room is poorly sealed. Update weather stripping around doors and windows.

Check for drafts around windows and doors by holding a tissue next to the jambs on a windy day. Fluttering indicates that the weather stripping is inadequate and should be upgraded or replaced.

Monitor energy usage and costs. Compare them year to year, taking into account changes in rate structures or general weather conditions. If changes seem significant, consider hiring a professional to conduct an energy audit.

Get a Clue

Before you can decide whether you need more insulation, you have to determine how much you have currently. The most important areas to check are basement walls, exterior walls, floors above unheated spaces and ceilings below unheated spaces.

In an unfinished area such as an attic, it's easy to see the type of insulation and measure its thickness. It's more difficult to check insulation in finished areas, but it is possible:

Shut off the circuit and remove a switchplate cover along an outer wall. Use a plastic crochet hook to probe the area around the electrical box, checking for insulation type and depth.

Drill holes directly into an outer wall in a closet or other hidden area. Using a keyhole or reciprocating saw, cut a 1 to 1½" hole in an outer wall to check insulation.

Have an energy audit conducted by your utility company or an independent energy contractor. Ask about infrared photography, furnace efficiency instruments and a blower door test, which identifies areas of heat loss and air leaks in walls and ceilings.

Recommended Insulation Amounts

Resistance value (R-value) measures the ability of a material to resist heat flow. In simple terms, it describes the ability of an insulating material to act as a heat barrier.

The first chart below shows minimum R-values for different areas (R-values may be obtained by combining two layers of insulation). Use the second chart to determine how much insulation you can install in a specific area.

Recommended R-Values

	Cold Climate	Moderate Climate
Attic:	R-38	R-26
Wall:	R-19	R-19
Floor:	R-22	R-11

Insulation Thickness Chart

Fiberglass		Open-cell foam	
R-11 (faced)	3½"	R-4	1"
R-13 (unfaced)	3½"	R-6	1½"
R-19 (unfaced)	6"	R-8	2"
R-21 (high density)	5¼"		
R-25 (unfaced)	8"	**Urethane foam**	
R-30 (unfaced)	10"	R-5	1"
		R-10	2"

Settling In

When checking finished walls for insulation, homeowners often get the idea that insulation may have "settled" into the lower parts of the walls. In truth, you'll get a reasonably accurate picture of the state of your home's insulation no matter where you look into outer walls.

Another important piece of information you can gather from probing exterior walls is whether there are obstructions built into them. In homes built before 1930, there may be internal diagonal blocking within the walls. If so, there might not be enough space within the walls to justify the expense of adding insulation.

SAFETY FIRST

According the the U.S. Department of Energy, fiberglass, cellulose and rock wool particles can irritate the lungs if inhaled. When you add insulation, wear a dual-cartridge respirator.

If insulation fibers are drawn into your home's air-distribution system, they are circulated within your home.

To avoid potential problems, seal any bypasses where insulation could leak out of wall or ceiling openings.

SAFETY FIRST

Insulation can irritate your skin and airways, so avoid direct contact with it. Wear protective clothing—long sleeves, heavy pants, boots and gloves. Consider buying a disposable coverall to wear over your clothes. Use a respirator or face mask.

When handling cellulose, remove contact lenses and wear eye protection such as goggles.

When fiberglass fibers get onto your skin, gently pat the area with duct tape to remove them. Shower as soon as you finish your project.

Smoke Gets in Your Eyes

Sealing attic bypasses reduces moisture problems and prevents the formation of ice dams.

To locate drafts surrounding attic bypasses, carefully hold a smoking stick of incense near pipes, flues, light fixtures and other openings. If the smoke drifts in response to air movement, caulk or seal the bypass. Although incense does not have a flame, use common sense when handling it near flammable materials.

Adding On

In most homes, the attic is the biggest area for energy loss and the most common target for additional insulation. If you add insulation to an attic, keep these ideas in mind:

Seal air leaks and attic bypasses before you insulate an attic. Install vapor barriers where necessary, and make sure the attic is adequately ventilated.

Use unfaced rolls with no vapor barrier when adding fiberglass to existing insulation. A facing acts as a vapor barrier, and placing it on top of existing insulation will trap moisture and reduce the efficiency of the lower layer.

Install the new rolls of insulation perpendicular to the existing rows to ensure a good seal.

Holding Back

If insulation gets too close to an electrical fixture that generates heat, such as a recessed light or vent fan, the fixture can overheat, creating a short circuit or fire hazard.

To avoid this problem, install insulation dams between ceiling joists, at least 6" away from the fixtures. Or, use fixtures rated IC (Insulation Covered), which indicates they can be covered without creating a fire hazard.

Insulating Tops of Cabinets

If your cabinets are cold in the winter, check the insulation batts over the soffit. In many cases, dropped soffits above kitchen cabinets are open to the attic above. As a result, the ceiling insulation batts over the soffit tend to shift.

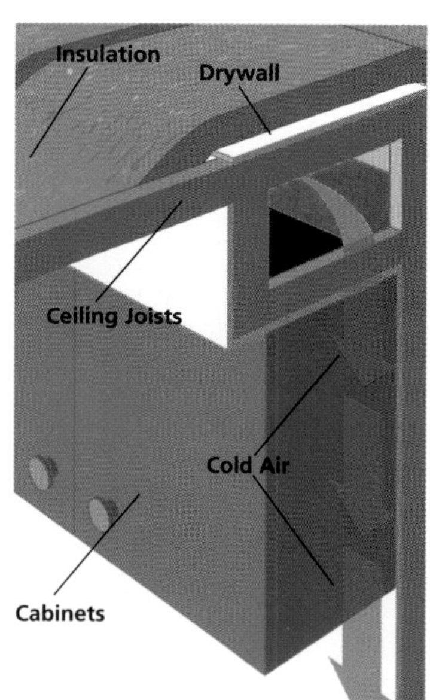

Solve the problem by installing a top on the soffit in the attic. This way, insulation batts won't fall into the open area.

A second option is to fill the soffit with insulation. Before insulating a soffit that contains recessed lighting fixtures, make sure they are rated IC, as described above.

Insulating a Crawl Space

The floor above an uninsulated crawl space can get very cold in the winter. There are several ways to solve this problem.

One is to insulate the crawl-space walls. Attach foam board or insulation batts to the walls and the rim joist. An easier, less expensive approach is to install insulation between the floor joists. Simply place unfaced fiberglass batts between the joists and hold them in place with pieces of stiff support wire, or use new insulation products designed for insulating floors without "keepers."

Closing the crawl-space vents during the winter will also help prevent the floor from getting cold.

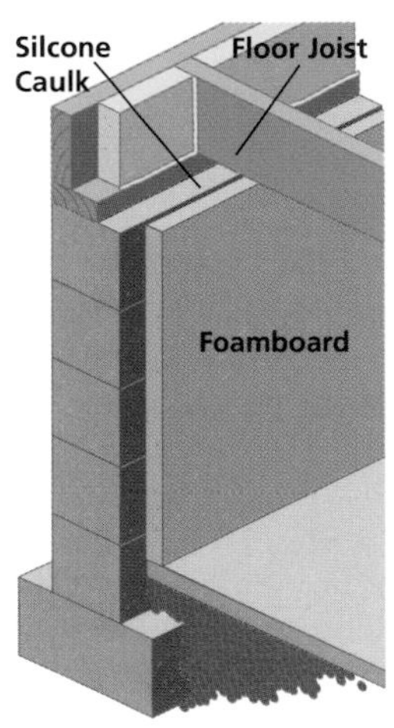

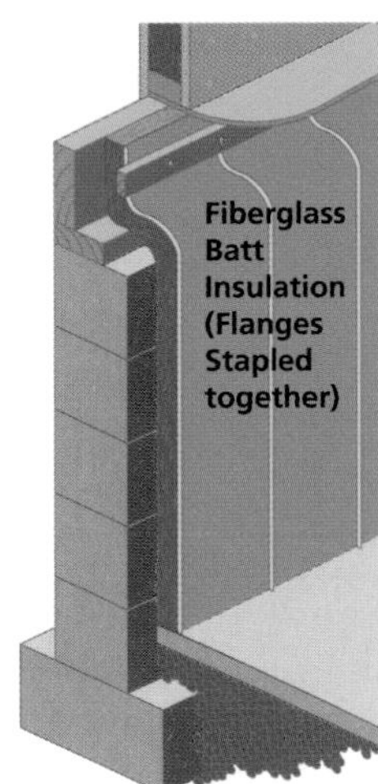

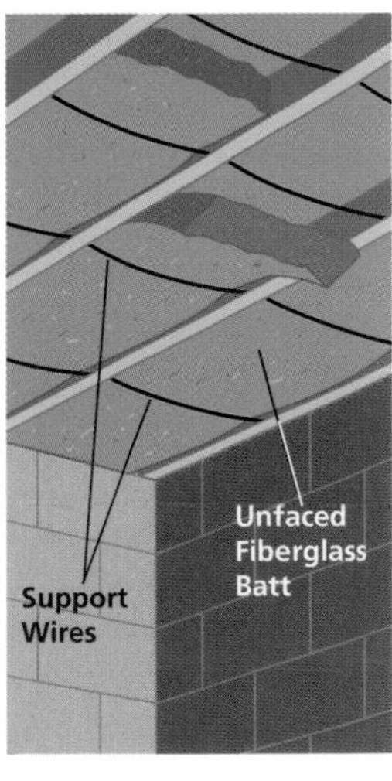

Fill It Up

Two door frames, each with a 1/8" gap, can leak as much air as a small window left open all winter. Closing those gaps with caulk can pay for itself in one heating season or less. Here are some simple things to remember about caulking:

Survey your home for areas that need caulking. Check at least these areas: door and window frames, dryer vents, pipe and wire entrances, seams between masonry and siding, chimneys, inside corners and the joints between a porch and the house.

Select caulk suitable for the size and type of crack to be filled.

Remove old caulking completely, which will help new caulk adhere. Clean the area, removing paint buildup, dirt, loose materials and grease or oil. Wipe surfaces with rubbing alcohol and let them dry completely before you begin caulking.

Use expandable polyurethane foam or a backer material, such as rope caulking or foam backer rod, to fill cracks that are larger than 3/8".

Practice until you can create a uniform bead that adheres to two sides and the back of the crack. Without this three-point contact, the caulking will quickly crack.

Counting Up

When buying caulk, estimate half a cartridge per window or door to be caulked, four for an average-size foundation sill and at least one more to close gaps around vents, pipes and other exterior openings.

Lost in Space

Houses act like big chimneys. Warm air rises to the top, increasing air pressure near the ceiling. The difference between indoor and outdoor pressure is what drives warm air through cracks, gaps and crevices. The high pressure at the top also creates low pressure near the bottom of the house, which pulls cold air in through openings around the foundation or slab.

The first step to reducing this air loss is to seal the gaps that lead from living space into the attic (see page 104). Next, insulate the rim joist, the area where the house meets the foundation. Caulk the sill plate; then, fill the rim joists with fiberglass insulation. Pack batt insulation in just tightly enough that it doesn't fall out, or cut foam board to fit.

Acrylic Latex

Siding

Realtors often talk about "curb appeal," the first impression made by a home. Few elements impact a home's curb appeal as directly as siding and trim.

Quick Reference

A well-maintained exterior welcomes you home and invites friends and neighbors into your domain. On the other hand, unrepaired damage or deterioration is both unattractive and an invitation to further problems. The maintenance of your siding and trim directly affects the appearance and value of your home.

Despite the claims of some "low-maintenance" or "no-maintenance" products, most homeowners recognize that all types of siding and trim require maintenance and repair from time to time.

Wood siding can be easily repaired by anyone with a little woodworking experience. New, easy-to-use products bring masonry repair within the range of the average homeowner's abilities as well. And although the repair of aluminum, vinyl and steel siding was once done exclusively by contractors, a wide range of replacement parts and repair products is now readily available, making it possible for do-it-yourselfers to perform many simple repairs.

Helpful Terms

Fiber cementboard: A thick, rigid siding made of a mixture of cement and fiber; resembles boards

Masonry veneer: In many parts of the country, "masonry (or brick) veneer," is used to describe a facing of masonry over a stud wall (often sill height or less) that imitates a brick foundation or solid brick wall

Metal lath: Mesh screening used as a base for stucco siding

Molding: Sections of trim that seal a home's exterior walls and protect against moisture and insects

Shingle siding: Wood roofing shingles (usually cedar) used to side a home's exterior; shingles are sawn to uniform thickness and length

Shake siding: Like shingles, only thicker and less regular; often nailed in a saw-tooth (irregular) pattern

Tuckpointing: Technique used to repair old, failing mortar; old morter is scraped out and replaced with new mortar

SAFETY FIRST

Many homes built in the 1940s and 1950s were sided with milled cementboard asbestos shingles. These shingles, which look very similar to fiberglass shingles, usually have a rough, heavily ridged surface. Because asbestos is classified as a hazardous material, its handling and disposal are regulated. Contact your local waste management department before handling these shingles.

Cracks and Splits

Wood siding frequently develops cracks and splits as it ages. The good news is that almost everyone has the tools and ability to make lasting repairs to wood siding.

Apply epoxy wood glue to both sides of the crack; then, press the board back together. For best results, position a board under the bottom edge of the damaged board and press it upward to create even pressure until the glue sets. If you're working near the ground, wedge an upright 2 × 4 under the board.

After the glue sets, drive galvanized deck screws on each side of the crack to reinforce the repair. Clean off the excess glue, and touch up the repair with paint.

Reattaching Loose Trim

Trim pieces often serve a purpose beyond decoration. End caps and brick molding actually seal exterior walls and protect your house from moisture and insects. Here's a quick way to repair loose wood trim.

Drive new ring-shank siding nails near the old nail locations. Fill the old nail holes with paintable caulk; then, touch up the caulk and new nail heads with paint to match the surrounding area.

Just Filling In

The goal of most exterior repair projects is simply to keep minor problems from turning into major damage. Small to medium-size holes in siding are a perfect example of this concept. If you fill small holes, you can prevent the infiltration of moisture and insects, avoiding the damage that each can cause.

For wood siding, fill small holes with epoxy wood filler. Paint the repair to match the surrounding area.

For metal and vinyl siding, fill holes with tinted exterior caulk. If local building centers don't carry caulk in a matching color, call the siding manufacturer for specific suggestions.

Removing Decorative Trim

Decorative trim is often referred to as "gingerbread," possibly because it adds spice to the appearance of a house. Although it doesn't affect your home's structural soundness, damaged decorative trim makes your home look shabby.

If a piece of trim is badly damaged, it's usually best to remove it and repair it in your workshop—unless you must remove siding to gain access to the trim. You can fill small dents or holes with wood filler or epoxy glue. If damage is severe, make or buy replacement parts. If all else fails, take the trim to a custom millwork shop and ask them to duplicate it.

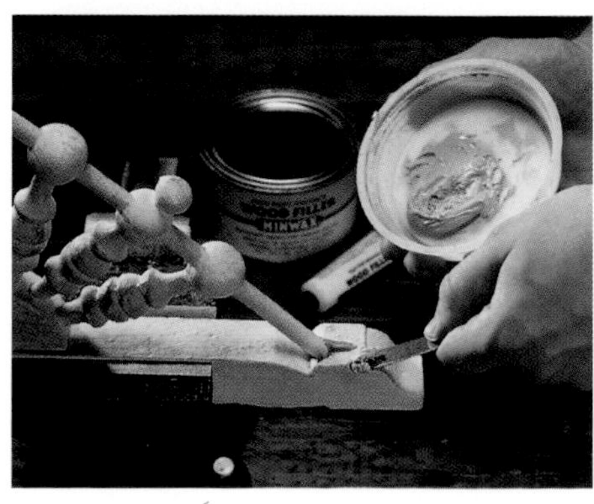

QUICK TIPS

If you plan to remove siding temporarily and then replace it, the job will be simpler if you reinstall the pieces in their original locations.

Give yourself a head start by numbering the siding pieces as you remove them.

If you're replacing siding that has cutouts for utility openings, use the old pieces as templates for cutting the replacement pieces.

Staggering Seams

If you have to cut out an area of damaged siding, remove it in a pattern that will allow you to stagger the vertical seams when you replace it. Create these seams along framing members so you have something solid to nail into when you replace the boards.

If the damage is near the end of a board that is longer than 4 ft., you simply can cut out the damaged area.

To remove damage confined to a small area in the middle of a long board, make two cuts, one on either side of the damage. Locate cuts well beyond all damage, stay at least 12" away from butt joints in the courses above and below, and center the cut on a wall stud.

Replacing Wood Shingles

As anyone with shingle siding knows, shakes and shingles are damaged fairly easily. Fortunately, they are easy to replace.

Split damaged pieces with a hammer and chisel, and remove them. Insert wood spacers under the shakes or shingles above the repair area.

Slip a hacksaw blade under the top board, and cut off old nail heads.

Cut replacement shakes or shingles to fit, leaving a 1/8 to 1/4"-wide expansion gap at each side. Immerse these shakes or shingles in wood preservative for a few minutes.

Starting at the lowest course of the repair area, slip the patch under the siding above. Drive ring-shank nails near the top of the exposed area on the patch.

Cover nail heads with caulk colored to match the siding, and wipe off any excess. Remove the spacers.

Spacing Out

Sometimes the most difficult part of spot-repairing siding is getting enough room to remove the old piece and attach the new one.

To simplify the repair process, insert spacers between the siding and sheathing above the work area while you make repairs.

Caution: Metal siding will buckle if you bend it too far.

Filling the Gap

Hail has a way of leaving its mark on siding. The damage usually isn't severe, but may be noticeable from certain angles.

If you have hail damage, take advantage of raw wood's ability to retain water.

Gently wire-brush the area to remove any finish; then, wet the siding thoroughly with soap and water. If the wood fibers are crushed but not broken, they may expand enough to fill the dents. Let the siding dry completely, and apply paint or stain.

Patching Siding

Vinyl and metal siding are popular because they are inexpensive and can last for decades. However, the materials are susceptible to dents, holes and fading. You can repair this type of minor damage, but major repairs are probably best left to the contractor who installed the siding. To find replacement siding, contact the original contractor or the siding manufacturer.

Patching Vinyl Siding

Use a zip tool to unlock the interlocking joints, starting with the seam nearest the damaged area. Install spacers underneath the row of siding above the damage. Using a flat pry bar, pry out the fasteners in the damaged pieces.

Using a straightedge and a utility knife, cut out the damaged area. Next, cut a replacement piece that is 4" longer than the open area. Trim off 2" of the nailing strip from each end of the replacement piece in the overlap area. Slide the piece into position.

Attach the replacement siding. Because the nailing strip is difficult to reach with a hammer, press ring-shank siding nails in the slots of the nailing strip, then position the end of a flat pry bar over each nail head. Drive nails by rapping on the neck of the pry bar with a hammer. Slip the J-channel over the nailing strip.

Patching Metal Siding

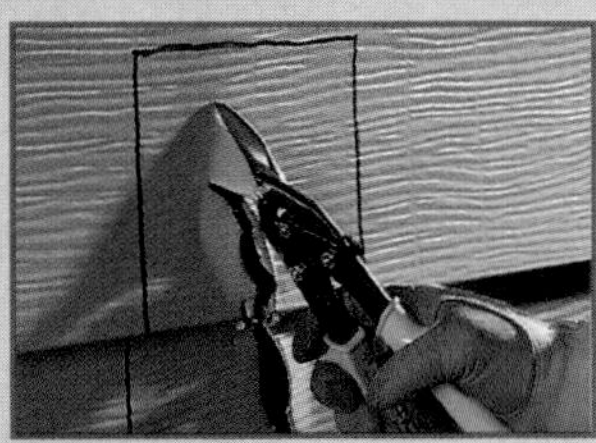

Cut out the damaged area with aviation snips and a hacksaw blade. Leave some exposed surface area at the top of the uppermost piece you remove, to serve as a bonding surface for the siding patch.

Cut patches 4" wider than the repair area, using matching siding material. Cut off the nailing strip from the top patch piece. Make sure all edges are smooth, deburring them with metal sandpaper, if necessary.

Nail lower patches in place by driving ring-shank siding nails through the nailing strips, starting with the lowest piece. To install the top piece, apply roof cement to the back, and press the patch in place, slipping the J-shaped locking channel over the nailing strip below. Caulk the seams.

BAD REACTION

When wasps or hornets try to build a home in the eaves, your response may be to spray first and ask questions later.

Be particularly careful when using insect sprays near vinyl siding. These petroleum-based products may react with the chemical components of vinyl, permanently discoloring it.

If you've already stained the vinyl siding, you might be able to lighten the discoloration. Dampen a white cloth with naptha or mineral spirits, and dab at the stains. When you're finished, rinse the area thoroughly with water.

No More Mildew

It's quite common for mildew to grow on siding in humid climates, despite exterior paints and stains that contain mildewcides. Every spring, inspect areas that are prone to mildew, and remove it with this hardworking formula:

Combine 3 quarts of warm water, 1 quart of chlorine bleach, ⅔ cup of trisodium phosphate (TSP) and ⅓ cup of powdered laundry detergent. Protect your hands with rubber gloves while you work.

Thoroughly water surrounding landscaping before you start. Wet plants will not absorb as much of the cleaner, but you should still try not to splash on surrounding plants. Spray the cleaner onto the siding, and scrub with a medium-bristled brush, if necessary. When the mildew is gone, rinse the siding thoroughly and water the plants again as well.

Clinging Vines Beware

If you want the shade and homey appearance that vines provide but don't want to expose your siding to the damage they can inflict, build a trellis to keep the vines a few inches away from the house.

Build the trellis from pressure-treated wood, vinyl lattice or metal fencing. Bolt the bottom of the trellis uprights to fixed 4 × 4 posts. Hold the bottom of the uprights away from the house with U-shaped brackets and bolts. In this way, the top can be disconnected and the trellis folded down and away from the house when you need to clean or repair the siding.

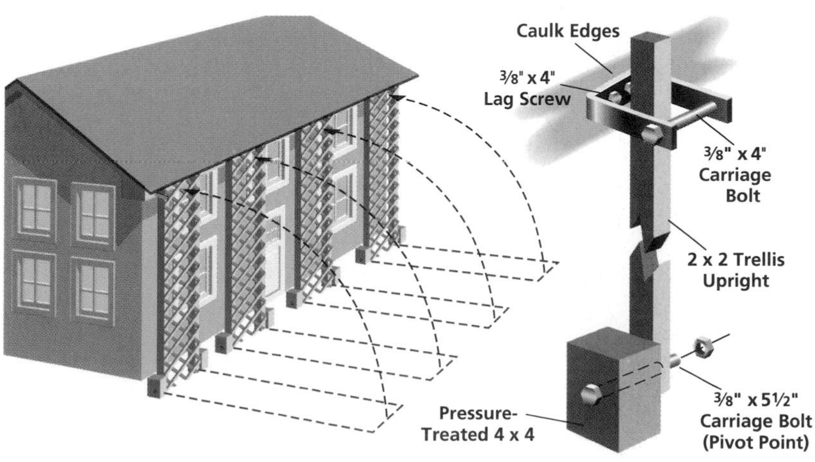

Hit and Run

Dented aluminum siding looks shabby, and it may seem that replacement is the only answer.

Actually, most small dents will become invisible if you fill them with auto body filler and paint them to match the siding.

Past Its Prime

If your home has cementboard asbestos siding, contact the Environmental Protection Agency before making extensive repairs.

If the siding is cracked and all the pieces are still in place, glue or caulk them together. If there are small holes, fill them with wood filler and tool the filler to blend into the siding. Don't sand the repairs—abrading the material in any way releases asbestos fibers into the air.

Your best bet is to replace cementboard asbestos siding. It will undoubtably become more brittle (and therefore more hazardous) as it continues to age.

Tuckpointing Mortar Joints

The most common brick and block wall repair is tuckpointing—the process of replacing failed mortar joints with fresh mortar. Tuckpointing is a highly useful repair technique for any homeowner. It requires only a few tools and is easy to master if you follow these simple suggestions:

Clean out loose or deteriorated mortar to a depth of 1/4 to 3/4". Use a mortar raking tool first (above, top); then, switch to a masonry chisel and a hammer (bottom) if the mortar is stubborn. Clear away all loose debris, and dampen the surface with water.

Mix the mortar, adding a latex concrete fortifier. Add pigment if the old mortar has discolored. Starting with the horizontal joints, push the mortar into the joints with a joint filler. Apply mortar in 1/4"-thick layers, and let each layer dry for 30 minutes before applying another. Fill the joints until the mortar is flush with the face of the brick or block.

Moving to the vertical joints, scoop mortar onto the back of a joint filler and press it into a joint. Work from the top of the area downward. After the final layer is applied, smooth the joints with a jointing tool. Smooth the horizontal joints first; then, the vertical. Let the mortar dry until it is crumbly; then, brush off the excess with a stiff-bristled brush.

Solvents for Brick & Block Stains

Egg splatter: Dissolve oxalic acid crystals in water, following manufacturer's instructions, in a nonmetallic container. Brush onto the surface.

Efflorescence: Scrub surface with a stiff-bristled brush. Use a household cleaning solution for surfaces with heavy accumulation.

Iron stains: Spray or brush a solution of oxalic acid crystals dissolved in water, following manufacturer's instructions. Apply directly to the stain.

Ivy: Cut vines away from the surface (do not pull them off). Let remaining stems dry up; then, scrub them off with a stiff-bristled brush and household cleaning solution.

Oil: Apply a paste made of mineral spirits and an absorbant inert material, such as sawdust.

Paint stains: Remove new paint with a solution of trisodium phosphate (TSP) and water, following manufacturer's mixing instructions. Old paint usually can be removed with heavy scrubbing or sandblasting.

Smoke stains: Scrub surface with household cleanser containing bleach, or use a mixture of ammonia and water. (Note: Never mix products containing bleach with ammonia or products containing ammonia.)

Repairing Brick and Block

When moisture trapped inside bricks is subjected to repeated cycles of freezing and thawing, damage is inevitable. This type of damage, called spalling, occurs when freezing water or other forces cause enough directional pressure to fracture the brick.

The first step to a permanent repair is eliminating the moisture. Check the mortar joints—mortar is softer than most bricks and is prone to damage. If the mortar joints are deteriorated, tuckpoint them as described on page 112. Also, damaged gutters may be letting water drain onto the bricks, or the slope of the adjacent landscape may be directing water toward them. If necessary, repair gutters or regrade landscape.

The next step is to remove damaged bricks. The easiest way to remove bricks is to score the surface and surrounding mortar joints with a power drill and a masonry-cutting disc, then break them along scored lines with a mason's chisel and hammer.

For walls with extensive damage, remove bricks from the top down, one row at a time, until the entire damaged area is removed. Do not dismantle load-bearing brick structures like foundation walls; consult a professional mason for these repairs.

For walls with internal damaged areas, remove only the damaged section, keeping the upper layers intact if they are in good condition. Don't remove more than four adjacent bricks in one area. If the damaged area is larger than this, it will require temporary support, which is a job for a professional mason.

Replace bricks using standard brick-laying techniques.

All Cracked Up

Concrete is very durable, but it occasionally requires repair and maintenance. If you prepare cracked surfaces properly and use the right products for the job, your repairs should be permanent.

Loose material or debris left in a crack results in a poor bond and an ineffective repair. Use a wire brush or a portable drill with a wire wheel attachment to clean out loose material from the crack.

Create an angled cutout shape to keep the repair material from pushing itself out of the crack. Use a cold chisel and hammer to chisel out a backward-angled cut (wider at the base than at the surface) surrounding the crack.

Bonding adhesive keeps the repair material firmly attached to the sides. Paint a thin layer of bonding adhesive onto the entire repair area.

Vinyl-reinforced patching compound is perfect for small cracks because it's somewhat flexible.

Vinyl-reinforced concrete or hydraulic cement is appropriate for large cracks. Slightly overfill the crack, then feather the material even with the surface. If the crack is deep (over 1/2"), trowel in successive layers 1/4 to 1/2" thick. Pack in the repair material, let it dry, and repeat.

Master of Disguise

Since concrete repairs should be as unobtrusive as possible, try these disguises:

- Add concrete pigment to your patching compound to match the original concrete's color. Experiment with different mixtures of pigment and repair cement until you get just the right color, but remember to compare the color of dried samples, not wet compound.
- Use masonry paint to cover repairs. Keep in mind that high-traffic surfaces will need more frequent touch-ups.

SAFETY FIRST

Concrete products must be handled with care and disposed of properly. Concrete and mortar mix contain silica, which is a hazardous substance in large quantities. These products also contain skin irritants.

Wear a particle mask, protective goggles and gloves when handling or mixing dry concrete materials. Use the same protection when cutting concrete, brick or block. To avoid skin irritation, wear gloves any time you handle wet concrete or masonry products.

QUICK TIPS

Before you purchase replacement bricks, chip off a piece of the damaged brick to use as a color reference in your search.

Mortar is softer than bricks or blocks and is more prone to damage. Deterioration is not always visible, so probe joints with a screwdriver to see if they're sound.

Write down the brick color and manufacturer whenever you have new brick installed. This will save you valuable time if you ever need to replace bricks.

Patch It Up

You can repair holes and chip-outs in concrete in much the same way you repair cracks, so it's quite simple. But here are a few specific ideas to help you fill holes with ease:

Use a masonry-grinding disc mounted on a portable drill to cut a 15° bevel around the perimeter of the damaged area. Remove any loose concrete within the repair area.

Use vinyl-reinforced concrete patcher for holes less than ½" deep. For deeper holes, use sand-mix concrete with an acrylic or latex fortifier. Sand mix can be applied in layers up to 2" thick.

Quick Face-lift

Many homes have a stucco veneer (see page 107) around the foundation. Damage to this veneer leaves a home vulnerable to moisture and pests. But with the right tools, materials and techniques, you can repair this masonry veneer like a professional. Just follow these simple steps:

Use a cold chisel and hammer to remove crumbled, loose or deteriorated stucco. Chisel the damaged veneer until you have a good, solid surface remaining, but take care not to damage the wall behind the veneer. Clean the repair area with a wire brush.

If the metal lath is in good condition, you're ready for the next step. If not, cut it out with aviation snips; then, secure new lath to the wall with masonry anchors.

Mix fortified sand-mix concrete (or a specialty concrete blend for wall repair), and trowel it over the lath until it is even with the surrounding surfaces. Re-create the surface texture to match the surrounding area. Textures can often be duplicated by stippling the surface with a stiff-bristled brush.

Pest Control

Insects, rodents and other assorted pests belong outside. Here are some simple steps you can take to deny pests access to your home.

If telltale signs of infestation point to a large-scale problem, call an exterminator or your local agricultural extension agent.

Stuff caulking backer rope in gaps between the siding and the foundation to keep crawling insects on the outside. Check the top of the foundation walls, and caulk between the concrete and the rim, or band joist, if necessary.

Look for anthills, tunnels, hives and nests around the exterior of your home. When you find their living quarters and identify the pests, block access points near the nesting area. Avoid using chemical pesticides, except as a last resort.

Install protected dryer vents. Standard vents offer attractive entry points, especially for small rodents. Designed to be one-for-one replacements for flap-style vents, protected vents also reduce energy loss.

Add a chimney cap to keep birds, bats, insects and squirrels out of your chimney. A chimney cap with a cover and screening, sized to fit your flue, also sheds rainwater. Read manufacturer's recommendations—some chimney covers can impede air movement in the chimney or furnace.

Replace damaged screening in windows and over air vent covers, using new insect screen (a 1⁄16" mesh). CAUTION: If vent covers were previously screened with coarser mesh, add another vent to compensate for decreased air flow.

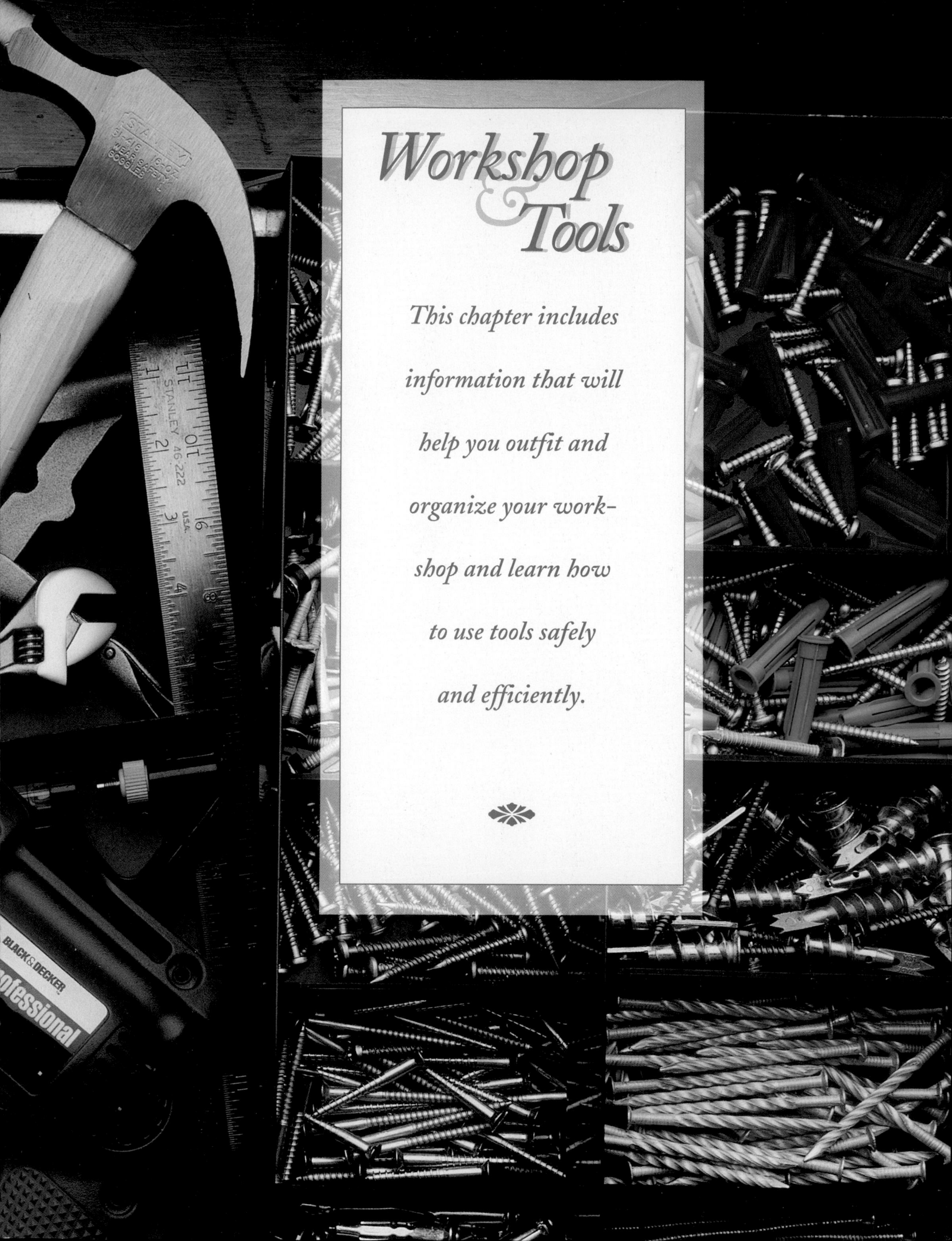

Workshop & Tools

This chapter includes information that will help you outfit and organize your workshop and learn how to use tools safely and efficiently.

Workshop

A well-equipped, well-organized workshop forms a base of operations for all types of home maintenance as well as for creative projects.

Quick Reference

Working with your hands can bring you personal satisfaction, reduce stress and provide an outlet for creativity. A workshop often represents more than just a place to house tools, materials and projects in progress—it can be a treasure trove and a retreat from the outside world.

Whether you're an experienced woodworker with a vast tool collection or a do-it-yourselfer with a small-but-growing tool kit, workshop space is probably at a premium. This chapter offers suggestions that will help you get the most from your workshop and the work you do there. You'll also find ideas gathered by hobbyists, woodworkers and professional builders over years of working with workshop and construction materials. These tips and techniques, which cover many aspects of workshop planning and organization, tool use and project craftsmanship, will save you time and money.

Essential Workshop Items

Safety Equipment:
- Fire extinguisher
- Smoke detector
- First aid kit
- Eye-wash kit
- Disposable gloves
- Telephone
- Window fan
- Flashlight

Protective Gear:
- Ear plugs
- Safety goggles
- Respirator
- Dust mask
- Stripping gloves
- Study work boots or shoes

Helpful Items:
- Bench vise
- Clip lights
- Heavy-duty extension cords
- Peg-Board® with hooks
- Rubber antifatigue mat
- Power strips
- Dehumidifier
- Yellow Pages

SAFETY FIRST

Wear safety goggles whenever you are sanding or using power tools.

Keep lenses free of sawdust and other airborne particulates by wiping them with a used fabric-softener strip (the kind you put into a clothes dryer). The softener helps prevent static electricity, which attracts the dust.

Stick 'em Up

If you own many hand tools, locating the tools you use most often in a drawer or toolbox can be a nuisance. A practical storage alternative is to attach magnetic strips to the front of a workbench or the stand of a stationary tool. The strips allow you to safely hang any metal tool or part. Powerful magnetic strips are available at hardware or cutlery stores.

Making the Most of Limited Space

Organizing large stationary power tools, such as table saws or bench grinders, in a workshop with limited space can be a real challenge. To give yourself more flexibility, try installing locking casters on the bottom of these tools. The casters allow you to roll your tools around the workshop and position them where you need them. Another benefit of this solution is that it allows you to position the tools near open doors or windows when you need extra space for working with long lengths of lumber.

Cord Clamps

Dangling extension cords can clutter your work area and impose a hazard when you're using power tools. Keep extension cords out of the way by clamping them with clothespins. Attach the clothespins to workshop walls and ceiling with screws or hot-melt glue.

Rust Prevention

Moisture can rust hand tools stored in an unfinished basement or garage. To help absorb the moisture and prevent spotting and corrosion, wrap a few charcoal briquettes in a piece of cloth and toss them into your toolbox or tool drawer. Replace the briquettes every several months.

A coating of light machine oil will also prevent hand tools from rusting. Lining your tool drawer with a piece of scrap carpet moistened with a few sprays of light machine oil will keep your tools oiled. The carpet will also help prevent tools from being scratched or nicked.

Clear the Air

One of the most important considerations in the layout of your workshop is ventilation. Refinishing wood, for instance, can create many hazards, including dangerous vapors and sanding dust, which impair breathing.

Try to locate your workshop in a well-ventilated area, such as a basement with several windows, or a garage. When you are doing projects that involve sanding, varnishing, painting or gluing, use electric fans to improve air circulation. If possible, direct at least one fan outside through an open door or window to remove vapors and dust, and direct another fan into the room to supply fresh air.

Choose the Right Extension Cord

When using extension cords with power tools, make sure the cords you're using are capable of carrying the amount of electricity required. Cords that are too small will overheat and cause an electrical short.

Use only heavy-duty extension cords with power tools. Extension cords are rated by wire gauge, watts and amps. The smaller the wire gauge, the higher the amp and watt ratings. Make sure that the ratings of the extension cord are equal to or greater than the tool's ratings. For extension cords longer than 50 ft., choose the next larger wire gauge. Use the chart below to help you determine what size cord you'll need for your tools.

WIRE GAUGE	WATT RATING	AMP RATING	TYPICAL USE
#18	600	5	Power drill, jigsaw, hand sander
#16	840	7	Reciprocating saw, belt sander
#14	1440	12	Router, circular saw, miter saw, table saw
#12	1920	16	Radial arm saw, large table saw

QUICK TIPS

Extension and power tool cords often become knotted and tangled. Try creating a sleeve for coiled cords from plastic motor oil bottles. Thoroughly clean the bottles; then, use a utility knife to cut the ends off, creating a square plastic sleeve. Slip the sleeve over the coiled electrical cord.

Storing Sharp Tools

You probably have a number of small sharp tools, such as chisels, awls and utility knives, loose in your workshop. To keep these tools organized and sharp, and protect yourself from injury, build a small box to hold them.

Take a shallow wood box (a small cigar box works well) and cut a piece of 2"-thick foam insulation board to fit inside. Insert your tools point-side-down in the foam.

When the foam becomes chewed up, either flip the foam over and use the other side, or cut a new piece.

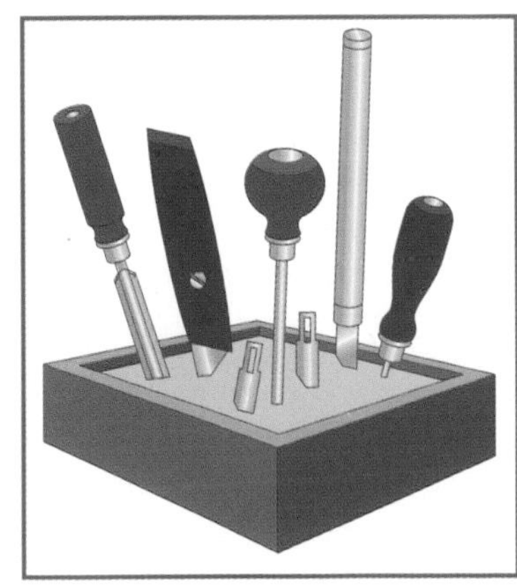

BUYING LUMBER BY THE BOARD FOOT

If you're planning to build a deck or any other project that involves buying a sizable quantity of wood, consider purchasing your wood in bulk from a lumberyard rather than buy the piece from a home center.

When purchasing wood from a lumberyard, keep in mind that they sell wood in board feet, rather than by actual measurements. A board foot is a unit volume equal to 144 cubic in. or a 1-ft.-square, 1-in.-thick piece of wood.

Dimensional lumber is always listed as thickness × width × length. Make sure the numbers you have are inches × inches × feet (they usually are). Then multiply your dimensions together and divide that figure by 12 to determine board feet. If you're paying by the board foot, you pay for the listed, "nominal" size, not the actual size (which in the case of a 2 × 4 is 1½ × 3½, on a good day). Use the chart at the right to get an idea of how actual measurements convert to board feet.

Converting Actual Measurements to Board Feet
1 in. × 12 in. × 1 ft. = 1 b.f.
2 in. × 4 in. × 8 ft. = 5.33 b.f.
2 in. × 4 in. × 12 ft. = 8 b.f.
2 in. × 6 in. × 8 ft. = 8 b.f.
2 in. × 8 in. × 10 ft. = 13.33 b.f.
4 in. × 4 in. × 8 ft. = 10.66 b.f.

Inequivalent Lengths

Different tape measures do not necessarily measure equally. The hooks on the end of tape measures are not always attached in the same place and can work loose. This difference can measure as much as 1/16" between two tapes, even if they are the same brand and style. If possible, use only one tape measure while working on a project. If you must work with two tapes, check them to make sure they give the same measurements.

Handy Hammer Measuring

Sometimes you won't have a tape measure on hand to take rough measurements. Use this carpenter's tip the next time you find yourself in this situation.

Turn your hammer into a ruler. Measure exactly 12 inches from the head of the hammer and mark the handle with a piece of colored electrical tape. Place another piece of tape 6 or 8 inches from the head. If you have a long-handled framing hammer, you may be able to add a tape strip at 16 inches, too. This technique is especially helpful when doing repetitive nailing, such as driving evenly spaced nails along the edge of a plywood sheet.

Tale of the Tape

The older your tape measure gets, the more likely it is to stick or jam. To keep your tape measure retracting smoothly, coat the blade with a small amount of paste wax applied with a soft cloth. The wax keeps the tape retractor working smoothly and prevents dirt and grease from sticking to the blade.

Choosing the Right Glue

Many types of glue are available, each with its own characteristics and appropriate applications. The chart below describes various types of glue and their uses. If you have a choice between water-based (latex) adhesives and solvent-based adhesives, always choose latex, which is less toxic, not flammable and does not emit harmful vapors.

Types	Characteristics	Uses
White glue	**Strength:** moderate; rigid bond **Drying time:** several hours **Resistance to heat:** poor **Resistance to moisture:** poor **Hazards:** none **Cleanup/solvent:** soap and water	**Porous surfaces:** Wood (indoors) Paper Cloth
Yellow carpenter's glue	**Strength:** moderate to good; rigid bond **Drying time:** several hours; faster than white glue **Resistance to heat:** moderate **Resistance to moisture:** moderate **Hazards:** none **Cleanup/solvent:** soap and water	**Porous surfaces:** Wood (indoors) Paper Cloth
Two-part epoxy	**Strength:** excellent; strongest of all adhesives **Drying time:** varies; depends on manufacturer **Resistance to heat:** excellent **Resistance to moisture:** excellent **Hazards:** fumes are toxic and flammable **Cleanup/solvent:** acetone will dissolve some types	**Smooth and porous surfaces:** Wood (indoors & outdoors) Metal Masonry Glass Fiberglass
Hot glue	**Strength:** depends on type **Drying time:** less than 60 seconds **Resistance to heat:** fair **Resistance to moisture:** good **Hazards:** hot glue can cause burns **Cleanup/solvent:** heat will loosen bond	**Smooth and porous surfaces:** Glass Plastics Wood
Cyanoacrylate (instant) glue	**Strength:** excellent, but with little flexibility **Drying time:** a few seconds **Resistance to heat:** excellent **Resistance to moisture:** excellent **Hazards:** can bond to skin instantly; toxic, flammable **Cleanup/solvent:** acetone	**Smooth surfaces:** Glass Ceramics Plastics Metal
Latex acrylic panel adhesive	**Strength:** good to excellent; very durable **Drying time:** 24 hours **Resistance to heat:** good **Resistance to moisture:** excellent **Hazards:** may irritate skin and eyes **Cleanup/solvent:** soap and water (while still wet)	**Porous surfaces:** Framing lumber Plywood and paneling Wallboard Foam panels Masonry
Water-based contact cement	**Strength:** good **Drying time:** bonds instantly; dries fully in 30 minutes **Resistance to heat:** excellent **Resistance to moisture:** good **Hazards:** may irritate skin and eyes **Cleanup/solvent:** soap and water (while still wet)	**Porous surfaces:** Plastic laminates Plywood Flooring Cloth
Silicone sealant	**Strength:** fair to good; very flexible bond **Drying time:** 24 hours **Resistance to heat:** good **Resistance to moisture:** excellent **Hazards:** may irritate skin and eyes **Cleanup/solvent:** acetone	**Smooth and porous surfaces:** Wood Porcelain Fiberglass Plastics Glass

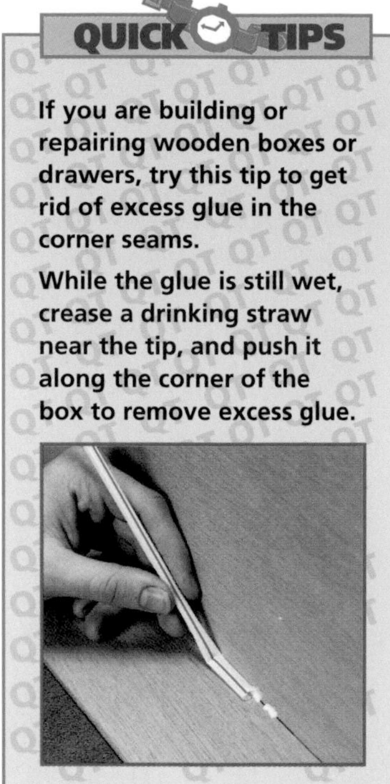

QUICK TIPS

If you are building or repairing wooden boxes or drawers, try this tip to get rid of excess glue in the corner seams.

While the glue is still wet, crease a drinking straw near the tip, and push it along the corner of the box to remove excess glue.

In the Bag

Most workshops have dozens of small containers holding screws, nails, bolts and other hardware. To locate items quickly and easily, try storing lightweight items in paper lunch bags. Use a hot glue gun to secure a sample of the contents on the outside of each bag.

TOOL BOX

Carpenter's glue is nearly invisible when it dries—until you stain the wood. If excess carpenter's glue is present when the stain is applied, it leaves an unsightly light-colored streak.

Remove dried carpenter's glue by scraping it with a sharp chisel, held bevel-side-down. To prevent gouges, round off the corners of a chisel with a file or bench grinder.

Ready-to-Go Glue

Workshop glues have a tendency to not work well when you need them the most. You're often struggling to hold together a project and squeeze the glue from the bottom of the bottle at the same time. Avoid this situation by storing glue bottles upside down so the glue is ready to pour whenever it is needed. Make a glue bottle holder by drilling holes in a scrap 1 × 4 and attaching it to a wall or a Peg-Board® storage panel.

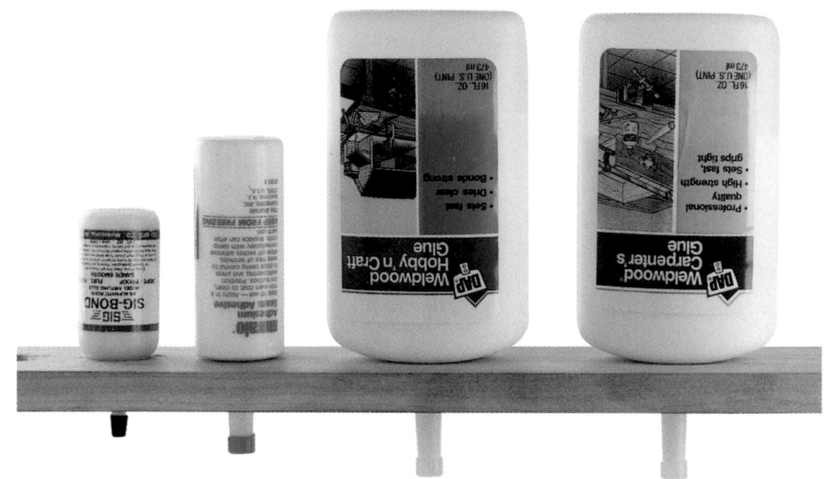

Regluing Loose Veneer

Loose or blistered veneer is common on old furniture and doors and is relatively simple to repair. In some cases, the veneer can be reglued by covering the damaged area with a towel, then pressing it with an iron, which can reactivate existing glue. If the iron doesn't work, use the steps below to make the repair:

Use a putty knife to gently pry up the edge of the loose veneer. Carefully scrape away the old glue.

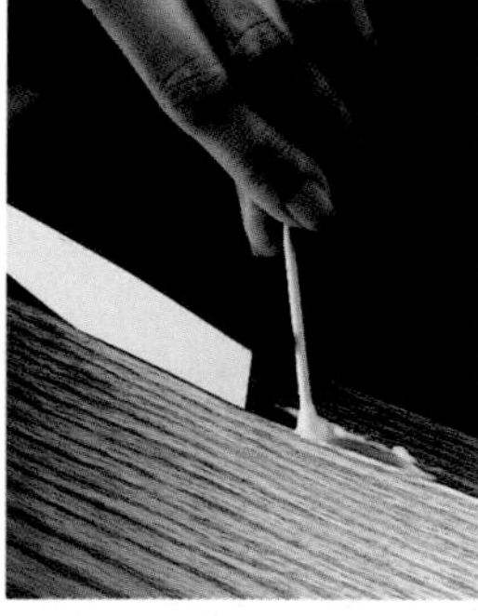

Apply a thin coat of yellow carpenter's glue to the surfaces, using a cotton swab or craft stick. Press the veneer in place, and wipe away any excess glue with a damp cloth.

Cover the glued area with wax paper or a scrap of rubber, and clamp it with a block of wood and a C-clamp. Let the glue dry overnight.

Don't Split Yet

Having boards split as you're nailing them together is a common workshop frustration. To ensure that it doesn't happen to you, try these techniques:

If you're using hardwood, drill pilot holes to avoid splitting. Use a finishing nail instead of a drill bit for quick and accurate hole sizing.

For any wood projects, try staggering the placement of nails so they do not enter the same spot in the wood grain. Angling the nails will also provide better holding power than driving them straight in.

QUICK TIPS

Use emery boards to sand tight areas where a sanding block or power sander will not fit. Emery boards work well on tight corners and on decorative spindles.

You can also sand hard-to-reach crevices with narrow strips cut from cloth-backed sanding belts.

CREATIVE CLAMPING

Sawhorse Stirrup

It can be difficult to balance long workpieces on a pair of sawhorses. Use a bicycle inner tube to hold them securely. Slide the inner tube over the workpiece, and use your foot to stretch the inner tube and hold the lumber in place while you saw.

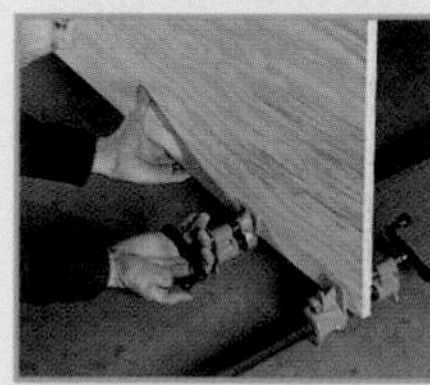

Upright Support

When painting or cutting plywood or paneling, support the sheet in an upright position by attaching a pair of pipe clamps to one edge with the pipes facing in opposite directions. This technique also can be used to hold a door when drilling for locks, chiseling mortises or planing an edge.

Hold It

Hand power tools such as drills and sanders can be anchored temporarily to a workbench with handscrew clamps. This technique is good for sanding small workpieces. Clamp the tool securely so it does not move, but do not overtighten the handscrew, which can damage the tool. A pad of foam rubber under the handscrew jaw will help grip the tool without damaging the tool casing.

C-Clamp Miter Mate

For accurate mitering of decorative moldings, the wood must be clamped securely in the miter saw. Ordinary clamps can damage the contours of wood molding, but you can make a simple miter clamp from a C-clamp, an old tennis ball and a plastic cap from a film canister.

Cut a small slice from the side of the tennis ball, then hot-glue the film cap to the side opposite the slice, as shown here. When the miter clamp is attached to the miter saw, the tennis ball holds the workpiece tightly without damaging the wood, and the film cap keeps the C-clamp pad from slipping.

Tools

A basic collection of hand and power tools may be all that's necessary for most projects, but few people can resist the temptation of obtaining the perfect tool for the job.

Quick Reference

You don't need an extensive collection of tools in order to successfully complete a wide range of projects. With the right techniques and proper care, a simple set of tools will carry many people through a lifetime of household projects. But with each success, you just might find yourself taking on more difficult projects and buying additional tools with specialized features.

The tips collected in this chapter will help you care for and get more accurate results from the hand and power tools you already own, and give you ideas for other useful tools you may want to add to your collection. Many of the ideas here illustrate techniques professionals use to perform tasks faster, more safely and more efficiently. There are also several suggestions for using these tools for new and different applications as well as ideas for inexpensively modifying your tools to perform additional functions.

Essential Tools

Ideal Starter Set:

- 16-oz. claw hammer
- Wood mallet
- Phillips screwdrivers
- Standard screwdrivers
- Power screwdriver
- 3/8" power drill
- Assorted drill bits
- Circular saw
- Wallboard handsaw
- Crosscut handsaw
- Hacksaw
- Adjustable wrenches
- Slip-joint pliers
- Wood chisels
- Ratchet wrench and sockets

Intermediate Tool Set:

- Router
- Jigsaw
- Reciprocating saw
- Palm sander
- Belt sander
- Miter saw
- Glue gun
- Plane
- Hole saw drill attachment

Hammer Helpers

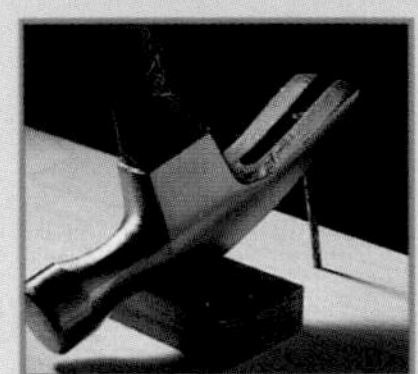

More Power to You

Remove stubborn nails by placing a block of wood under the hammerhead for added leverage. Use a block big enough to distribute the pressure from the hammerhead.

Thumbs Up

To avoid hitting your thumb when hammering a small nail, push the nail through a piece of stiff paper. Or, hold the nail with a needlenose pliers or tweezers.

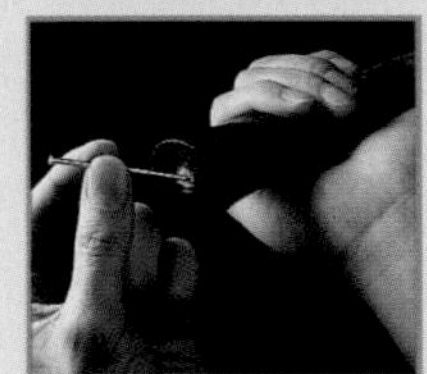

Easy Driver

Drive nails into hardwoods more easily by lubricating the nail points with beeswax. Keep a supply of wax handy by drilling a ¼"-diameter, ½"-deep hole in the end of your hammer handle and filling the hole with wax.

Surface Saver

Protect surfaces from hammer misses by slipping a piece of scrap Peg-Board® over the nail and against the workpiece. When the nail is flush to the surface of the Peg-Board, remove it and finish the job with a nail set.

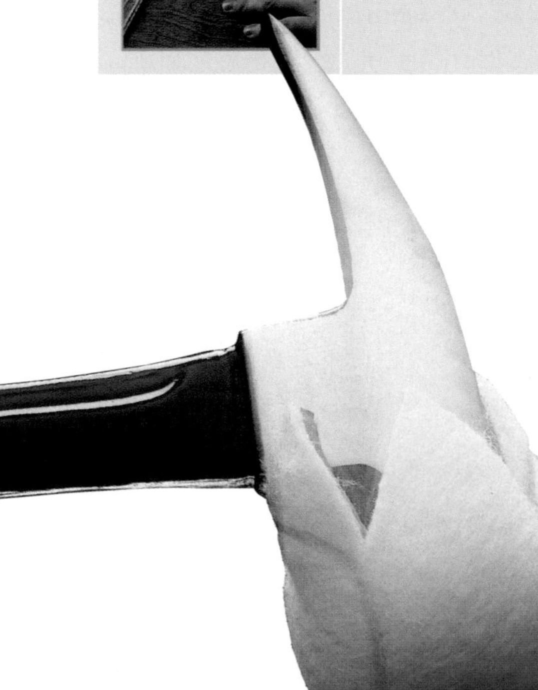

Soften the Blow

Using a standard metal hammer to tap wood joints into place can damage the workpiece.

To avoid marring workpieces, convert your hammer into a soft-headed mallet with the help of a tennis ball.

Cut an X-shaped slit in a tennis ball and slip it over the striking face of the hammer.

To keep a wood hammer handle from breaking when you're removing a stubborn nail, lever the hammer to the right or left—onto its side—rather than straight back.

Clean hammer faces periodically by rubbing them with fine sandpaper. Wood resins and nail coatings may build up on the face, causing the hammer to slip and damage the work surface or bend the nail.

KNOCK ON WOOD

A woodworking mallet is a good tool to own—it won't damage your chisels or workpieces the way a hammer will. Surprisingly enough, you may not even need to buy one, provided you own an old croquet set.

Simply cut off all but 12" of the handle on an old croquet mallet. To finish your woodworking mallet, sand the cut end and wrap the "grip" portion of the handle with cloth or vinyl tape.

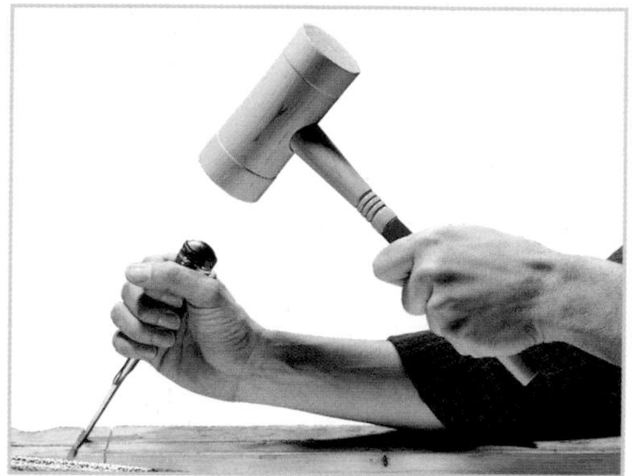

A Hammer by Any Other Name

When nailing wallboard, always select a wallboard hammer. Unlike other hammers, wallboard hammers have a convex face, which allows you to set nails below surface without marring the wall. These hammers also have an offset handle, which allows you to hammer nails without hitting your knuckles against the wall. To keep the face of your wallboard hammer from slipping off nails, try this carpenter's trick: file a cross-hatch pattern on the face of the hammer. The grooves help the hammer face grip the nail.

Check the end grain before buying a new tool or tool handle. The strongest wooden tool handles have wood grain that runs parallel to the tool head (left). Handles with the grain running perpendicular to the tool head (right) are more likely to break. Tool handles that are cracked or loose should be replaced.

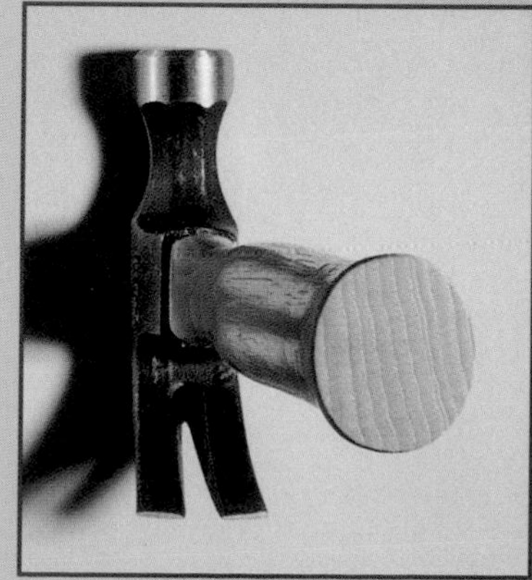

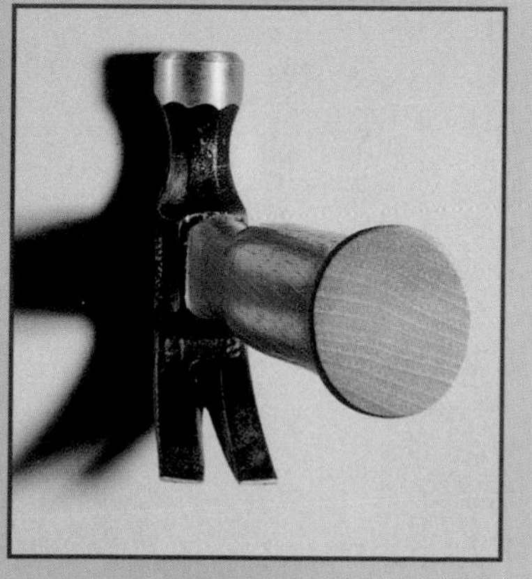

Get a Grip

Holding your hammer incorrectly won't just make your hand sore or tired. Over time, a bad hammer grip can cause carpal tunnel syndrome.

When hammering, don't grip the handle too tightly or place your thumb on the top of the handle as you work. A bad grip allows vibrations to travel through the hammer to your wrists and arms.

It's also a good idea to use hammers with wooden, rather than metal or fiberglass, handles. Wood absorbs more shock and will cut down on the harmful vibrations.

Don't Get Pushy

When using a wrench, keep in mind that it's better to pull than push. If a nut becomes stuck and you're pushing the wrench, your hand may slip off the wrench—and into a wall or pipe.

If you're working with an adjustable wrench, push toward the open side of the wrench, if possible. This will give you a better grip on the nut and prevent damage to the adjustable jaw.

Removing Damaged Screws

Slotted screwheads are easily ruined, especially those made of soft brass or aluminum. Boring a pilot hole before inserting a screw can prevent most damage.

But if you have already damaged the screwhead or if the head is badly corroded, removing the screw can be virtually impossible.

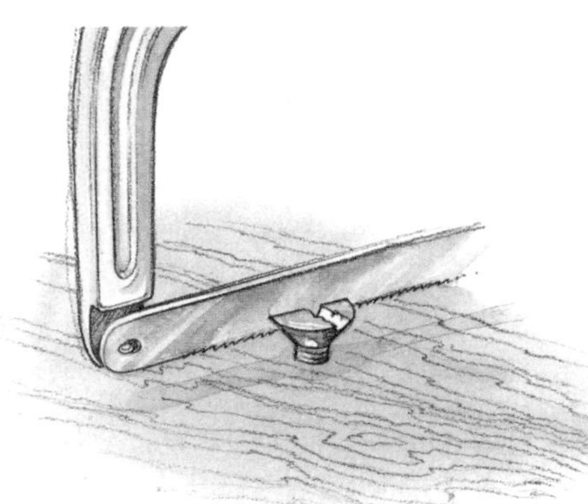

One trick is to deepen the existing slot or cut a new one perpendicular to the original with a hacksaw. Then simply remove the screw with a screwdriver. This technique can also be used on stripped Phillips-head screws.

Nice Threads

Shortening a screw or carriage bolt with a hacksaw or a reciprocating saw often mars the threads, making it impossible to thread a bolt onto the screw.

The next time you need to shorten a fastener, try this: Put the nut onto the threaded end of the fastener before making the cut. Once you have sawed through, remove the nut, using a wrench. The nut will reform the threads and shear off any burrs.

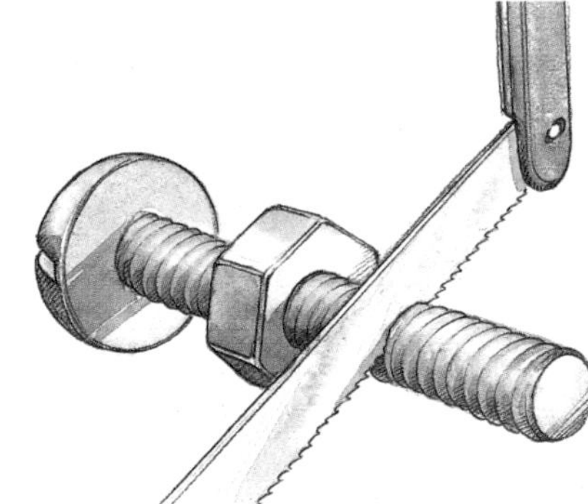

QUICK TIPS

To keep handsaws in top condition, wipe the metal blade after each use with a rag coated in light machine oil. You should also protect the teeth with a protective cover to prevent them from dulling or damaging other tools. If your saw did not come with a blade cover, make one from a length of an old garden hose.

Many people use a coating of soap on the ends of screws to help them go in easier. However, candle wax or paraffin is a better choice for lubricating screws. The salt in soap attracts moisture and can eventually cause the screws to rust and stain surfaces.

TOOL BOX

The blade in your hacksaw should be tight but have some flex. Tightening your blade too much won't allow the blade any leeway when cutting—resulting in a broken blade.

When cutting thin metal with a hacksaw, reciprocating saw or sabre saw, choose a metal-cutting blade that has at least three teeth contacting the edge of the workpiece. A blade with too few teeth will catch on the edge, dulling the blade and possibly damaging the workpiece.

Magnetic Attraction

A magnetic screwdriver is handy when trying to install a screw in tight quarters. You can magnetize an ordinary screwdriver by drawing one pole of a magnet down the shaft of the screwdriver four or five times, moving in one direction only. To demagnetize the screwdriver, draw the magnet along the shaft in the opposite direction two or three times.

Going Against the Grain

As a rule, you should always sand with the wood grain to prevent crossgrain scratches. But when you're using a belt sander to remove a lot of wood or smooth a rough board, you can save some time by bending the rule a bit.

Instead of holding the sander parallel with the grain, start by holding it at a 45-degree angle. Move it straight up and back, keeping the tool canted. The aggressive angle of the belt will quickly cut through even the toughest varieties of hardwood.

Once you're satisfied with the surface, turn the sander parallel with the grain and smooth out the diagonal scratches. Continue sanding, using progressively finer-grit belts, until the board is smooth.

Gang-Sanding Technique with a Belt Sander

Next time you need to belt-sand the edges of several boards, clamp them together with the edges flush, then sand them all at the same time. Known as gang-sanding, this technique saves a lot of time and ensures uniformity because the same amount is removed from each board. The wide surface of the ganged boards also makes it easier to keep the sander flat.

Gang-sanding is ideal for sanding a single board, too. The technique prevents the sander from rounding the board's edges. Simply clamp the workpiece between two pieces of scrap lumber.

TOOL BOX

Glue gums up belt sanders, but an old pair of sneakers can solve the problem. Simply clamp your belt sander upside down on a workbench. Turn the sander on and press the sole of a tennis shoe to the running belt. The shoe's sole will remove the glue.

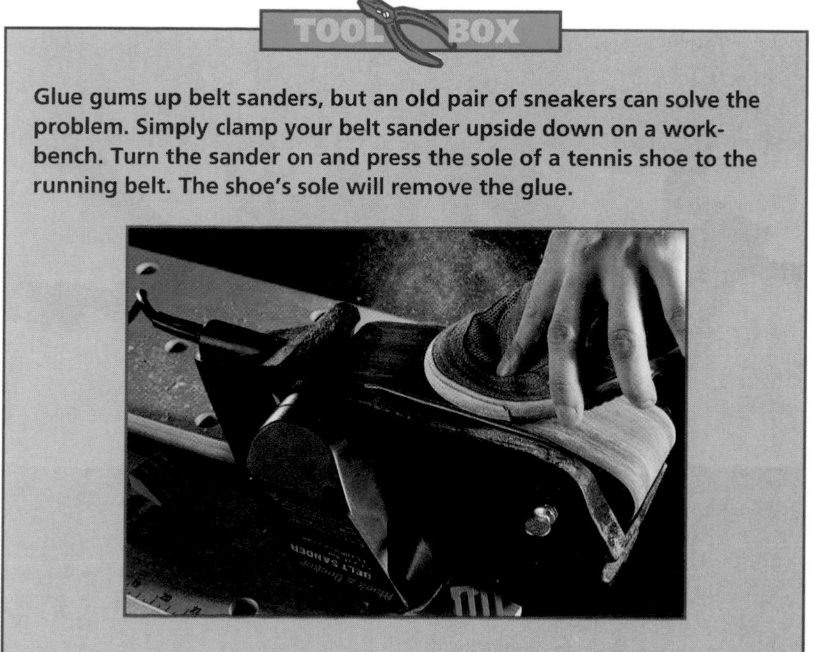

SAFETY FIRST

Prevent children from using power tools by making sure they can't plug the tool into an outlet.

Insert spring–metal key rings or small, key-operated luggage padlocks through the holes in the prongs of the plug.

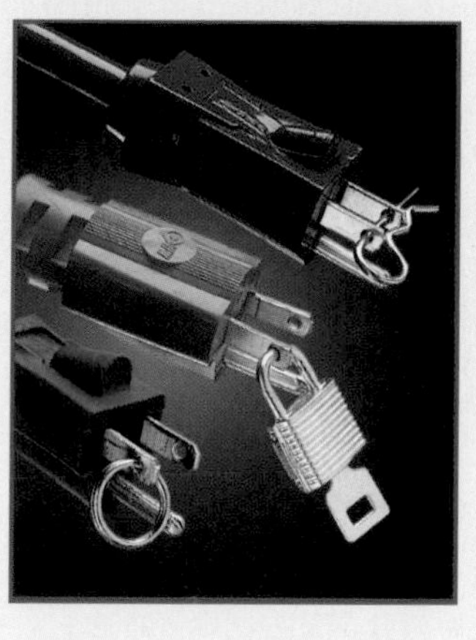

Flush It Out

Sabre saws are versatile tools that routinely handle nearly any cutting job. But with standard blades it's impossible to cut flush against a vertical surface. That's because the saw shoe extends past the blade by roughly an inch. Angling the saw upward doesn't work, because the tip of the blade can damage the workpiece, break the blade or even break and cause injury.

Instead, buy a special flush-cutting blade. The teeth of this oversized blade protrude beyond the front of the saw shoe so you can easily cut up to a vertical surface.

Take a Bigger Bite

A typical 10-inch power miter saw can crosscut a board up to about 5½" wide. But what if you need to cut 6"-wide baseboard or 6½" crown molding?

Widen the cutting capacity of the saw by about 1" putting a 2 × 6 board beneath the workpiece. This raises the piece so the widest part of the blade can cut it. For safety, securely clamp both the workpiece and the support board to the saw table.

Going in Circles

A router is one of the most versatile power tools you can own. It allows you to cut virtually any shape or pattern out of wood. But cutting perfect circles in wood can be difficult.

To easily cut circles with a router, all you need is a screw and a short length of chain. Drive the screw in the centerpoint of the circle, then attach one end of the chain to the screw. Attach the other end of the chain to the router handle.

Cut the circle by stretching the chain taut against the center screw. Lower the bit into the surface and move the router slowly around the perimeter of the circle, keeping the chain taut as you go.

Perfect-Cut Paneling

A circular saw provides a fast, safe way to cut plywood paneling. But, it's nearly impossible to keep the narrow blade cutting straight when sawing the thin sheets. The best solution is to build a straightedge jig to use as a guide. Made from two plywood strips, the straightedge guide has a thin base that allows easy positioning on a workpiece. The base also keeps the foot of the circular saw from scratching the paneling you're cutting.

To build the straightedge you'll need a ¼" plywood base (10" × 96") and a ¾" plywood cleat with a perfectly straight edge (try to use a piece with a factory edge). Assemble and use the straightedge following the steps below:

Apply carpenter's glue to the bottom of the ¾" plywood cleat (A); then, position the cleat on the ¼" plywood base (B), 2" from one edge. Clamp the pieces together until the glue dries.

Position the circular saw with the foot tight against the ¾" plywood cleat. Cut away the excess portion of the plywood base with a single pass of the saw. Use sandpaper to smooth any rough edges.

To use the straightedge guide, position it with the edge of the base flush against the marked cutting line on the workpiece. Clamp the guide in place with C-clamps.

Using a Hole Saw on Wood

Cutting a large-diameter hole through thick wood with a hole saw can strain your wrist and the drill motor. Here's a way to ease the strain and speed the process.

Use the hole saw to cut just enough to score the surface of the wood. Next, remove the saw and bore four or five 1/4"-diameter holes around the inside edge of the scored circle. Then continue cutting. The holes provide chip-clearing spaces, which keeps the saw cutting cooler and cleaner with less chance of binding.

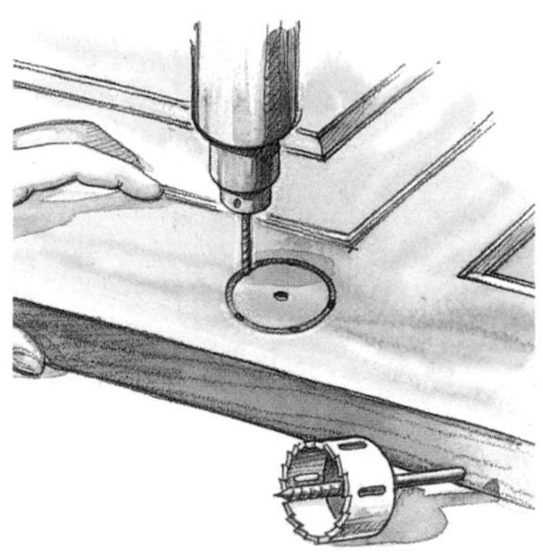

Holes Through Steel

If you need to drill a large-diameter hole through a metal door or stainless-steel sink, a hole saw is the answer. The tiny teeth on this tool are specially engineered to cut through the toughest materials. Unfortunately, the heat created by the spinning saw may dull the saw teeth and discolor the workpiece. To avoid this damage you'll need to lubricate the saw as you work. The following tip will help you keep the saw lubricated:

Use the saw to cut through a sponge. Remove the "plug" from the saw, coat it in cutting fluid or machine oil, and slip it back inside the hole cutter. Oil will seep from the sponge as you cut, lubricating the saw so it cuts cooler and quicker.

SAFETY FIRST

When using a circular saw, always set the cutting blade 1/4" deeper than the thickness of the board you want to cut. This precaution will help prevent the saw from bucking or sticking, a common cause of circular-saw-related injuries.

Knowing the Drill

Drilling straight, accurate holes with a power drill can be difficult. Here are two methods professionals use to make these tasks easier:

To drill perfectly straight holes, use a square wooden block as a visual guide. Place the block directly behind the area you're about to drill, and keep the drill bit shank parallel to the corner of the block when drilling.

Drilling a hole to the right depth—not too deep and not too shallow—can be difficult, as well. To drill the right depth quickly and easily, mark your drill bit.

Measure from the tip of the bit the length you need to drill. Then apply a piece of tape to the bit to mark this measurement. Drill the hole until the tape is flush with the surface.

DRIVE
A
B
C
M
D
N
O
E
L
P
K
F
J
I
FLAG STO

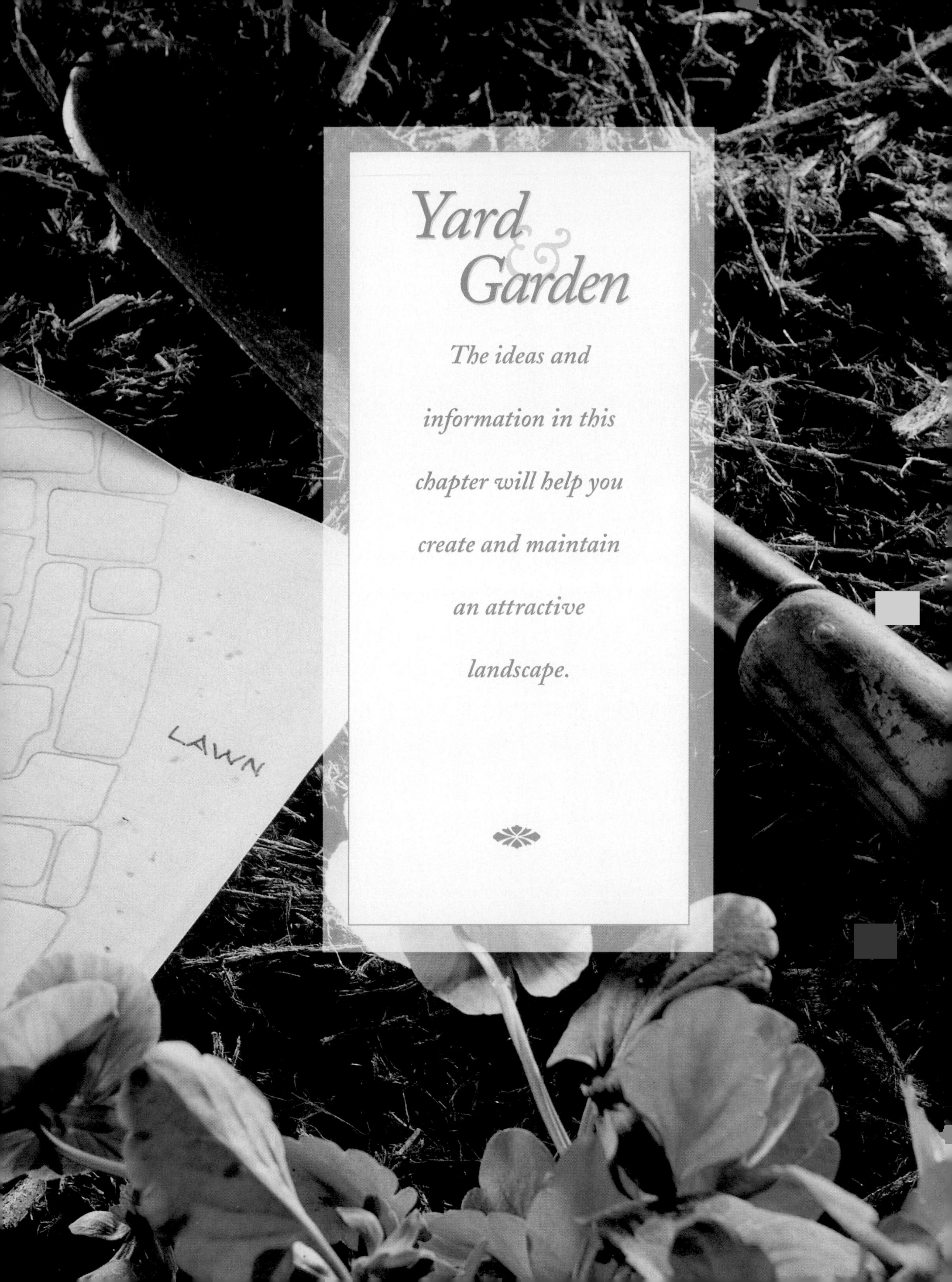

Yard & Garden

The ideas and information in this chapter will help you create and maintain an attractive landscape.

Gardening Basics

Gardens add color and texture to your yard, improving both the appearance and value of your home. They also provide a source of pleasure and pride for the gardener.

QUICK REFERENCE

Planning
pages 138–141

Plant Care
pages 142–145

Trees/Shrubs
pages 146–147

Successful gardens are a result of careful planning, adaptation to climate and soil conditions, and balance between the abilities of the gardener and the needs of the garden.

More than 61 million people, about one in four Americans, currently identify themselves as gardeners. The burgeoning interest in gardening is reflected in the recent explosion of periodicals, retail space and catalogs dedicated to the subject. Almost everyone enjoys the sight and smell of plants and flowers, but not everyone is interested in committing time and energy to gardening. Whether your goal is to limit the effort required to maintain your garden or to embrace gardening as a lifestyle, this chapter will help you enjoy success.

USDA Zone Map

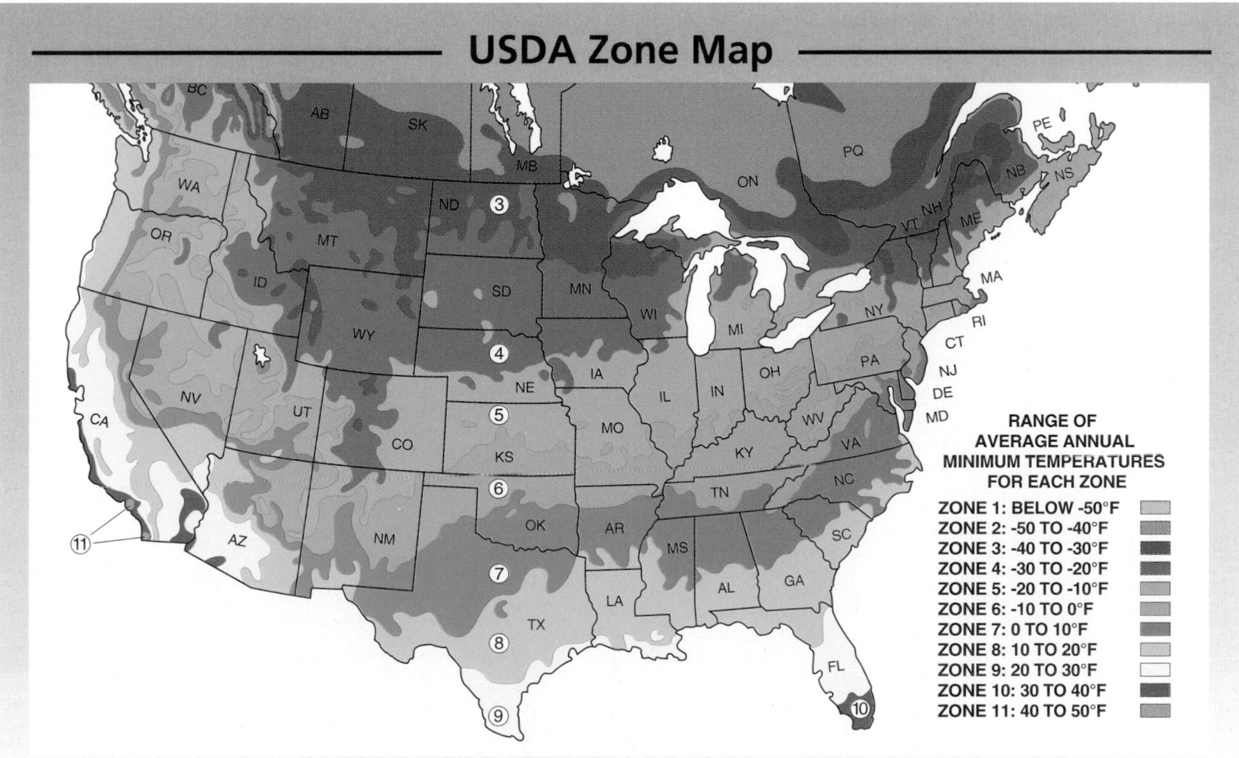

The Best-Laid Plans

Landscape designers and architects know that people enjoy spaces designed using familiar patterns. You can create attractive landscapes by remembering the principles of scale, balance, repetition and contrast.

Think about scale—the relative size of objects in a landscape. In the design shown in the illustration at right, the plantings are arranged so the larger lilacs and tall bushes are near the back, with smaller shrubs and flowers in front.

Create focal points by using contrasting colors and distinctive accents to draw visual attention to a few areas of your yard.

Repeat yourself. Good landscapes echo similar shapes, colors and textures to give a feeling of unity.

Create contrast by using textures, shapes, sizes and colors. In general, design your landscape so that large or coarse-textured items stand behind smaller items or those with more subtle textures. Use contrast selectively: landscapes with too many contrasting elements look random and unplanned.

Cost Control

For large landscaping projects, you may want to spread out the expense and time by dividing the project into smaller jobs that can be completed over a period of months or even years. If you choose to work this way, make sure you begin with a good overall landscaping plan. Consider these ideas:

Make accurate estimates of the materials you need because leftover materials like concrete, brick and stone usually cannot be returned to suppliers.

Try to coordinate landscaping projects with neighbors so you can take advantage of volume discounts on brick, stone, sod and other materials.

Collect free materials. For example, you can get wood chips from tree trimmers, power companies and other utility companies. Farmers or housing developers may let you collect rubble stone. Paving brick can be salvaged from demolition sites. If you are removing old landscaping structures, consider reusing the materials.

Haul material yourself with a pickup truck or trailer. Shipping charges for small volumes of gravel, sand or topsoil can be more expensive than the materials themselves.

Before mowing season arrives, get your mower blade sharpened. Keeping mower blades sharp helps you maintain a healthy lawn. Dull blades tear rather than cut the blades of grass, making your lawn look brown.

To ensure that you always have a sharp blade available, buy an extra one. When one blade gets dull, replace and immediately sharpen it so that you always have a spare.

Just a Test

Making sketches is the traditional method for testing landscape ideas, but you will get a better idea of how landscapes would look if you model your plans in the yard itself. For example, use stakes and sheets of cardboard to demonstrate how a fence, trellis or freestanding wall will look.

While testing your ideas, look at the landscape from many different angles. View the yard from downstairs and upstairs windows, from the street in front of the house and from neighboring yards. Consider how time-of-day and seasonal changes will affect shade patterns in the yard. Try these modeling ideas:

Buy or borrow sample materials, like interlocking blocks or brick pavers, and arrange them on site to see which materials complement the existing materials in your yard and house.

Use brown wrapping paper to model patios, walkways and other paved surfaces on your yard. Test different paver patterns by tracing the designs on the paper with colored chalk.

Use a garden hose to test the layout of walkways, patios, planting beds, ponds and other landscape features. When planning a curved walkway, use pieces of wood lath cut to even lengths to maintain an accurate width (photo below).

Test layouts for planting areas, using potted plants and shrubs. This can also help you determine which plant species look best in your yard.

Hedge-Planting Guidance

When planting a hedge, it can be difficult to determine the proper spacing of the plants.

First, ask a nursery professional or check reference books to find the mature size of the plants you're considering.

Once you've selected plants and know their spacing requirements, simply divide the total distance of the area you're planting by the space requirement to determine the number of plants you'll need.

QUICK TIPS

If you want a wide, dense hedge, set the plants in staggered rows. Before digging, measure and mark the holes to ensure even spacing.

For a narrow hedge, dig a straight trench and set plants close together.

Methods for Estimating Landscaping Materials

This chart can help you estimate the materials you need for landscaping projects, including appropriate waste. Sizes and weights of materials may vary, so consult your supplier for more detailed information.

ESTIMATING MATERIALS	
Sand, gravel, topsoil (2" layer)	surface area (sq. ft.) / 100 = tons needed
Standard brick pavers (4" × 8")	surface area (sq. ft.) × 5 = number of pavers needed
Poured concrete (4" layer)	surface area (sq. ft.) × .012 = cubic yards needed
Flagstone	surface area (sq. ft.) / 100 = tons of stone needed
Interlocking block (6" × 16" face)	area of wall face (sq. ft.) × 1.5 = number of blocks needed
Retaining wall timbers (5"× 6" × 8 ft.)	area of wall face (sq. ft.) / 3 = number of timbers needed
Cut stone for 1-ft.-thick walls	area of wall face (sq. ft.) / 15 = tons of stone needed
Rubble stone for 1-ft.-thick walls	area of wall face (sq. ft.) / 35 = tons of stone needed
8 × 8 × 16 concrete block for freestanding walls	height of wall (ft.) × length of wall × 1.125 = number of blocks

Good Dirt

Properly prepared soil is essential to landscaping. Soil anchors your landscape and provides nutrients, air and moisture to plants.

Dig a hole about 1 ft. deep and 1 ft. wide. Fill the hole with water and time how long it takes the water to drain into the ground.

Good loamy soil will generally drain at a rate of about 1 inch per hour. Sandy soil drains faster, while clay soil drains much slower.

Pipe Down

If you need to drain water from a low-lying lawn area, try this:

Dig a trench that extends from the flooded area across a long expanse of your yard. Line this trench with gravel.

Set perforated pipe in the gravel bed, pitching it down to a valley. Cover the gravel above the pipe with landscape fabric to keep dirt from clogging the pipe over time; then bury the pipe.

Water will find its way into the pipe and drain across a broad area, eliminating soggy spots.

Patience Pays

Ornamental vines are often used on fences or arbors to enclose outdoor-living areas and provide shade and privacy. If you plan to use vines in this way, you should recognize that they will take several years to fully mature.

As the old saying goes, "The first year, vines sleep; the second year, they creep; the third year, they leap."

Among the vines you might consider for this purpose are clematis species, climbing hydrangea, Dutchman's pipe, silver lace vine, trumpet vine and wisteria.

Goodbye, Deer

Deer are notorious for nibbling on young trees and shrubs, and they have been known to virtually destroy vegetable gardens. Experts agree that the best way to keep deer away is to surround your yard with a 10-ft. fence.

If this method isn't practical for you, there are many homespun defenses you can try.

Surround plantings with human hair or dog hair trimmings.

Scatter scraps of bar soap around the perimeter of plantings.

Play a radio 24 hours a day.

Try one of the new battery-operated motion and heat sensors. When a deer moves within range, the sensor flashes bright lights and sends out a loud whistle. In short, it scares the deer right out of your yard.

Rearranging the Flowers

Once you've planted your perennials, you don't have to leave them in the same spot year after year. Like furniture, perennials can be moved or rearranged to suit your changing taste and needs. Don't be afraid to divide and replant perennials that have grown too large—you can also share any extras with neighbors or friends. Remove any plants that don't work well in a particular bed, and try them in another spot. If you don't like the results, you can always move them again.

Take the Test

Take the guesswork out of treating your lawn and garden by having your soil tested. The results of the lab test will tell you what nutrients you'll need to add to your soil to grow a healthy lawn and have productive gardens.

To get an accurate reading, collect soil plugs from several areas of your yard. Send these separate samples to your local university extension service or soil testing lab.

Energy Plants

Energy-conscious homeowners have learned that low-e windows, high-R-value insulation and efficient heating and cooling systems will help cut energy consumption and costs. An overlooked but excellent way to reduce energy use lies right outside those low-e windows—landscaping.

According to studies conducted by the U.S. Department of Energy (DOE), strategically planted trees and shrubs can reduce utility bills by up to 25 percent. The studies found, for example, that the proper placement of just three trees can save the average household between $100 and $250 per year.

During the summer, trees, vines and shrubs can serve as sunscreens to keep a home cool. Shading and evapotranspiration (the process by which trees actively release water vapor) can reduce the surrounding air temperature by nearly 10°F.

In winter, properly placed evergreen trees, hedges and thick shrubs will protect a home from biting winds. A study in South Dakota found that planting windbreaks along just the windward side of the house cut fuel consumption by 25 percent. When extended to three sides (north, west and east), the plantings reduced the heating bill by a whopping 40 percent.

Simple Translation

The three numbers on fertilizer packages indicate the percentage by weight of nitrogen (N), phosphorus (P) and potassium (K) contained in the package. The three numbers always stand for N-P-K, in that order.

In the illustration at right, the 5-lb. box of 10-10-10 fertilizer contains 10% nitrogen, 10% phosphorus and 10% potassium. Therefore, this box contains 1/2 lb. (5 lb. × .10 = .5 lb.) of nitrogen, 1/2 lb. of phosphorus and 1/2 lb. of potassium, for a total of 1 1/2 lb. of fertilizer. In this example, the remaining part (3 1/2 lb.) is filler material, such as sand, which helps spread the fertilizer more evenly. If a fertilizer contains nutrients in addition to N, P and K, the label will list them, along with their percentage by weight.

10-10-10

GUARANTEED ANALYSIS
Total Nitrogen (N) 10%
2.1% Ammoniacal Nitrogen
7.9% Urea Nitrogen
Available Phosphoric Acid (P_2O_5) . . . 10%
Soluble Potash (K_2O) 10%
Primary Nutrients from Urea, Ammonium Phosphate and Muriate of Potash.
Chlorine, not more than 8.5%
84-1079

CAUTION: Keep out of reach of children. May cause eye irritation. Avoid contact with eyes.

Solar Weeding

You can use the summer sun for more than getting a tan. In fact, the sun can help eliminate weeds. It's called "solarization" and the idea is simple: Trap the sun's heat under sheets of plastic, raising soil temperature enough to destroy weeds and disease-producing fungi.

First, till or spade and level the soil as you would for planting (there's no need to remove all growing weeds). Moisten the soil to a 1-ft depth; then, cover the area with clear plastic sheets. Smooth out the plastic so it makes contact with the soil, and bury the edges in 4"-deep trenches. In windy areas, lay bricks on top of the plastic to keep it in place.

In clear weather, with the average maximum temperature ranging between 85° and 90°F, allow six to eight weeks before uncovering the soil. When you remove the plastic, work only the top several inches of soil so you don't churn up any healthy weed seeds.

Solarization is most effective on many cool-season weeds and grasses. Tough grasses, such as Bermuda and clover, will be weakened, but probably won't be eliminated.

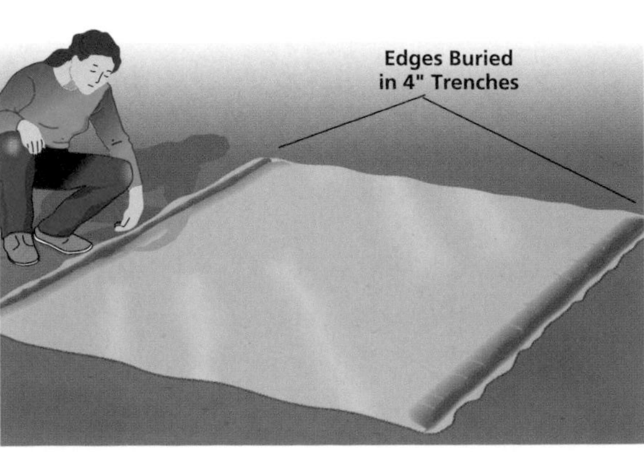

Cut Down on Salt

In cold climates, homeowners often throw rock salt on driveways and sidewalks in the winter. Salt may keep you from slipping on the ice and snow, but too much of it can harm even salt-tolerant plants, especially when the soil in the area is compacted, poorly drained or dry.

Here are some ways to minimize salt damage to plants:

Build an earth berm or other barrier to shield plants.

Saturate the area with water each spring to wash the salt down through the soil.

Choose alternate deicers. Try potassium chloride or calcium chloride or consider using fertilizer, such as urea or ammonium nitrate instead of salt. Used in moderation, the fertilizer won't harm plants, though urea is slightly corrosive to metal, and ammonium nitrate can damage concrete.

Sprinkle ash and cinders to create a nonslip surface. Neither will damage plants, but they will raise the soil pH, making it less acidic. Keep ash and cinders away from acid-loving plants, such as azaleas and rhododendrons.

How Does Your Garden Grow?

If a healthy crop of weeds is growing where you want to create a garden or flower bed, you probably don't need a soil test. The fact that a good variety of plants is already growing there is proof that most ornamentals or vegetables will grow there, too.

Effective Watering

No two yards have the same irrigation needs. Climate, soil type, slope and plant type all determine when, how often and how long you should water. Nevertheless, there are some basic guidelines for watering wisely:

Reduce evaporation. Even before water from your sprinkler hits the ground, some is lost through evaporation from sun and wind. On a warm day, more than 30 percent of the water evaporates before entering the ground. Minimize evaporation by watering when the air is calm and the ground and air are cool; typically, in the early morning.

Don't overwater. With established plants, let the top 2 to 3" of soil dry out between waterings. Soil that is constantly saturated doesn't provide enough oxygen for healthy root development and adequate nutrient absorption. What's more, organisms harmful to roots thrive in a wet environment.

Water deeply. Deep watering promotes strong downward-growing roots. Light watering causes roots to stay near the soil surface. Because soil dries from the surface downward, shallow roots need to be watered that much sooner.

Prevent overspraying. To avoid watering paved areas along with your plants, match the spray pattern of the sprinkler with the area you're watering.

Ground Rules

There is no such thing as a no-maintenance garden, but if you plant the right plants in the right places and prepare the soil properly, your garden will require less maintenance and be more successful.

Stick to lawn grasses, flowers and woody plants that have been proven successful in your climate. Otherwise, you'll spend lots of time planting and replanting or struggling to keep stressed plants alive. Also be sure the plants you're considering fit the location chosen within your yard. For example, a sun-loving plant will struggle in shade.

Prepare the soil before planting. Even the most carefully chosen and tended plants won't thrive unless the soil provides the nutrients, air and water they need. Have soil tested by your local extension service; then apply the amendments they recommend to correct pH or nutrient deficiencies in your soil.

Eliminate weeds before planting. The more weeds you remove before you plant, the fewer you'll have to deal with later. Also, put down a porous landscape fabric to inhibit weed growth and soil erosion. After planting, hide the fabric with mulch.

Automate irrigation. A simple, affordable way to do this is with timers that attach to the faucet. Some designs turn the water off, while others can be programmed to turn the water on and off at set intervals throughout the day or week. The ultimate irrigation systems are automated pop-up sprinklers for lawns and drip irrigation for trees, shrubs and flower gardens.

Keep your gardening gear in top shape by following these basic tips:

To keep tools free of rust, clean metal parts with an oil-soaked rag. Most oils work, including vegetable oil, but stay away from used motor oil. Remove encrusted dirt by plunging tools into a box filled with a mixture of sand and oil.

To get a good edge on pruning shears, trowels and hoes, remove dirt and rust with a wire brush, and sharpen them with a 10" to 12" all-purpose mill bastard file.

To clean sticky sap off hand-held pruning shears, scrub the blades with an old toothbrush that's been dipped in distilled vinegar.

Free Fertilizer

Whenever you bag lawn clippings, you're disrupting the natural cycle of growth and decomposition. Clippings have nutrients your lawn needs to grow and stay healthy.

There are some rules you need to follow, however. The clippings must be fine enough that they don't mat down on top of the lawn; they should filter down to the soil level. Mow often, so the clippings won't be too long; better yet, invest in a mulching mower.

Spraying chemicals on your lawn kills off bacteria, worms and microbes, which aid the decomposition of grass clippings.

NURSERY SCHOOL

Summer-flowering annuals, such as marigolds, petunias, portulaca, salvias and zinnias, are a great way to perk up flower beds and containers, even late in the season.

For great performance and the most value for your dollar, look for the healthiest specimens you can find at a nursery or garden center. As a general rule, these places take better care of plants than do discount stores. Let the following tips guide you through the nursery aisles:

- Nurseries carry the same types of plants in different sizes of containers. Healthy plants in small containers, if not root-bound, suffer less transplant shock, grow faster than large plants and cost less.
- If you have a choice, buy plants before they flower. They will bloom for a long season—in your garden, rather than on the store rack.
- Look for compact plants with good leaf color—leaves should be perky and richly colored. Tall, spindly plants are probably stressed from crowding or insufficient light.
- Avoid plants that have roots growing through the drainage holes of the containers; they are probably root-bound.

Cow Manure Fertilizer

While the highest concentration of nutrients is found in fresh livestock manure, aged or composted manure is safest for plants. Soluble salts in fresh manure can damage plant roots, and the nitrogen it contains is in the form of ammonia, which can also hurt growing plants.

Get manure in the fall, and work it into empty garden beds. Or, collect the manure and compost it for use in the spring. One benefit of composting is that if the compost pile heats up sufficiently—110° to 140°—the process kills most weed seeds mixed with the manure.

Manure increases the organic content of the soil, which improves its structure and stimulates bacterial and fungal activity, making other nutrients more available to plants.

Putting Down Roots

Nurseries commonly sell "bare-root" plants—dormant trees, shrubs, cane berries and perennials, with the soil removed from their roots. Although these scraggly, lifeless-looking sticks lack the shelf appeal of container plants, several factors make them attractive:

Bare-root plants cost 15 to 25 percent less than container plants. Although that might not amount to much on a single tree, it adds up when you're buying many trees or shrubs for a backyard orchard or a new hedge.

Bare-root plants take up less space than container plants, so nurseries can offer more varieties. And, they will often special-order plants you can't find.

Bare-root trees and shrubs are easier to maneuver because they don't have the bulk and weight of soil.

Bare-root plants adapt more easily to garden soil because they don't have to make the transition from the artificial soil mix in nursery containers. They also develop strong roots. And unlike container plants, which can arrive with their roots cramped and overgrown, bare roots are free to spread out through soil.

Long-Lasting Roses

If you have a rose garden, you've probably experienced the disappointment of seeing the heads of your freshly cut roses drooping after the first day.

To prepare cut roses so they last longer, cut them early in the morning, while they're still dewy. Plunge the stems into a vase of tepid water immediately. This may not seem as romantic as carrying them about in a basket, but the idea is to minimize the amount of time the roses are without moisture.

Trim the stems again under running tepid water and remove any greenery that's below water level. The greenery rots, producing mold that invades and decays the flower stems. Change the water daily to reduce mold.

There are a variety of powdered products that are intended to lengthen the life of cut roses. The jury is out on these, but most of the old tricks, like putting a spoonful of sugar in the water, don't really work.

Garden Deadheads

Removing the faded flowers or flower stalks from annuals and perennials is called deadheading. It can keep the plants blooming longer and improve their appearance. Once blossoms die and seeds start forming, deadheading prevents plants from putting all their energy into fattening up seeds at the expense of flower production.

To deadhead large-flowered annuals like zinnias or marigolds, simply pinch off or cut fading flowers back to the next branch.

For mat-forming plants with small flowers, such as alyssum and lobelia, it's easier to shear them off with garden scissors or pruning shears. Just don't remove more than a third of the plant or you risk stunting its growth.

Pruning Roses

To stimulate growth and create attractive bushes, roses should be pruned in the early spring, before growth starts. Don't be timid about taking off too much; rose bushes grow quickly and will become leggy unless they're well trimmed. As a rule, you should leave 8 to 9" of green stem.

During the growing season, remove spent blooms and shape the plant by cutting back to the nearest five-leaf shoot. Autumn pruning isn't necessary because you'll eliminate dead canes and dieback in the spring pruning.

For best results, use a bypass pruner, available from a number of garden-tool manufacturers. Sharpen your pruning shears frequently—dull blades can mash the canes.

Share and Share Alike

Once you get into the swing of gardening, you'll often find that you have extra plants or seedlings. And you'll probably make gardening friends who also have extras.

Swapping plants with friends and neighbors is a great way to expand your garden and your plant collection. Or, join a garden club and participate in their periodic plant exchanges.

Another inexpensive way to expand your collection is to attend plant sales sponsored by church groups, nonprofit gardens, and arboretum groups. Low prices at these sales can provide you with amazing bargains and unique additions to your gardens.

(Above left) Clusters of small insects and sticky deposits on buds are signs your roses are infested with aphids.

(Above right) Black spots and yellowing leaves are signs of fungal diseases, common when leaves are damp for an extended time.

(Left) Black or brown canes indicate winter dieback, the result of exposure to severe cold weather.

QUICK TIPS

Keep the blades of hedge trimmers sharp and in proper adjustment. Always wear eye, face and ear protection as well as nonslip gloves when using a hedge trimmer.

Tilt the blades of a hedge trimmer into the foliage for the best cutting performance. Cut from the bottom up when shaping the sides of hedges, and always taper vertical cuts to make the bottom wider than the top.

Keep the trimmer's blades clean, free of resin and lubricated with a light #10 oil. Sluggish blades will quickly drain battery-powered machines.

Christmas All Year Long

A cut fir or spruce makes a great gift for the yard once the holidays are over. Instead of having your tree hauled away, recycle it.

Place the tree along the edge of the yard or near a bird feeder to give birds cover and shelter.

Remove boughs and place them over perennials to help collect snow, which insulates plant roots. Or, prop boughs against evergreens to protect them from winter wind and sun.

Save the main trunk to support pole beans or other annual vines in summer gardens.

Shred the tree and use it as mulch. Add some nitrogen fertilizer when using fresh chips. Or, compost the chips and then work the finished compost into the soil.

Direct Pipeline

The biggest concern after planting or transplanting trees is making sure that water and fertilizer are getting to the roots, where they'll do the most good. Here's a quick and simple trick that doesn't require much extra effort, but will guarantee that newly planted trees get the water and nutrients they need.

You can deliver water and fertilizer directly to the root ball through lengths of PVC pipe planted right beside the tree. Dig the appropriate size hole for the root ball; then, carve out more space for the pipes on either side (see illustration below). Backfill the hole, leaving each piece of pipe sticking up about 2 inches out of the ground. Fill the pipes with gravel; then, water and fertilize the tree through the pipes—as well as around the entire tree—according to your garden center's instructions.

This method also works well for an existing tree. Use a posthole digger or power auger to excavate the holes, but be careful not to dig so close to the trunk that you damage the root system. Use the drip line of the lower branches as a guideline for safe hole placement.

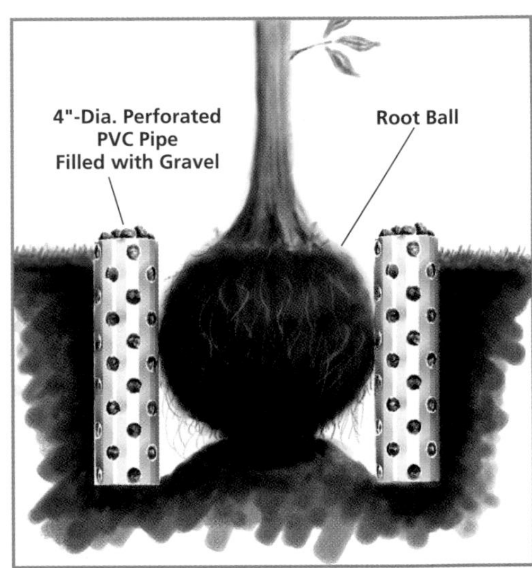

Fruit Stand

Fruit trees can be a wonderful addition to your yard or garden, but you have to select the right varieties if your goal is a bountiful crop.

For example, consider the "chilling requirement"—the actual number of hours of exposure to cold temperatures that fruit trees need each winter in order to produce fruit. If you garden in the warmer regions (zones 7 to 11), select fruit varieties that don't require a period of cold weather for good spring blossom and leaf growth.

Another factor to keep in mind when selecting fruit trees is pollination. Some fruit trees and other fruit plants need to be cross-pollinated with other related varieties in order to produce fruit. Apples, pears, pecans, Japanese plums and blueberries, for example, need to be cross-pollinated with other varieties to produce their best fruit. On the other hand, peaches, nectarines, almonds and apricots are all self-pollinators that produce big yields without cross-pollination.

Read plant catalogs and label information carefully to determine whether your fruit trees and plants have special pollination needs.

Trim and Tidy

When you're trimming a tree, it's important to remove limbs without tearing the tree's bark. By following this simple procedure, you'll work more effectively and protect the tree as well.

First, cut upward, halfway through the branch about 6" out from the main trunk. Next, cut downward just outside the lower cut. These two cuts will remove the greatest part of the limb. Finally, cut the limb stub off just outside the collar that joins the branch to the trunk.

Mulch Ado

Do your yard a favor—spread a layer of loose organic mulch, like ground bark, shredded leaves or straw, over the soil surface around trees, shrubs and plants. Mulch saves water by reducing evaporation, and it inhibits weeds. When you water, mulch stops mud from splashing onto plants, preventing some soil-borne diseases.

What's more, when mulch is applied regularly over several years, your soil gets richer and richer as the mulch decomposes.

Apply a 3 to 4" mulch layer. Keep it a couple of inches away from the base of woody plants; this allows air to circulate freely, thus discouraging disease.

Use only weed-free mulches (straw instead of hay, for example).

Use fresh sawdust or wood chips with caution: Soil bacteria that break down these materials consume nitrogen from the soil in the process, reducing the nitrogen available to plants. To prevent nitrogen deficiency, increase the amount of nitrogen fertilizer regularly used by 25 percent. Or, before mulching with sawdust, incorporate 2 to 4 lbs. of a nonnitrogen fertilizer, such as 10-0-0, per 100 sq. ft. of area to be mulched.

Turn leaves into mulch. Gather them from different kinds of trees for a wider acid/alkaline range that will produce a healthier soil pH. Run the leaves through the mower or a shredder to chop them up; then, put them in garbage bags. Sprinkle the leaves with water, and seal up the bags. Mix two cups of agricultural lime into each bag of leaves. Lay the garbage bags on the garden bed in full sun for the entire winter. In spring, you'll have bags full of free mulch.

Avoiding Winter Sunburn

The intense light on a bright, sunny winter day can damage, or sunscald, some trees. The bark can crack, become mushy or slough off in patches, revealing dead tissue.

According to the Colorado State University Cooperative Extension, sun rays heat south-facing branches and the southwest side of trees, raising bark temperature above freezing and causing some cells to become active. When the temperature suddenly drops again, these cells freeze and die. Sunscald occurs most frequently on newly planted trees with thin bark, like birch, silver maple and many fruit trees, and usually appears on the southwest side of trees.

To prevent it, plant susceptible trees on the east side of structures or shade them from late afternoon sun. Commercial tree wrap, a heavy paper that is applied like a spiraling bandage around the tree trunk, also protects trees. Wrap trees in October or November; remove the paper in April so it doesn't restrict growth, girdle the trunk or become a haven for pests.

Outdoor Structures

Decks, patios and fences give form to your yard, offering outdoor living space your family can enjoy all year long.

For many people, outdoor structures figure prominently in childhood memories. If you have enjoyed long afternoons on a porch swing, picnics on the patio or barbecues on the deck, you know just how much pleasure these structures add to your life.

Many homeowners are constantly improving or adding to their outdoor structures. Sturdy decks, attractive patios and rustic fences add character and value to your home, so building and maintaining them makes good financial sense.

Helpful Terms

Ashlar: Natural stone that has been cut into cubic shapes; also known as cut stone; may be marble, hard limestone or granite; expensive, top-quality building material

Batter: Backward slant that provides additional stability to a retaining wall

Bonding adhesive: Compound used primarily in concrete repair to improve adhesion of repair materials

Deck screws: Galvanized screws, typically 3" long; preferable to nails because they can easily be removed and don't rust or stain decking

Flagstone: Uncut sedimentary stone that has naturally flat surfaces; limestone, slate and shale are common types; durable paving material

Heartwood: Wood from the inner, older part of a tree; when purchasing cedar or redwood, landscape professionals often specify heartwood because it's more resistant to insects and decay than the sapwood

Pressure-treated lumber: Wood, usually pine, that has been treated with preservatives to make it last longer; traditionally green that weathers to gray, now also available in dark-brown color; must be sealed to prevent water damage

Rubble stone: Irregular, uncut rock collected from fields or stream beds; can include boulders, glacial debris, rough quartz or granite and random pieces of sandstone; less formal and less expensive than cut stone

Swale: Shallow ditch that provides drainage for runoff water

Wood sealer: Compound used to prevent water damage; typically applied to all exposed surfaces of a board, including ends and edges

Weight Lifting

Retaining walls are subject to enormous pressure from the weight of the soil behind the wall. To offset this pressure, build retaining walls so each row of material is set slightly behind the previous row.

Retaining walls built with this backward angle (at least 1" for each foot in height) are called "battered walls."

A Little Setback

Setback regulations keep you from building any structure too close to property lines. You need to consider these regulations when you're planning fences, walls and other landscape structures.

Call your local building department office to learn about local rules and restrictions.

SAFETY FIRST

Underground utility lines can be very dangerous. Before starting any yard or garden project that requires digging or excavation, you must make sure you will not encounter or interfere with them.

You are required by law to locate buried utility lines before you dig. All public utility companies will inspect your site and mark their locations.

A Swale Deal

Dense soil that does not drain well can create real problems for retaining walls. Excessive water pressure will topple a wall in time, so installing a drainage system is a must.

If you recognize a drainage problem during the wall's planning or construction phase, backfill the area at the base of the wall with 4 to 5" of gravel and install a perforated drainpipe near the bottom of the backfill. Vent the pipe to the side or bottom of the wall, where runoff water can flow away from the hillside without causing erosion.

To solve a drainage problem surrounding an existing retaining wall, dig a shallow ditch, called a *swale*, 1 to 2 ft. away from the top of the wall. Cover the swale with fresh sod.

For severe problems, dig a 1-ft.-deep swale angled slightly downward to the outlet point. Line the swale with landscape fabric and spread a 2" layer of coarse gravel over it. Lay perforated drainpipe over the gravel, cover the pipe with a 5" layer of gravel; then wrap the landscape fabric over the top of the gravel. Cover the swale with soil and fresh sod. Set a splash block at the outlet to distribute the runoff and prevent erosion.

Tall Timbers

Despite the fact that landscape timbers are commonly used for retaining walls, they are not particularly easy to work with. Here are some ideas that will make building a timber wall easier:

Draw a detailed plan for your project and determine the exact length of each timber. Order them cut to length rather than trying to cut them yourself.

Predrill holes for spikes so they don't split as the timbers dry out. To further reduce the risk of splitting, place spikes at least 6" from the ends of the timbers.

Use metal reinforcement bars instead of spikes to connect the timbers if you have heavy, dense soil that drains poorly. Drill pilot holes at 2-ft. intervals. Cut 12 to 24" lengths of bar, then drive them into the holes.

Note: The chemicals used in treated lumber are toxic, so wear a particle mask, gloves and long sleeves when cutting or handling them, and don't burn scraps.

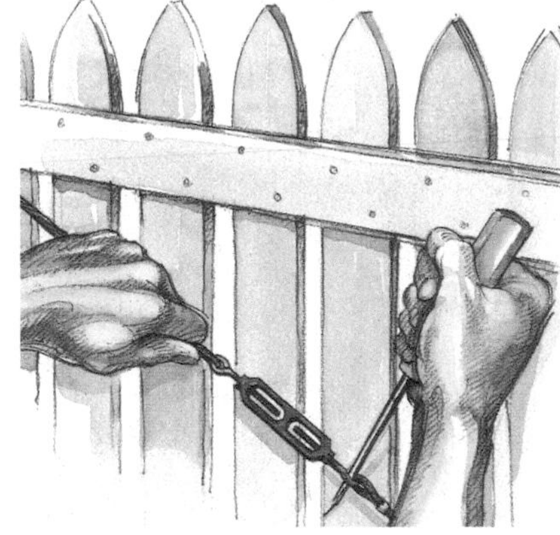

Gate Straightener

Gravity and joyriding kids can make swinging gates sag over time. To square up a droopy gate, mount an eye screw into the gate frame near the upper hinge. Fasten a length of steel cable to the screw with a U-bolt clip. Place another eye screw diagonally across at the lower corner of the gate and fasten a second length of cable. Connect the two cable ends with a small turnbuckle. Then rotate the turnbuckle shackle with a screwdriver to draw the two cables together until the gate is square.

Interlocking-Block Walls

Interlocking-block retaining walls have become quite popular in recent years. They're attractive, relatively inexpensive, and the materials are readily available at building and outdoor centers.

If you plan to build an interlocking block wall, investigate the various styles. Some are held together with a system of overlapping flanges that automatically set the backward angle (batter) as the blocks are stacked; others use a pinning system.

Before you buy blocks, talk to your neighbors to see if anyone is interested in coordinating a project with you. Suppliers often offer substantial discounts when interlocking block is purchased in large quantities, so you may be able to save money if you order blocks together.

Making Half Blocks

Even with careful planning, you can't avoid the need for half blocks when building an interlocking block wall. Half blocks are used when making corners and to ensure that vertical joints between blocks are staggered between rows.

You can score a line across a block with a maul and cold chisel and pound away until the block breaks in half, but there is an easier way.

Score the block with a circular saw and masonry blade; then use the maul and chisel to break the block along the line.

Repairing Fence Rails

Here's a quick and easy fence-repair tip from the folks at the Housing Resource Center in Cleveland, Ohio: If the horizontal rails of a utility fence keep coming loose from the posts, don't renail them. Instead, install joist hangers.

Nail or screw the hangers to the posts. Then slip the rail ends into the hangers. To secure the fence section, screw through the hangers and into the rails. Or, skip the last step and you'll be able to lift off the fence section for painting, repair or to drive a truckload of topsoil, firewood or lumber into your yard.

At the Post

When fences lean, sag or wobble, the problem can usually be traced back to the posts. Common post problems include rot, cracked footings and improper alignment.

Evaluate fence posts early in the spring when the ground is still damp but not muddy. Dig down about 6" to check for rot. Next, make sure the posts are plumb. If not, gravity will continue to loosen them until the fence tilts and wobbles.

To realign a post, dig away the dirt around the footing and reposition the post to plumb. Fill the hole with gravel and new concrete to maintain the post's plumb position.

Cut back any plants that surround posts. They hold moisture and promote rot. Remove plant roots, too, so their growth doesn't exert pressure on the posts.

Resurfacing Concrete

Spalling and pop-outs, common in old concrete surfaces, make sidewalks and patios look shabby. If the damage is extensive, replacement is the only answer. If the surface is damaged but the concrete is still structurally sound, it can be preserved by resurfacing—applying a thin layer of new concrete over the old surface.

If you mix your own repair material for the new surface, use sand-mix concrete and make it slightly stiffer (drier) than normal. If you're ordering ready-mix concrete, specify that the aggregate in the mixture be no larger than 1/2".

Clean the surface thoroughly. Scrape it to dislodge as much loose concrete as you can; then sweep the surface clean. You also need to dig a 6"-wide trench around all sides of the concrete to create room for 2 × 4 forms.

Stake 2 × 4 forms flush against the sides of the slabs, 1 to 2" above the surface. Drive stakes every 3 ft., and at every joint in the forms. Mark control joint locations onto the outside of the forms, directly above existing control joints. Spray the inside faces of the forms with vegetable oil.

Following the product directions carefully, apply a thin layer of bonding adhesive over the entire surface. Spread the concrete over the surface; then press the mixture down with a shovel or 2 × 4 to pack it into the forms. Smooth the surface with a screed board.

Float the concrete with a wood float; then tool it with an edger. Re-create the surface treatment, such as brooming, used on the original surface. Cut control joints in the original locations. After the concrete is fully set, cover the surface with plastic, and let it cure for one week.

Coloring Concrete

To color existing concrete surfaces, your best bet is a concrete stain. It works like a penetrating wood stain by soaking into the concrete. The specially formulated stain won't peel like paint and it dries to a dead-flat finish. The easiest way to apply it is with a long-handled roller.

The preferred method of coloring new concrete is to add a liquid dye to the mix before it's poured. That way, the color goes all the way through the slab. The next-best method is to sprinkle a powdered dye onto the wet concrete surface after it has been poured and floated, but before it cures.

Concrete stains are available at home centers and lumberyards in a wide variety of colors.

Bleached Out

Weeds often seem to find their way into the control joints of sidewalks and patios. They're unattractive and the roots exert pressure on the concrete.

One way to get rid of weeds without using pesticides is to carefully pour full-strength bleach into the joints.

Throw Like a Pro

If your plans for outdoor structures include masonry surfaces, you're almost sure to find yourself "throwing mortar" to lay bricks or blocks. Although throwing mortar is an acquired skill, a beginner can use the basic techniques with just a little practice.

The most critical element is the mixture. If the mortar is too thick, it will fall off the trowel in a heap. If it's too watery, the mortar will be impossible to control. Experiment with different water ratios until you find a mixture that you can deliver in a controlled, even line that holds its shape after settling. Take notes, recording the best mixture.

Don't mix more mortar than you can use in 30 minutes. Once mortar begins to set up, it's hard to work with and yields poor results.

Bracing Wobbly Handrails

Weak, wobbly handrails on a deck or porch are dangerous. An easy, effective fix is to cut a 6"-long wood block from a length of 2 × 2 or 2 × 4. Bevel the bottom end of the block and fasten it to the post directly beneath the handrail with two galvanized screws. Then drive a third screw up at a 45-degree angle through the block and into the underside of the handrail. To prevent splitting the wood, prebore shank-clearance holes for all the screws.

Deck Brightener

It happens every spring—you take a good look at the deck and make plans to clean and protect it. There are many commercial deck cleaning formulas on the market, but they're often expensive. And pressure washing can be effective, but if the deck is mildewed, the pressure can actually drive the mildew spore into the wood, allowing it to reestablish itself quickly.

Cleaning the deck doesn't need to be complicated or expensive. To begin, hose down the deck to remove loose dirt. Use a putty knife to remove debris trapped between decking boards.

Water plants near the deck to dilute any cleaning solution that may fall on them. Mix one gallon of water with two cups of household bleach and one cup of laundry detergent. Use this cleaning solution and a stiff garage broom to thoroughly scrub the deck. Make sure you remove all moss, mold, mildew and dirt. Work in sections, rinsing each within 10 minutes of applying the solution.

Allow two weeks for the deck to dry completely, then apply deck sealer. Even if your deck is made of pressure-treated lumber, it needs to be sealed. Pressure-treated lumber is protected against rot and decay; sealer protects it against checking and cupping.

QUICK TIPS

If you're repairing brittle deck boards, grind the sharp points off the nails you're driving or blunt the points by striking them with a hammer. Blunt nails will cut through brittle wood while sharp nails just part the grain, leading to splitting.

No matter how carefully you select lumber, you find bowed boards as you build. If a deck board is slightly bowed, install it bow up. Gravity and the weight of furniture and people will eventually flatten it.

Straightening Warped Decking

A warped deck board isn't just unsightly. It's also dangerous because it creates uneven spacing between boards that catches heels and trips the unwary.

To straighten a warped board, insert one or more wedges between it and the next board. Use a hammer to drive in the wedges until the board straightens out. If necessary, remove the nails or screws within a few feet of either side of the warp; then drive two 3"-long deck screws through the straightened board at each joist location. When you're done, remove all the wedges.

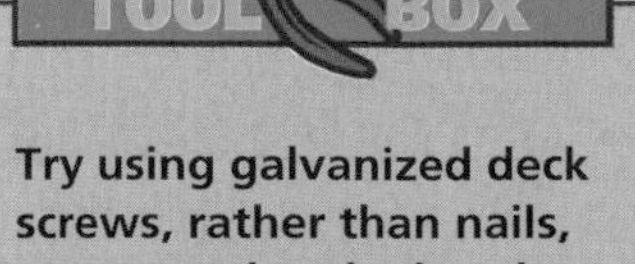

Try using galvanized deck screws, rather than nails, to secure the planks when building a deck. It will be easier to remove and replace damaged sections in the future. The screws are also less likely to loosen over time.

Helping Hand

Supporting a heavy floor beam or holding a long ledgerboard in place is often necessary when building a deck, adding on or doing major repairs. Unfortunately, so is the strain associated with these tasks. You'll never find a stronger, more tireless assistant than an automobile scissor jack.

The long crank handle and threaded mechanism on the jack lets you raise or lower heavy objects with surprising precision. And unlike some hydraulic bottle jacks, a scissor jack won't "leak" and suddenly drop while under pressure. Keep the jack from sinking into the ground by putting it on top of a 2×8 support board. If necessary, dig out the ground so the board is level.

Deck Flashing

Standing water is one of your deck's natural enemies. Flashing prevents water from flowing into joints and becoming trapped beneath decking where it can cause rot.

You can flash the joint between a deck ledger and its joists, even after they are installed. First, run a thick, continuous bead of 25-year elastomeric caulk over the top edge of the ledger. Then slip in the flashing behind the siding and bend it down over the top edge of the ledger. Extend it out another inch or so to cover the ledger-to-joist joints. Snip the flashing between the joists and bend it down slightly to divert water away from the ledger.

Flash the top edges of the joists with strips that are about an inch wider than the joist tops. Bend down the edges of the strip to shed water away from the joist sides. Tuck the ends of the joist flashing under the ledger flashing.

It's simple to flash the joint between the ledger board and the house siding before the deck boards are nailed down as shown here. Position an aluminum-coated modified bituminous strip against the siding, and bend it down over the ledger board. Finish by nailing joist hangers over the flashing and installing the joists.

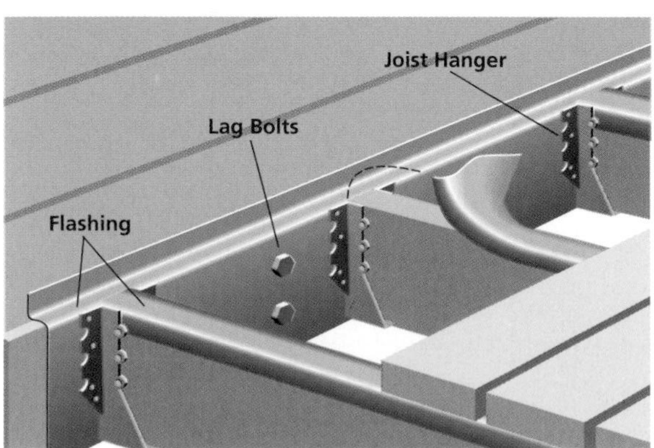

Repairing Damaged Decking and Joists

Inspect your deck every spring, checking for signs of damage and deterioration. Early detection is important—wood rot can spread, weakening surrounding boards.

If you find signs of damage, remove decking and inspect the underlying joists. If you see soft, discolored areas, the joists need to be reinforced. The photos below will guide you to a professional deck repair.

Use a hammer and chisel to remove rotted portions of joist.

Apply a thick coat of sealer-preservative to the damaged joist. Let the sealer dry, and apply a second coat. Then cut a reinforcing joist (sister joist) from pressure-treated lumber. Apply sealer, and let it dry.

Position the sister joist tightly against the damaged joist and attach it with 10d nails driven every 2 ft. Then toenail the sister joist to the ledger and header. Cut, seal and attach new decking boards to the joists with galvanized deck screws or nails.

On the Level

To combat freeze-thaw upheavals that can unsettle your deck and cause it to list, follow these instructions. First, support the weight of the deck temporarily with two vertical 4 × 4s and a double 2 × 8 crossbeam. Cut the post 6" above the ground, dig out the bottom portion of the post, and excavate the hole down to the frost line. (Check with your local building department for the frost-line depth in your area. If you live outside the snow belt, dig post holes to at least 30" deep.)

Next, bore a 1$^1/_{16}$"-dia. hole into the end of the 4 × 4 post (see illustration). Then cut a piece of 6"-dia. PVC pipe 3" longer than the depth of the hole. Also cut a length of 1"-dia. galvanized threaded rod to equal three-quarters of the pipe length plus an extra 6".

Put a hex nut and a 2"-dia. washer onto the threaded rod (positioning them 3" from one end), place the rod in the PVC pipe and stand the pipe in the hole. Insert the rod up into the posthole and then backfill around the pipe with dirt. After ensuring that the rod is plumb and centered in the pipe, fill the pipe with concrete. Once the concrete is cured, level the deck by turning the nut to raise the post. Any future frost-heave problems can be easily adjusted with a wrench.

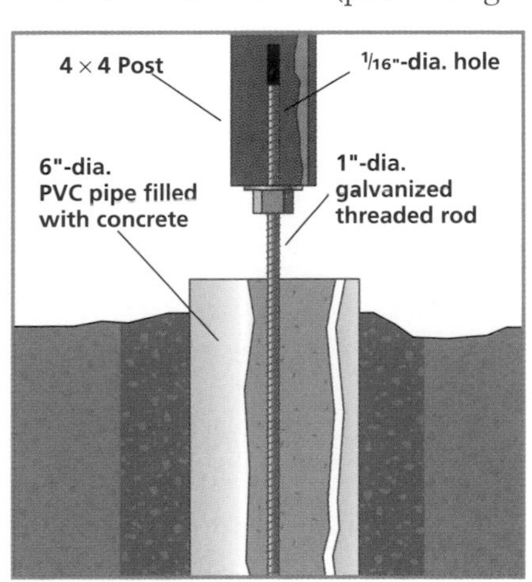

Deck-Railing Brace

Long handrail runs on decks and porches tend to sag in the middle. A prop block made from a cedar, redwood or pressure-treated pine 2 × 6 will shore up that sagging rail.

Measure the distance between the decking and the underside of the railing at one of the posts. Cut the block to that length. Then use two 2 × 4s as a lever and fulcrum to raise the railing enough to slide the block in. Remove the lever, and screw or nail the block top and bottom.

INDEX

T

U

V

W

Illustration Credits:
Andrew Christie: 111, 154 bottom
Brian Chrisyie: 27 top, 60 bottom, 142
Mario Ferro: 12 bottom, 59 left, 66 top, 77
Trevor Johnston: 146
Narda Lebo: 9, 11, 12 top, 15, 20, 21, 22 bottom, 23, 26, 50, 54, 55, 56, 60 top, 66 bottom, 69, 87, 92, 96, 130, 131, 132, 133, 151, 153, 154 top
Tom Moore: 145
Chad A. Peterson: 147
Richard Stromwell: 8, 13, 22 top, 24 top, 42, 59 right, 102, 104, 105, 121, 155
Ian Warpole: 27 bottom

Photo on p. 115, second from top, courtesy of J. Walter Thompson

Creative Publishing international, Inc. offers a variety of how-to books.
For information write:
Creative Publishing international, Inc.
Subscriber Books
5900 Green Oak Drive
Minnetonka, MN 55343